P9-AGV-027

SCIENCE AS WRITING

DAVID M. LOCKE

Science as
Writing

Yale
University
Press
New Haven
and
London

Designed by Nancy Ovedovitz and set in Janson Text type by Brevis Press, Bethany, Connecticut. Printed in the United States of America by BookCrafters, Chelsea, Michigan.

Library of Congress Cataloging-in-Publication Data
Locke, David M. (David Millard), 1929–
    Science as writing / David Locke.
    p. cm.
    Includes bibliographical references and index.
    ISBN 0-300-05452-1
    1. Scientific literature.   2. Communication in science.   3. Technical writing.   I. Title.
    Q225.5.L63   1992
    808'.0665 – dc20   92-7824
                                        CIP
                                        Rev.

A catalogue record for this book is available from the British Library.
The paper in this book meets the guidelines for permanence and durability of the Committee on Production Guidelines for Book Longevity of the Council on Library Resources.

10   9   8   7   6   5   4   3   2   1

CONTENTS

PREFACE

HERE ARE NO IDEAS THAT DO NOT IMPINGE ON A WORLD OF OTHER ideas, and that is certainly true of the ideas expressed here. Thus, within literary studies, there has been a continual extension and broadening of the boundaries of the canon in the twentieth century. Much to the chagrin of those dedicated obstinately to the preservation of "standards," literary scholars have turned their attention from the classical to the vernacular literatures, from the ancients to the moderns, even the postmoderns. The literatures of the third world have for some time been in vogue, and a generation of feminist critics has challenged the patriarchal monopoly of the canon. There are many now who no longer feel constrained not to examine even the popular, the ephemeral.

Similarly, from the perspective of literary studies, and also within the disciplines themselves, the various bodies of professional, functional discourse have come increasingly under scrutiny as language, not as the mere conveyors of ideas. For philosophy, language has always been a fit subject for study, and philosophers long ago learned not to exempt their own discourse from their analyses. Now they have redoubled their attention. History, as is well known, is undergoing its own convulsive reconsideration of its methods, including the problem of writing. Paramount, here, of course, is concern over the character of historical narrative, but the matter of style, too, plays its part; one thinks at once of historian Peter Gay's 1974 *Style in History*. The human sciences — to borrow the European term — find their discourses coming increasingly under examination. Indeed, Donald McCloskey's 1985 *Rhetoric of Economics* is one of the first in a projected series, Rhetoric of the Human Sciences.

In such a climate, it is hardly surprising that the languages of the hard sciences should come finally to lose — or at least to find questioned — their privileged position as pure functional notation, as mere shorthand records of observations made and experiments performed. That such questioning, such challenging, is currently underway, is the raison d'être for this book, and it is intended to make its own contribution to the argument.

If, as it seems, no body of discourse is especially privileged — is able to operate simply as a vehicle for the untrammeled expression of its ideas — any text which makes that argument suffers from the debilitating paradox that it employs language it assumes operates precisely as it argues language cannot operate. Short of silence, or self-conscious reference to this dilemma with every statement made, there seems little choice but to proceed, as this work does, knowing that the argument is problematized by its very existence as discourse, but knowing also that, like all argument, however problematized, it is worth making if it wins assent. Discourse, imperfect though it may be, proceeds if human activity is to proceed.

To present the argument, I have selected material from a variety of sources, choosing scientific writings from various disciplines, times, and places, including some of those classic scientific texts that have entered the realm of key cultural documents, variously designated as "great" books. The argument can be made — has been made — that such texts, like Darwin's *Origin of Species*, in surviving to become classics no longer are read strictly as scientific documents but rather have acquired a special status as literature, a status that supposedly sets them apart from the ordinary, functional works of science. We will return to this point, but let me say here that I do not believe that any special qualities of such texts can be divorced from the essential features that permitted them to function effectively in their own time and place. Although it is true that readings vary with readers — that every age, as they say, reads Shakespeare in its own way — that is not to say that new readings give old texts qualities they did not always possess in posse. The musicianship in Bach's church music does not spring into being only when those works are played in the modern concert hall; that musicianship is what made them successful, functional works in their original environment. Similarly with scientific works: the text of the *Origin* we read with so much appreciation today is not entirely different from the text perused with such avidity by Darwin's contemporaries. Nonetheless,

I have tried to include a variety of illustrative materials because my argument is a general one, which applies whenever and by whomever scientific texts are read. I do not contend that every scientific document is read the same way, nor that any one scientific document is read the same way by every reader, but I do assert that every scientific text must be *read*, that it is *writing*, not some privileged verbal shorthand that conveys a pure and unvarnished scientific truth.

There is an increasing number of scientists for whom this argument will not be news; there are historians and philosophers of science who have been making essentially the same point for some time; and a number of literary scholars are now bringing to bear on scientific texts precisely the kind of scrutiny that is called for here. It is not to these persons that this volume is addressed, though I hope they will welcome a general statement of the basic assumptions on which, in many cases, their own work is based. Rather, it is directed toward those who are not yet convinced — that body of scientists who continue to believe that their language does not much matter, that it is merely the empty vessel into which the content of their scientific thought is poured; and those literary persons who see scientific texts as something else, something apart from the texts they examine, those patterns of signs, those intricate interpenetrating laceworks of codes, which they, and we, characterize as literary works.

I should like to acknowledge here my debts to those who have made the preparation of this text possible. A sabbatical year from the University of Florida permitted me to complete the first draft of the manuscript. A number of colleagues, namely Alistair Duckworth, John Leavey, Jack Perlette, Ellie Ragland-Sullivan, and my old friend John R. Nabholtz have thoughtfully commented on individual chapters of an earlier version of the text. I am extremely grateful to Melvyn New for plowing through that longer and considerably more cumbersome manuscript in its entirety and giving me his trenchant and helpful criticism. I also am much indebted to my new friend Roald Hoffmann for his helpful advice, as I am to several anonymous reviewers of the manuscript. I am especially grateful to George Levine for his detailed and helpful critique. David Loewus of *Angewandte Chemie* provided numerous editorial suggestions, and my colleague John Van Hook abundant bibliographic assistance. And I thank Marie Nelson and Muriel Burks for coping with several equally untidy versions of the manuscript and wedging them into those tiny disks. That I have managed to err in spite of the assistance and the corrections of these individuals I trust will not be held against them.

Finally, I must note that like many others writing in a field that is suddenly deluged with newly published material, I have had to include only citations to new works that ideally would have found their way more integrally into my discussion.

SCIENCE AS WRITING

CHAPTER ONE

Introduction: Science and Literature

N DECEMBER 1817, AT A DINNER THAT THE HOST, PAINTER BENJAMIN Robert Haydon, has characterized as "immortal," Charles Lamb bibulously chided his host for including the visage of Sir Isaac Newton in his *Jerusalem*. John Keats promptly joined Lamb in declaring that Newton had "destroyed all the poetry of the rainbow by reducing it to the prismatic colours." The tipsy company then drank "Newton's health, and confusion to mathematics," affirming once again the great gulf between poetry and science.[1]

Science and poetry. Which two human endeavors can be more unlike? The one, cold, precise, factual; the other, warm, impressionistic, imaginative. And their practitioners: the poet—impassioned, frenzied, inspired; the scientist—aloof, calculating, deliberate. Or so the stereotypes go. And, though like all stereotypes they do not represent the truth, like all stereotypes they seem to carry more than a touch of the truth with them.

For three decades it has been fashionable to deny, or at least, to decry, C. P. Snow's division of the learned world into two camps, two "cultures," science and the humanities.[2] That the denial still seems necessary is because the thesis still appears to most of us so patently, so obviously, true, and its consequences—for anyone concerned about the humanness of our existence—so profoundly troublesome. It is unthinkable that our best intellectual efforts should be so forever split. Unthinkable; but inevitable?

Perhaps not. The long tradition of a great, impassable gulf between science and literature[3] is accompanied by another tradition — equally venerable, though less prominent — that sees the two as sister occupations, proceeding as it were hand in hand in their pursuit of the secrets of the world. Thus, William Wordsworth was present at Haydon's immortal dinner but was, as Haydon reminded him in a letter years later, reluctant to join in the toast of "confusion" to Newton.[4] Indeed, in the famous Preface to the *Lyrical Ballads*, Wordsworth is at some pains to reconcile science and poetry: "If the labours of Men of science should ever create any material revolution . . . , the Poet will be at [their] side, carrying sensation into the midst of the objects of science itself."[5]

Indeed, the writing in verse of natural philosophy — science — constitutes virtually a literary genre of its own, with such notable practitioners down the years as Empedocles (Aristotle warns us not to consider him a poet comparable to Homer);[6] Lucretius, the laureate of the atom; and the redoubtable Dr. Erasmus Darwin, grandfather of Charles Robert. Our own age favors the bellettristic scientific essay, penned by, say, Loren Eiseley or Lewis Thomas, suggestive evidence in any case that scientific writings *can* be literature.

A tradition, then, and a countertradition: one asserts that science and literature are opposed; the other — of growing significance, this book will argue — that they are akin.

2

If, as the tradition asserts, scientist and poet do inhabit different cultures, live different lives, then their respective writings — the papers of the scientist and the poems of the poet — are, it would seem, incommensurable, that is, so unlike one another in every respect that they are simply not to be compared. Such a judgment should surely, one might think, end the matter. But often, in fact, within the tradition, scientific writings and poetry (imaginative literature generally) are compared or contrasted, each in effect being used to define, delimit, and characterize the other.

Thus, it has long been something of a commonplace in literary studies to begin by marking off the language of literature from that of science, the purpose being to describe literature more precisely, to lay out its particularities for further study. In such discussions, scientific language is taken as the opposite extreme, most remote from, and in its characteristics most opposed to, literary language. The point is best illustrated perhaps by a passage from René Wellek and Austin Warren's *Theory of Literature*, a 1940s text that helped shape the thinking of several generations of English graduate students (many of them the literary theorists and practicing critics of today):

> Scientific language tends toward such a system of signs as mathematics or symbolic logic. Its ideal is such a universal language as the *characteristica universalis* which Leibniz had begun to plan as early as the late seventeenth century. Compared to scientific language, literary language will appear in some ways deficient. It abounds in ambiguities; it is, like every other historical language, full of homonyms, arbitrary or irrational categories such as grammatical gender; it is permeated with historical accidents, memories, and associations. In a word, it is highly "connotative." Moreover, literary language is far from merely referential. It has its expressive side; it conveys the tone and attitude of the speaker or writer. And it does not merely state and express what it says; it also wants to influence the attitude of the reader, persuade him, and ultimately change him. There is a further important distinction between literary and scientific language: in the former, the sign itself, the sound symbolism of the word, is stressed. All kinds of techniques have been invented to draw attention to it, such as metre, alliteration, and patterns of sound.[7]

The essential distinction between the two uses of language is still being drawn in some circles today. Thus, in an essay entitled "Literature and Science," published in 1982 in the Modern Language Association's *Interrelations of Literature*, George Slusser and George Guffey begin by differentiating the two modes of discourse on the basis that one, the literary, is primarily perceptual (that is, interesting to perceive), whereas the other, the scientific, is largely conceptual (that is, valuable for the message it conveys).[8] Nor is this an isolated instance. In an article entitled "Art and Science: Do They Need To Be Yoked?" Leo Steinberg's answer to his own rhetorical question is "no," suggesting that the two are simply too different to be "yoked."[9] And in presenting "The Rhetorical Case against a Theory of Literature and Science," Mark Kipperman argues that the two bodies of discourse "not only cannot be 'reconciled' but also that they must not be." He adds, "While both literature and science may . . . use metaphor and share similar linguistic structures, the rhetorical directions of the two activities are not only different, they are opposed."[10]

And, just as the traditional literary scholar seems intent on marking off the literary domain from the writings of science, so the traditional scientist appears not reluctant to return the compliment. From its beginnings, modern science has sought to achieve a mode of discourse conspicuously free of literary affectations. Although Thomas Sprat was not in any sense of the term himself a scientist, his often-cited remarks from the *History of the Royal Society* surely reflect the intention, if not quite the practice, of his confreres in that august body. After heatedly (and at some length) denouncing the "superfluity of talking" that has "overwhelm'd most other *Arts* and *Professions*," Sprat goes on to praise the custom of the Royal Society:

> They have therefore been most rigorous in putting in execution, the only Remedy, that can be found for this *extravagance*: and that has been, a constant Resolution, to reject all the amplifications, digressions, and swellings of style: to return back to the primitive purity, and shortness, when men deliver'd so many *things*, almost in an equal number of *words*. They have exacted from all their members, a close, naked, natural way of speaking; positive expressions; clear senses; a native easiness: bringing all things as near the Mathematical plainness, as they can: and preferring the language of Artizans, Countrymen, and Merchants, before that, of Wits, or Scholars.[11]

Today's college or university student of science (or technology) is likely to take a course labeled "technical writing" intended not, as the name might suggest, to train students for employment as technical writers but rather to prepare them for the writing they will do as part of their professional activities. Significantly, textbooks for such courses often begin by drawing the same kinds of distinctions between scientific and literary writing that traditional textbooks of literature draw. Thus, a typical textbook differentiates literature and scientific writing in terms that are reminiscent of those of Wellek and Warren:

> This important distinction [between the subjective and the objective] corresponds to the difference between literature and technical writing. Literature is an interpretive record of human progress and is based on imaginative and emotional experiences rather than the factual record of human achievements. Technical writing, however, is not history. (History is a record of our past; it subjectively interprets and offers value judgments about the past.) Literature is concerned mainly with our thoughts, feelings, and reactions to experiences. Its purpose is to give us insight. Technical writing concerns itself solely with factual information; its language does not appeal to the emotions nor to the imagination, but to the intellect. Its words are exact and

precise, and its primary purpose is to inform. Its information is the activity and progress of science and technology.[12]

Although the Whiggish attitude of this passage toward scientific progress and its blanket attribution of subjectivity to historical writing may not meet with universal approbation, it probably reflects the attitude toward their language of traditionalist scientists of our day, as well as those of Thomas Sprat's. Roland Barthes has perhaps best described this view of the scientist's attitude toward his or her writing:

> As far as science is concerned language is simply an instrument, which it profits it to make as transparent and neutral as possible: it is subordinate to the matter of science (workings, hypotheses, results) which, so it is said, exists outside language and precedes it. On the one hand and *first* there is the content of the scientific message, which is everything; on the other hand and *next*, the verbal form responsible for expressing that content, which is nothing.[13]

Yet, this by now familiar view of science versus literature, which one sees in both literary and scientific circles, has, as already noted, its strong counterview, science *and* literature, akin in aims and methods. This counterview — this countertradition — is being increasingly enunciated, and it is the thesis of this book that the counter-tradition deserves the attention of scientist and humanist alike, as well as of all who are simply interested in the makings of our culture.

3

In the literary critical world, the countertradition, like the tradition, has its venerable side. The Renaissance literary critic, for example, responding to the "new science," was likely to note something of the ambiguous kinship of literature and science. Thus, Sir Philip Sidney likens (and differentiates) poetry and science. The poet, Sidney says, "yields to the powers of the mind an image of that whereof the philosopher [scientist] bestows but a wordish description."[14]

With many contemporary critics the tendency to liken literature to science, or at least to downplay their differences, is even more marked. Not that such critics would speak for the scientific objectivity of literature, but rather that they would proceed from a judgment necessitated in some areas of science — most notably quantum mechanics — that the ultimate objectivity of certain classes of scientific observation cannot be maintained. As

Wayne Booth says, "Now that the scientists have given up the claim that they are seeking one single formulation of a firmly constituted reality, unaffected by the limitations and interests of the observer, perhaps we [in literature] should once again pack up our bags and follow after."[15]

Indeed, it is part of the countertraditional argument that historically the discourses of literature and science were not conceptually severed until relatively modern times — "no earlier than the mid-eighteenth century," Stephen Weininger asserts.[16] "The bifurcation," G. S. Rousseau says, "is a figment of our post-Kantian imagination."[17]

Thus, within literary studies, early and late, a countertradition seeks to liken, not differentiate, science and literature. Turning now to science, we find the story is much the same: here, too, a countertradition minimizes the differences of science and literature, to as great a degree perhaps as the tradition maximizes them.

To begin with, some branches of science have themselves become increasingly self-conscious of their own use of language.[18] Thus, as noted, in quantum physics it has become firmly established that the findings are not independent of the system that yields them, including the apparatus of the science and the conceptualizations of the scientist. Here, even the "facts," those ultimate bits of "truth" the scientific method grinds out like sausages, become only quasifacts (queasy facts?) David Bohm, a theoretical physicist, speaks of the field: "Here, it is important to note that facts are not to be considered as if they were independently existent objects that we might find or pick up in the laboratory. . . . In a certain sense, we 'make' the fact. That is to say, beginning with immediate perception of an actual situation, we develop the fact by giving it further order, form and structure with the aid of our theoretical concepts."[19] Thus, quantum physicists have been forced to become self-conscious about their own formulations, to believe that what they *think* determines in some measure what they *perceive*. (All I would add to this view is that it is the *language* of their formulations that helps determine the shape of their pictures of the world.)

Much of the peculiarity of quantum mechanics stems from the fact that the machinations of the experimenters inevitably disturb the system with which they are experimenting. Similarly, in the social sciences there is a long tradition of uneasiness over the impact of the scientist-observer on the society under observation. Classically, in their discourse, social scientists have sought to minimize this effect by adopting an objective, impersonal tone and explicitly noting only in certain stylized ways the incidental effects of their impacts on their informants. Now, however, some ethnographers at least, troubled by the artificiality of this procedure and above all by its failure to deal with the complex realities of the interaction between the observer and the observed, are rethinking the nature of their texts and are experimenting with alternate modes of presentation. As a case in point, the recent *Writing Culture: The Poetics and Politics of Ethnography* presents a group of symposium papers dealing with ethnography essentially as *writing*. Collectively, the contributors to *Writing Culture* assert that ethnographic discourse, and presumably much of the discourse of social science, is not the bare, unselfconscious record of observed social circumstance the standard view of scientific discourse would claim it to be. As James Clifford, one of the editors of the collection, observes of the contributors: "Their focus on text making and rhetoric serves to highlight the constructed, artificial nature of cultural accounts."[20]

Both social science and quantum mechanics, however, may seem to be exceptional cases. Everyone knows that the world of the quantum is most peculiar (in terms of our everyday experience) and that the methodology of social science is soft compared to that of the hard sciences, like physics and chemistry. It is perhaps not surprising then that their respective bodies of discourse should themselves seem peculiar, unscientific. But even among the "regular" sciences there exists, alongside the positivist view of the scientific document as the factual record of things done, another, rather more sophisticated view, which recognizes the scientific report as, if not the equivalent of a literary work, at least something of a construct, a contrivance.

Here, for example, is the advice of chemist-writers Louis and Mary Fieser to a neophyte chemist on how to compose a scientific paper:

> Proper organization of a paper is of key importance, but no simple formula exists for achieving a forceful scheme of presentation. However, one approach which is to be avoided is narration of the whole chronology of work on a problem. The full story of a research may include an initial wrong guess, a false clue, a misinterpretation of directions, a fortuitous circumstance; such details possibly may have entertainment value in a talk on the research, but they are probably out of place in a formal paper. A paper should present, as directly as possible, the objective of the work, the results, and the conclusions; the chance happenings along the way are of little consequence in the permanent record. . . . Any simplification that can be achieved will certainly increase clarity and lighten the burden of the reader.[21]

Nor is this practice of manipulation of the material in scientific papers something new that twentieth-century science has introduced. Newton, in the *Opticks*, confesses that the experiments he presents have been, at best, selected to make his points: "In the Description of these Experiments, I have set down such Circumstances, by which either the Phaenomenon might be render'd more conspicuous, or a Novice might more easily try them, or by which I did try them only."[22] This seems to imply that some of the experiments described never were performed precisely as reported; certainly it says that considerable selection has occurred in what is presented.

Both Newton and the Fiesers justify their decisions on the ground of clarity and simplicity. But some scientists are now willing to admit that this kind of artful presentation has a rhetorical effect, if not a consciously rhetorical purpose. Thus, one recent Nobel laureate, Sir Peter Medawar, remarks, "In retrospect we tend to forget the errors [committed in scientific research], so that 'The Scientific Method' appears very much more powerful than it really is, particularly when it is presented to the public in the terminology of breakthroughs, and to fellow scientists with the *studied hypocrisy* expected of a contribution to a learned journal" (emphasis added).[23] It is this "studied hypocrisy," this selecting, shaping, organizing, and arranging of the material to produce an effect — even an effect of clarity and directness of presentation, if not of "power" and infallibility — that certain scientists have come to recognize as signaling the nature of the scientific document.

The scientific paper, in this judgment, is not a simple tale of what was done in the laboratory, not a direct presentation of research carried out, but a crafted, shaped object, formulated within rules and conventions, some spoken (or written on the backs of scientific journals) and some tacitly understood. Or, as another recent Nobel laureate, Roald Hoffmann, puts it: "What is written in a scientific periodical is not a true and faithful representation (if such a thing were possible) of what transpired. It is not a laboratory notebook, and one knows that that notebook in turn is only a partially reliable guide to what took place. It is a more or less . . . carefully constructed man- or woman-made *text*."[24]

Thus, even within the body of science there are signs of a different, non-"standard" view of the texts of science, a view becoming increasingly widespread as those inside and outside science turn their attention to the discourse of science itself. Indeed, as historians, philosophers, and sociologists direct ever-closer scrutiny at the entire enterprise of science, they are bringing the discourse of science under new, more critical examination.

4

For some time, historians have eschewed the old-style history of science, with its Whiggish retrojection of the present, "perfect" state of science into the past and its hailing of the "discoverers" and "pioneers" who first enunciated and defended present views. What new-style historians of science seek to do is better understand the science of the past in its own terms, rather than judge it by how well it anticipates modern science.

Historians are coming, also, to focus on the discourse of science as significant, itself of interest. Thus, in his 1975 study, *The Chemists and the Word: The Didactic Origins of Chemistry*, Owen Hannaway examines the central role played by competing views of the "role of language in the explication of nature" in the emergence of chemistry as a discipline in the sixteenth and seventeenth centuries.[25] Similar attention to scientific language as a determinant of scientific content is given by Frederic L. Holmes, who demonstrates how Lavoisier's early notebook formulations of his ideas actually influenced the development of his research program.[26]

Philosophically, the edifice of positivist science has been under attack since the 1930s, when Karl Popper effectively challenged the notion that scientific hypotheses are proved, or verified, by the work that scientists do. Arguing that scientific statements can be only disproved, never proved, Popper makes falsification, not verification, the work of science. The best scientific statement has not been proved, it has simply been repeatedly tested and never falsified.

However it is viewed, the methodology of science has traditionally been sharply differentiated from that of the humanities: on the one hand, scientific discovery; on the other, hermeneutic inquiry. But now certain philosophers — in rather different ways, for example, Paul Ricoeur and Stephen Toulmin[27] — are bringing scientific methodology under the rubric of "hermeneutics," a label that, in spite of its current usage as referring broadly to the activity of deriving the meaning inherent in texts, still carries some connotation of its initial reference to biblical exegesis. It is, of course, the problematizing of the old scientific method, supposedly consisting of hypothesis and proof, that allows that method to reappear as a hermeneutic schema characterized by notions of guesswork and validation, or noninvalidation. As Toulmin says, "Once we recognize that the natural sciences too are in the business of construing reality, we shall be better able to preserve the central insights of the hermeneutic method, without succumbing to the misleading implications of its rhetorical misuse."[28] In such a view, both science and the humanities are engaged in the activity of interpretation, or the practice of hermeneutics. Indeed, philosopher Gyorgy Markus presents the beginning of a detailed humanistic analysis of scientific discourse in a paper provocatively titled "Why Is There No Hermeneutics of Natural Sciences? Some Preliminary Theses."[29]

If scientific "truths" are always "framework dependent," as claimed by the movement initiated by Thomas Kuhn and Paul Feyerabend, then the framework, or paradigm, is the enabling structure that determines what the scientific facts can be taken to mean, and indeed how they can be determined. Between competing paradigms there is no commensurability; without some overarching paradigm to give a context for comparison, events construed within each paradigm must make their own kind of sense. In the most extreme version of framework-dependence, no one framework can be preferred over another, and the movement of science from one paradigm to another represents merely change, not progress.

In Kuhnian terms, that movement from paradigm to paradigm is construed as a series of scientific revolutions, dramatic shifts in scientific thought and practice as scientists switch their allegiance. In this view, the long, steady march of science, with the past as a series of ever-closer approximations to the present, is simply an illusion. The periodic paradigmatic revolutions, the wrenching frameshifts, become inapparent, however, as science surveys its past, simply because the past is always seen from, and rewritten within, the prevailing paradigm. The "past" is the past the paradigm needs in order to account for its own present.

The Kuhnian conception of scientific revolutions has been extremely popular with literary critics because its picture of periodic scientific change so much resembles the conventional view of literary change: broad literary periods each governed by a single, conventional sensibility and bordered by abrupt changes of convention — the Augustan Age, say, terminated by the Romantic Rebellion. Such comparability suggests at once a kinship in the two modes of discourse, one hardly possible under the traditional view of slow and steady scientific progress. To be sure, as every student of literature knows, the more closely one examines the literary periods, the more the distinctions between them blur and the more artificial the boundaries seem. But so too has the post-Kuhnian history of science found the original notion of abrupt revolutionary paradigm shift something of an oversimplification. In any case, however, the historical periodicities of the two bodies of discourse emerge as not totally dissimilar and certainly not the marked differentiating feature the traditional view would insist them to be.[30]

5

Science, in addition, is now seen from certain perspectives as a collective affair. Rather than proceeding by the accumulation of singular discoveries of basic truths by isolated individuals, science is, in this view, an ongoing series of negotiations among groups of scientists variously competing and cooperating, seeking to arrive at views that will be acceptable to as much of the community as possible. As physicist (and philosopher) John Ziman says, *"The goal of science is a consensus of rational opinion over the widest possible field."*[31]

Determining the ways in which such consensus views are arrived at is a goal of the new sociology of science. The traditional sociology of science, begun in the 1930s by Robert Merton and his school, concerned itself with the organizational behavior of scientists and the impact of external social structures on the scientific enterprise.[32] The Mertonians deliberately excluded from their purview the substantive content of science — that is, they studied how scientists work together and how they are influenced by society at large, but not how these factors affect their accumulation of scientific "knowledge." It is precisely to this area that the newer sociologists of science — led by David Bloor, Barry Barnes, and others — have turned.[33]

Thus, these new sociologists argue that scientific "knowledge" is knowledge not because it correctly relates the true state of the natural world but because it has been accepted as knowledge by the working body of scientists involved. The causes of scientific knowledge, then, are to be sought in the social relations by which scientists achieve consensus rather than in the physical constraints of the external world. In achieving consensus scientists perforce accept some beliefs as true and reject others as false, and it may well be, the new sociologists hold, that the reasons they do so are themselves largely social. Perhaps for strategic reasons — it being less challenging to traditional views of what constitutes scientific knowledge — the new sociologists early on sought to examine the social causes that compel holders of "false" or "marginal" beliefs to maintain them. Thus there were sociological studies of such phenomena as ESP, UFOs, acupuncture, and so on.[34] But the "strong programme" of the new sociology, as laid out by Bloor, is symmetrical: it looks not only for the social causes of scientific beliefs but for the same kinds of causes for "true" and "false" beliefs.[35]

Indeed, a number of ethnographic studies of laboratory practice have now appeared, testifying to the growing interest in examining the social engagements of scientists as they go about their work of constituting scientific knowledge.[36] Thus, in *Laboratory Life: The Social Construction of Scientific Facts*, Bruno Latour and Steve Woolgar present an "anthropological" investigation of a neuro-endocrinology laboratory, which seeks to demonstrate how conditional and qualified observational statements — statements whose phraseology circumscribes their origin — eventually, through social processes, become taken as statements of unqualified scientific fact.[37] *Laboratory Life* is a real-time investigation, but the new sociological approach is applied to historical subjects as well. For example, *Leviathan and the Air-Pump*, by Steven Shapin and Simon Schaffer, examines the controversy between Robert Boyle and Thomas Hobbes over Boyle's air-pump experiments and their interpretation.[38] The study situates the dispute in the context of Restoration society and presents social and political reasons for the respective positions.

The paradigm-relativist and constructivist views of scientific knowledge on which the new sociology is based are not, needless to say, universally accepted. They run, for example, quite contrary to the instinctive thinking of most working scientists. And a number of philosophers of science hold, if not with the old positivism, at least with a new philosophical realism. Such philosophers — Richard Boyd, for example[39] — argue that scientific truths can be after all true (without quotation marks) and true of the real world (again, without qualification). Interestingly enough, the realist position has been used to "defend" literary criticism itself from the uncertainty and deconstruction introduced by the poststructuralists.[40] Although the realist position accords well with the operational thinking of most scientists, it has not won over the constructivists, who continue to insist that scientific knowledge is made, not discovered.[41]

The paradigm-relativist and constructivist positions cast scientific discourse in the countertraditional mold. Paradigm-relativism holds that the discourse within a paradigm is essentially autonomous and the choice between competing paradigms is a matter not of logic, but of rhetoric — though historians and philosophers may avoid the latter term. Thus, since considerations of scientific fact do not permit choices between paradigms, shifts in paradigmatic allegiance come about only when the discourse of one paradigm becomes more convincing to scientists than the discourse of another. Similarly when scientific facts are constructed, the constructivist holds, it is because the relevant scientists have found the discursive statements sufficiently convincing to be accorded the status of fact. In this view, the discourse does not record preexisting facts; rather, the discourse determines what become the facts.

If, then, scientific discourse is an organ of persuasion, like literature, and is an instrument for the construction of fact, as literature is of fiction, is there not a kinship between the two bodies of discourse? Presumably. As Latour and Woolgar say in a final footnote to *Laboratory Life*, "Our discussion is a first tentative step towards making clear the link between science and literature."[42] To a degree, Latour and Woolgar and the other new sociologists are joined, perhaps somewhat anticipated, in their "first tentative step" by certain literary critics, a number of historians of science, and some scientists themselves, all of whom speak not to the differences of science and literature but to their similarities.

And this leads us to the final question this chapter will address and the central topic of this book: what, precisely, are the similarities and the differences in the discourses of literature and science?

6

In the traditional comparisons of literary and scientific language cited earlier, there are not only assertions that the two bodies of discourse differ but indications as to how they differ. Thus, implicit in the discussion of Welleck and Warren, for instance, is what was for some time a standard formulation of the suitable perspectives from which one might view a literary text. That is to say that any literary argument could be – and at various times all literary arguments have been – validly based on one or more of these relationships of the text: (1) with the world it seeks to represent, (2) with the author whose views and feelings it aims to express, (3) with the reader whose acceptance it tries to win, and (4) with its own inner being, whose form it will embody.[43] Equally implicit in this traditional argument is the view that the scientific language, unlike the literary, is of significance only with respect to its subject matter. Its purpose is merely to convey that subject matter as clearly and simply as possible, and it is to be judged solely by how well it does so. Any trace of the author is considered accidental; any influence on readers, other than influence on their knowledge, is thought irrelevant; any self-awareness of the text, as text, is unthinkable.

Recent literary theory deemphasizes several of the classic perspectives and adds several new ones. Thus, it is argued that the literary work may function (some would say, *must* function) in an extraliterary milieu, namely in the political, social, and economic realm; it is, in this view, the milieu, through the author, that writes the text. Alternatively, another contemporary judgment asserts that the text, as multiple layers of signifying codes, serves — if I may so simply sum up a complex series of arguments — a constituting function. Thus, the codes of the text "write" the author (and not the reverse); the codes create the reader (and not the reverse); indeed, the codes construct the world the text purports to describe.

One might well anticipate that, since traditional literary criticism views literature variously while maintaining its singular view of the scientific text as "merely" representational, these newer literary critical modes too mark off the literary domain from the scientific — that is, extend neither social determinism nor textual constructivity to the discourse of science. And surely there are those who would hold such traditional views. To anticipate our argument, however, these contemporary critical modes are generally more congenial to the countertraditionalists and play an important role in the countertraditional argument that literary and scientific texts resemble each other more than they differ.

7

Traditional scientists are likely to agree with their literary critical counterparts that their discourse "represents" and that it bears none of the other hallmarks variously ascribed to literature. As Barthes has suggested, they regularly consider their writings as separate and distinct from their real, scientific work — making observations of and performing experiments with the real world and, on the basis of those observations and experiments, drawing inferences about the nature of that world. That the two kinds of activity are conceived to be separate and distinct can easily be seen. How else is one to interpret Darwin's often-cited remark, "A naturalist's life would be a happy one if he had only to observe, and never to write"?[44] A recent technical writing text is explicit on the same point: "Actually, they [scientists or engineers] are handed two very different problems when they are given a technical assignment and then asked to report on it. First, they must do the assigned technical work, make the study, gather the information, determine what it means. Next, they must report on that work to others."[45]

Scientists traditionally perceive the relation between what they do and what they write as "representation" or "mirroring," thereby agreeing with the literary critical characterization of their discourse. It is not difficult to find precise usage that supports this assertion. Thus one text on the writing of engineering reports makes the following comment, presumably as applicable to scientific as to engineering discourse: "In any report of engineering development the writing *reflects* the work itself" (emphasis added).[46] And an instructional volume for those writing papers for any professional journal says, "Organization in scientific writing is frequently a *reflection* of a specific scientific method" (emphasis added).[47]

Do scientists in the traditional camp, however, share the literary critical view that their work is devoid of those other qualities (expressivity, evocativity, and so on) variously assigned to the literary text? To begin with, such scientists surely do not believe that their writing is, like the poets', expressive. Of all the shibboleths that science promotes about its own enterprise, the most pervasive is this: that science is objective and impersonal. Indeed, we are repeatedly told, it is only through its objectivity, its impersonality, that science arrives at its ultimate truths. There is also a consensus among scientists that the objectivity of science must be duly reflected in the corollary objectivity of its discourse. As the Fiesers say in their *Style Guide for Chemists*: "We do not want our personality to emerge in our writing and divert attention from the story we are trying to tell. . . . Good writing, for us, is writing that is readable, clear, and interesting. We can do without style; indeed characteristics identifying a particular author are liable to be not marks of style but violations of principles of good usage."[48] As Albert Einstein noted in the introduction to his layman's account of relativity, *Relativity: The Special and the General Theory*, he "adhered scrupulously to the precept of that brilliant theoretical physicist L. Boltzmann, according to whom matters of elegance ought to be left to the tailor and to the cobbler."[49]

Many would go beyond the mere assertion of good taste or appropriateness in the choice of an objective voice for scientific discourse. For them the public verifiability of scientific findings is an essential part of the scientific method, and public verifiability demands a public, an objective, language. Linguist Leonard Bloomfield, in his *Linguistic Aspects of Science*, explains: "Science deals with the phases of response that are alike for all normal persons. Its observations and predictions can be tested by anyone. . . . Unique personal or communal behavior figures in science as an object, which may be observed like any other; but it does not figure as a part of scientific procedure."[50] Whether or not all traditional scientists today would endorse this view of precisely why their language is the way it is, most would almost surely agree that it is, as Bloomfield describes it, a language devoid of "private connotations."

It is also a language, they would agree, that eschews rhetoric. This idea is venerable. Thus, Robert Hooke, from his draft preamble to the statutes of the Royal Society: "The business of the Royal Society is: To improve the knowledge of natural things . . . (not meddling with Divinity, Metaphysics, Morals, Politics, Grammar, Rhetoric, or Logicks)."[51] Nor is this simply an old-fashioned attitude. Gunther Stent, a contemporary molecular biologist turned historian of science, accepts the traditional split between the objective language of science and the affective language of art. Thus, Stent says, science deals with "the outer, objective world of physical phenomena. Scientific statements therefore pertain mainly to relations between or among public events." Artistic statements, on the other hand, "pertain mainly to private events of affective significance."[52] The Bloomfieldian view of scientific discourse is that, just as the scientist-writer tries not to express individual, subjective, and affective material, the scientist-reader learns not to respond to or to ignore any such material that is unwittingly expressed. "As, by convention and training, the participants in scientific discourse learn consistently to ignore all private factors of meaning, the lexical, grammatical, and stylistic features of their informal discourse become indifferent: each scientist responds to each discourse only with the relevant operations or their linguistic substitutes."[53] Scientific language, in short, insulates itself from the provocation of any response other than operational understanding.

With respect to traditional scientists' view of the "artful" character of their writings, it probably coincides with the judgment about scientific documents given by the traditional critic, namely that they have no intrinsic interest as writing, that they merely serve — adequately enough, perhaps — their utilitarian purpose of having their scientific say. Indicative of this judgment is the phrase "Reconstruction of an Investigation," employed as a chapter title in one technical writing text to describe the report-writing process.[54] At the same time this view is entirely consonant with the scientific views that hold that the scientific work is merely a representation, that it is not expressive, that it has no rhetorical effect. Thus the scientist's paper is a kind of artless setting forth of what has been done, a transcript, a recording, a "mere" representation, writing that serves no purpose other than to transmit clearly whatever view lies behind it. Ideally, it is itself unseen, unobserved, undetected — certainly un-"interesting."

A central tenet of the "mystique" of science is that science is by virtue of its method insulated from any social, political, or economic pressures. Science, it is said, is dedicated to discovering the truth undeterred by extrascientific concerns; it is, in its essence, socially disinterested, ethically neutral, morally uncommitted, and pragmatically indifferent.

The scientific method itself is what is said to isolate, objectify, and neutralize science—free it from the curse of the human, individually or collectively. To make this possible, the scientist, or the apologist for science, often will divide the enterprise of the scientist into two portions, the phase of generation, in which the ideas are born, and the phase of justification, or verification, in which they are tested.[55] The scientific idea may come from anywhere—myth, ideology, the unconscious—and one need not be concerned, because the scientist at once moves on to the process of verification. Now the contaminated idea is tested in the crucible of the scientific method. The fire of scientific scrutiny burns away from the idea—the hypothesis or the theory—the stain of its origin. In this way, one can acknowledge the humanity of the scientist and yet maintain the ultimate objectivity of the endeavor.

In a similar view, the traditional scientist will insist on the freedom of science from contamination by the ends to which it is employed. Science may become a social tool, may do the world's work, but it remains untainted by that use. Science, in this official view, is an instrument; its blade can be used for life-saving surgery or human sacrifice and will wipe as clean in either case. One can acknowledge the misuse of science, its employment in unsavory ways (as in the Nazi concentration camps), while maintaining that science itself remains uncorrupted by such (mis)employment. Indeed, the traditional view will hold, science cannot long be misapplied because its method carries the mechanism to prevent such misuse, namely its own need for freedom of inquiry. The all-important verification procedures of science must be free to operate unchecked or the whole enterprise will cease to work.

Similarly, to much of the world of science, any reference to the "textuality" of its substance, any assertion that its language is operative in shaping its thought, in constituting its world, would be simply incomprehensible. To traditional scientists, the notion that their language is itself operative—a force, an instrumentality, that shapes the course of science—will, simply, not be believed. Such a scientist is, without consciously directing attention to the matter, convinced that scientific language is itself, as Barthes has described it, "transparent," the invisible, intangible, impotent carrier of the scientific thought. What matters is the substance of scientific thinking, not its formulation.

Traditionalist scientists, then, agree with their counterparts in the literary world not only in their judgment as to the dichotomy of their respective discourses — two cultures, two languages — but also in their delineation of scientific language as essentially representational and devoid of those other qualities — expressivity, affectivity, artfulness, social artifactuality, textual constitutivity — variously thought to give literary language its literariness.

8

The countertradition, needless to say, makes its own very different comparison of the respective discourses of literature and science. Neither within the scientific camp nor within literary criticism have the counterculturalists systematically developed modes of comparison of the two forms — a gap this book is intended in part to fill. But one can certainly make some observations as to the thinking that lies behind the various countertraditional critiques.

Within science, even the countertraditionalists will probably not trouble themselves to challenge the traditional view that scientific discourse is in considerable measure *representational*; after all, even nontraditional science is about something. Nor are countertraditional scientists likely to insist (contra tradition) that their discourse is *expressive*; traditional insistence on the objectivity of scientific discourse is very difficult to shake off. But the countertraditional scientist, as noted, will see a degree of *evocation* in scientific discourse and will not hesitate to acknowledge some rhetorical effect, if not rhetorical intent. Even the Fiesers advise their fellow chemists on how to "ease the burden of the reader." Furthermore, such scientists will concede that the scientific document is something of a construct — "a man- or woman-made text," as Roald Hoffmann says — not perhaps an art object, like a poem, but nonetheless something that is crafted and shaped.

Although modern science is a collective affair, and working scientists daily immerse themselves in the activities of their scientific culture — itself embedded in the social structures of the world at large — nonetheless, like most of us engaged in social practices, scientists are likely not to perceive the social constraints on their thought, but to see them simply as part and parcel of the content of the thought itself. Thus, even countertraditional scientists are not much given to pressing the case that their scientific discourse is *socially* shaped, let alone socially determined. It is true that ethnographers, as noted above, have been forced to consider their own subjective cultural frames as shaping their perceptions of the object cultures they encounter. And historians of science have for some time viewed social forces (in this case, largely external social forces) as shaping the scientific enterprise, Marxist critiques, in particular, having a quite extended history.[56] Recently, countercultural historian Robert M. Young, in arguing against the conception of separate "internalist" and "externalist" histories of science, has emphasized the mutual exchanges of influence between science and the social, political, and economic realm.[57] But it is largely the new sociologists of science who have made the countertraditional case that the scientific document is, in effect, a social artifact shaped by and functioning in the social milieu — the milieu of science and the milieu of the surrounding world.

Finally, countertraditional science, most notably quantum mechanics, in largely removing the privileged status of the scientist observer and forcing a consideration of the observer-observed as a single system, which must be judged in its entirety, has made the scientists' activities, as reported in their papers, in considerable measure *constitutive* of their results. In the quantum mechanical field, at least, scientists have been forced to concede that much of what they "find" they have themselves contrived or collaborated in. For many contemporary historians and philosophers of science, too — most notably the paradigm-relativists and the constructivists — the subject matter of any body of science is largely determined by the framework in which that science is conceived. Even these arch-countertraditionalists among the scientists and the historians of science, however, are unlikely to focus on the language formulations of science as themselves being determinative of scientific knowledge. Thus, the countertradition of science takes a step, but only a step, along the pathway from the traditional denial of the textually determinative character of scientific discourse. In sum, then, countertraditional science and historical, philosophical, and sociological students of science would modify the traditional view of scientific discourse as sharply marked off from literary discourse (in all but its representational aspects), particularly in emphasizing its rhetorical and social aspects and in recognizing, to a degree at least, its character as *text*, and indeed as constitutive text.

●

Within literary studies, the countertraditional view of the discourses of science and literature has in recent years made substantial headway, though it has yet to lay out a fully formulated comparison of the two modes. For long a minor, barely tolerated sidebar to "serious" literary study, the field of literature and science has in the decade of the 1980s virtually exploded. Testimony to the newfound popularity of this area was the formation in 1985 of the Society for Literature and Science, along with the growing number of conferences and publications dedicated to the field and to specific subsets within it.[58]

For much of its existence, this field has been dichotomized into studies of the influence of science on literary texts and, less common, literary studies of scientific texts. Much of the recent, impressive growth in the field has been in the latter area, and indeed, perhaps the most significant movement has been toward the analysis of nominally heterogeneous bodies of texts — texts whose usual attributions, "literary," "scientific," "technological," "political," seem finally irrelevant to their reading as documents growing out of a common mode of thought, designated often by Foucault's term "discursive formation."

Thorough reviews of these various bodies of work have recently appeared, and only a few comments need be made here.[59] Much of the literary study of the scientific literature has focused on the work of individual scientists, Darwin especially.[60] The first sustained close reading of Darwin was Stanley Edgar Hyman's *Tangled Bank: Darwin, Marx, Frazer and Freud as Imaginative Writers* in 1962.[61] And the most recent detailed examinations of his writings were Gillian Beer's *Darwin's Plots* in 1983 and George Levine's *Darwin and the Novelists* in 1988.[62] There are any number of possible reasons for the interest: Darwin's qualities as a writer, the accessibility of the major texts, and the importance of the Darwinian revolution in Victorian thought (there was hardly a Victorian writer who escaped its influence). But literary critics have scrutinized the writings of other scientists, too. Thus, another of Hyman's subjects, Freud, has attracted his share of attention, the most recent study being Patrick Mahony's *Freud as a Writer* in 1987.[63]

It is perhaps not surprising that in applying literary critical methods of scientific texts, many investigators should have followed literary critical practice and concentrated on individual works and authors. Common, too, are period studies like those of the literary world — for example, *Victorian*

Science and Victorian Values.[64] But also seen are generic and thematic investigations; thus, several scholars have analyzed the genre of the scientific paper.[65]

Thematic analysis of scientific discourse is most associated with the work of Gerald Holton, although the study of thematic usage that transcends traditional generic boundaries dates back to the 1930s and the history-of-ideas movement.[66] Its modern rebirth is largely the work of Michel Foucault,[67] with French historian of science Michel Serres contributing to the movement. Serres reads paintings, poems, novels, and fables, as well as scientific texts, in pursuit of patterns, themes, and metaphors that lie within thought and determine its shape.[68] Indeed, thematic analysis has its Anglo-American exponents as well.[69]

Critical modes that draw on disciplines outside the literary world, so-called extrinsic critical methods (Marxism, Freudianism, and the like) also have their adherents among the literary readers of scientific texts. Thus, there have been, for example, a number of Freudian readings of Darwin,[70] and, most recently, feminists have turned their scrutiny on the texts of science.[71]

Implicit, though not often made explicit, in these literary studies of scientific texts are certain assumptions about the general character of scientific discourse vis-à-vis literature. Clearly, these literary countertraditionalists, like their scientific counterparts, do not endorse the view of scientific discourse as pure representation. Nor do they argue to any extent for its expressivity. They, too, accept the evocational element in scientific discourse, as the many rhetorical studies of scientific texts demonstrate; Mahony's analysis of Freud's writing, for example, is in considerable measure rhetorical. Further, Hyman's New Critical studies of Darwin suggest that the art-object view of discourse is as applicable to science as it is to literature. The extrinsic critical readings of scientific texts, such as the Marxist and feminist ones, are quite indicative that such texts can be seen to bear the marks of their social determination. Indeed, period studies, such as those of Victorian science, often show the social influence on the scientific discourse of the time. Finally, those discourse analyses in the Foucaultian vein are testament to the reading of scientific texts as constitutive of the discursive worlds they bring into being. In these various respects, then, the countertraditional literary movement, much like that within science and its corollary disciplines, distances itself from the traditional view of the scientific text as devoid entirely of literary features. A fuller, more sustained development of these ideas is the aim of this book.

10

To proceed, we shall take up each of the six perspectives noted above as adopted at various times and under various circumstances for the reading of literary texts, investigating in turn the utility of each for the reading of scientific texts. (Even those approaches not currently in vogue in literary circles will prove relevant to the project.) In the argument, we shall adopt the convenient fiction that six discrete theories exist, each making its own competing claim for validity in the reading of the text: (1) representation theory, which sees the literary work as essentially a representation of the real world; (2) expression theory, which views that work as an expression of its author's thoughts and feelings; (3) evocation theory, which values it as an evoker of response from its readers; (4) art-object theory, which judges the work as an objet d'art, interesting in its purely formal properties; (5) artifact theory, which situates the work in its social milieu; and (6) instrumentality theory, which places the work among the signifying systems that organize, structure, indeed constitute, the world. Successive chapters will, in turn, briefly examine each theory for its general validity for scientific texts and with reference to specific texts seek to determine the value of the theory as an entrée to the fuller reading of the texts in question.

To anticipate the outcome, we shall see that the traditional judgment should be essentially reversed: that though scientific and literary discourses both represent, they do so in rather different ways, and that both bodies of discourse are approachable by methods suggested by other theories. Thus, we shall find, nothing in the literary critical armamentarium is per se to be ruled off-limits in the examination of scientific texts.

Indeed, each of the six theories will reveal something of importance about the reading of scientific texts: something scientists need to know if science is to proceed with full awareness of its own methodology; something the world of literary criticism needs to know if it is to understand fully its own modes of reading and their range of applicability; something all who dwell in the world science has made need to know if they are to understand that world and how it works. If there are two cultures, they interpenetrate. And if the world is to appreciate what the scientific culture is saying, and what it is *doing* by saying, it must employ the methods of the literary culture to discover how it is saying, and doing, it.

CHAPTER TWO

The Problematics of Representation

LTHOUGH TRADITIONAL SCIENTISTS ARE LIKELY NOT TO DEMUR AT THE suggestion that their writing is in some sense representation, they are less prone than the literary critic to refer to that representation as imitation (the famed *mimesis* of Plato and Aristotle). This may merely be because few scientists are raised on Aristotle's *Poetics*. More important, however, it suggests that scientists do not think that the markedly illusionistic effects commonly attributed to literary representation are important in their kind of discourse. Most people would probably agree that there is little scientific discourse that creates the kind of felt presence traditionally associated with literary representation; one would never expect the botanist's daffodils to "flutter and dance" before our eyes as Wordsworth's do. Scientists, to be sure, are expected to describe their experiments in enough detail to permit their replication by any other scientist similarly trained, but their descriptions are not required to create the illusion that the described events occur as real events before one's eyes, any more than the cook's recipes do.

Scientists, above all, hold that their representations are not fictive, as literary representations may frankly be; they report what, in fact, the scientists believe really to have occurred. At the same time, however, the scientists' representations need not be faithful to life or our expectations of life, as the classical view of mimesis holds that literature must be "probable," as Aristotle decrees,[1] because the scientists' events purport to be true. The most unlikely

23

or unexpected of scientific results may be thought to carry with them the stamp of truth, so that they need not be made to seem likely, just as they need not be made illusionistically real. Sir Alexander Fleming did not need to conceal his surprise that his bacterial cultures had died in the vicinity of *Penicillium* molds, nor did Otto Hahn and Lise Meitner seek to make "probable" the finding of light atoms among the products of uranium decay.

Yet, just as the classical and the neoclassical critics claim literary representation to be *generally* true, to assert a widely applicable truth,[2] so scientists, they would hold, aim ultimately at general laws. A scientist who does not uncover laws of general validity is not functioning as a true scientist. When scientists, however, arrive at general laws, they, unlike the poet, enunciate them. The job of the poet is to exemplify truths, not to formulate them in words. Poets clothe their insights in actions that show them to us; scientists give us their insights verbatim. Whereas Newton states his laws of motion, Shakespeare portrays his truths of the human heart by particularizing them. There are, indeed, literary traditions in which the authorial personae speak to us, direct our thinking, even dictate our judgments, but these must themselves derive from the experience presented, and there is clearly a tendency to favor—Jamesian realism indeed demands—the suppression of such overt instruction. "Showing," in the words of the English teachers, is preferred to "telling."

Further, the neoclassical view of literary representation typically holds that what is portrayed is to be shown as in some way better than what is real. There are suggestions of this even in Aristotle,[3] but it is the neoclassical critic who gives the idea full voice. Thus, Sir Philip Sidney asserts: Nature's "world is brazen; the poets only deliver a golden."[4] Traditional scientists, in their turn, would not think of improving on nature in what they represent; their only aim, they aver, is to find and depict what is really in nature. This view, to be sure, we must not let stand unchallenged, even provisionally, for every effort the scientist makes, as we will see, is to "improve" on nature: the curves have been artificially smoothed, the equations are merely approximate, and the laws hold only in some ideal Newtonian universe.

Traditional scientists, finally, do not trouble themselves to be "realistic," as literary realism proclaimed literature must be. Or, rather, it does not occur to them they can be anything other than realistic; they believe that they are setting down, representing, what really happened, and that that representation must be, on the face of it, realistic. Nor do they detect external conventions that might determine their view of how reality is to be experienced, like those that we have now come to believe affect the artist's view of reality. In this respect, the scientist joins with the artist in being largely unconscious of the social conventions that so heavily determine their respective views of reality. As to changing artistic conventions, however, here the artist and the scientist are likely to part company. Whereas the artist is likely to be aware of altering the conventions of the craft — or to feel that he or she is abandoning conventions of representation altogether — in the name of achieving greater fidelity to "nature" or to "truth,"[5] the scientist will likely feel no such impulse. To be sure, many scientists may believe that the "pictures" they paint of nature are a more faithful likeness than those of their predecessors, but only by virtue of the efficacy of their science, not because of the skill of their representation.

The scientist deals, science believes, with "eternal" truths. The discourse of science, to the scientist who holds to a traditionalist view, is a cumulative, ever-growing store of knowledge, not quite unchanging perhaps, but approaching asymptotically to the absolute truth. One well-known historian of science presents the traditional view of the working of science as follows: "The examination of records of observations by trained minds leads to classification; from classifications general rules or 'laws' are deduced; these laws may be applied to further observations; failures in correspondence between new observations and accepted laws may result in alterations of the laws; and these alterations lead to yet further observations; and so on. This is usually held to constitute the 'method' of science."[6] In this view, scientific representation can be only true and universal. Even when "records of observations by trained minds" give laws that need ultimately to be altered, the "records of observations" still stand; the altered laws must account for them as well as for the "new observations." Viewed thus, the discourse of science displays no counterpart of the changing conventions, the shifting notions of what constitutes realistic representation, that give the literary world its look of undergoing periodic waves of altered sensibility.

As to literature, it must be noted that representation theory is not a force in literary criticism today. The theory that played so leading a role in classical and neoclassical criticism, that formed the very credo of realism, has had but an exceedingly minor role to play in the theater of criticism since the coming of modernism and the New Criticism.[7] And, perhaps not coincidentally, epistemology, as Richard Rorty points out, has now abandoned its own version of representation theory — namely, that the mind represents, or mirrors, nature as it forms its mental images.[8] At the same time literary criticism (as noted in the previous chapter) has been happy to leave in place the ascription of representation to the discourse of science; science, it asserts, *merely* represents while literature no longer deigns to do so.

But science, traditional science, at least, has welcomed, as we have seen, this role. It has seemed entirely natural to traditional science to assert that in its discourse science represents what it learns of the world through its method. Implicit in this view of scientific representation, however, are three assumptions: (1) that there is an objective, real world, (2) that in some absolute sense this world becomes "known" to scientists through their efforts, and (3) and that what they "know" comes then to be translated into, and represented as, language. These assumptions the countertradition in its varied voices has called into question. The specific challenges it has made need not be rehearsed here, but we must examine these traditional assumptions from the standpoint of the operating procedures (including the writing) of science.

2

Epistemological problems aside, one must observe that the real world scientists believe they are studying is, with the steady expansion of the scientific enterprise, increasingly remote from the world of sensory impression and increasingly inexplicable in terms of everyday experience. To be sure, the modern scientist is not the first to separate appearance from reality. The pre-Socratics saw the ultimate reality variously in number, in stasis or flux, in fire or water, in atoms and the void. And Plato associated the world of appearance with *doxa*, opinion, not *episteme*, true knowledge of things.[9] But it was the "new science" of the sixteenth and seventeenth centuries that began the final subversion of the world of experience. First, it converted the earth from a massive, immobile bulk, squatting in the center of the universe, into a minute, fleeting mote, whirling endlessly through the heavens. Then it divorced the "secondary" world of sensation — the colors, the smells, the sounds of things — from the "primary" world of substance and seated that secondary world in the sensorium of man.

Yet it is the science of the twentieth century that has made the world the scientist explores truly incommensurable with the world of ordinary experience. Even the fundamental notions of time and space are quite swept away. In Newton's universe time and space are a proscenium stage, onto which the heavenly bodies appear to do their celestial dance, and from which they will someday disappear, leaving the empty stage to molder forever in the mist of eternity (or the mind of God). But the heavenly bodies of Einstein's universe are a group of strolling players, who bring their own time and space into being around them only as they begin their performance and take it away with them when they go. Nor is this the end to the wonders of modern physics: matter is energy, energy is matter; both are waves, both are particles. Everything exists as a field; matter is only perturbation in the field. In quantum mechanics — Einstein's protest (God does not play dice with the world) notwithstanding — individual events are not caused, they happen according to statistical principles; particles do not move in discrete paths, they are simply found at various spots in a smear of space; and spatially separate events are inextricably (and inexplicably) linked.

The logical positivists argued that the conclusions of science could be systematically joined through a series of logically and linguistically definable steps — sentence by sentence — with common, unexceptionable statements relating publicly demonstrable experiences. But the content of modern science is so abstruse, so explicable only in terms of its conceptual formulations, so far removed from any sense of everyday experience, that the connection between the two is, for all practical purposes, severed. This is not, of course, to challenge the validity of science; it is merely to assert that the subject matter of modern science is meaningful only in terms of its own conceptual schemes, not by direct appeal to ordinary experience.[10] To argue so is to accept a large part of the framework- or paradigm-relativist position. But it does not entail that position's ultimate point that competing paradigms ("conceptual schemes") are incommensurable, that science gives no procedures for deciding between them.

Here, I would only emphasize that the conceptual schemes of science, the patterns of thinking by which the scientist approaches the real world, are themselves fully embedded in systems of symbolization. There is no real world that scientists know independently of the linguistic, graphic, and mathematical formulations by which they conceive it.[11] One might at least imagine that sentient creatures without language know in some direct sensory way the world around them — that Helen Keller lived in something of a known world before she recognized the sign for water, that animals have a more or less coherent mental picture of the world they experience. But one can make no such leap of imagination about modern scientists and their world. One cannot conceive that the complex world of modern science could be directly accessible to the mind unmediated by language and mathematics. Ultimately, to claim that the scientist somehow explores the real world directly, without the mediation of language, and then represents, reflects, or translates into language this world picture is unthinkable. But that is precisely what scientific representation theory asserts.

Apparent exceptions spring to mind. One recalls the often told (and now perhaps suspect)[12] story of August Kekulé's daydreaming of the snake swallowing its tail and then conceiving of the ring formulation of the benzene molecule. Or Einstein's claim that he thought conceptually, and that the key relations in his ideas were perceived directly and only subsequently formulated in words and mathematical equations. Perhaps so. But Kekulé's daydream was the zoomorphizing of the conventional graphical symbolizations of molecular structures, and Einstein's perceived relations came into being in a mind already shaped by language and mathematics; it is hard to believe that they could have been inscribed on a tabula rasa or been understood in any sense had they been so inscribed.

3

But even if it is conceded that the real world the scientist studies is not the real world of everyday experience, and that the scientific real world is not even comprehensible outside the framework of science, may not the second of the assumptions implied in the traditional view of scientific representation hold — namely that through their efforts scientists come to know in some objective sense the real world they do study?

To begin with, the work of the scientist has always been more problematic than is commonly supposed. The general public assumes that scientific findings are black or white, positive or negative; that results are obtained or are not; that particular phenomena are observed or are not observed. But, in truth, about much of what they do, scientists are uncertain: the things they observe are in various shades of gray; it is their theories that demand they label them black or white.

Things *seem* to happen in the scientists' world, but they cannot always be sure. Or they are sure, but mistaken. After all, a generation of astronomers saw and drew pictures of canals on Mars. Or, for a more recent example, here is a 1984 Associated Press report on the launching of a satellite into space from a space shuttle: At first flight director Harold Draughon is quoted as saying the Westar VI satellite was released normally "within less than a second of the most accurate time," and that about an hour later a ground station reported a "partial acquisition" of radio signals. But: "It turned out sometime later, when we didn't get better acquisition, we questioned the first acquisition and they said they weren't real sure they had a real acquisition." And with respect to the rocket burn that supposedly sent the satellite into its assigned orbit, after first reporting that the burn was "normal," Draughon later confessed that there was "a real question whether or not there was a first burn or not [sic]."[13]

The fact that much of what the scientist does is quantitative seems to the public to give the results a special status of certainty. Can measurements be wrong? In fact, of course, they can. As every scientist knows, every measurement has its probability of error. Eyes are tired, instruments are faulty, samples are impure, standard materials have deteriorated. Further, scientists must depend not only on their own often unreliable results but on those of others, with which they are even less likely to know what might have gone wrong. In fact, it is becoming increasingly clear (the whole matter is something of a scientific scandal) that not only may the results a scientist gets from others be inaccurate; they may be fraudulent. More and more cases in recent years have come to light revealing scientists who, unable to meet the pressure to produce results, simply fake them.[14]

To be sure, science has its vaunted self-checking procedure: before scientific results are accepted as valid they must be replicated in other laboratories. But this takes time, and spurious results may go unchallenged for long periods. Furthermore, checking procedures conducted by different workers bring new problems of prejudice, preconception, and experimental unfamiliarity. Because written descriptions of complex procedures may be sketchy, and factors not known to be significant may simply be ignored, results from one lab sometimes cannot be replicated in another until its workers visit the first to learn the procedures (and the errors?) directly. There is, thus, a considerable degree of ambiguity in this business of replication. Valid results are those that have been replicated, but when replication fails, is it because the original experiment was faulty or the attempt at replication? The situation often involves much expenditure of time and money and effort in experimentation as well as in negotiation, until a sense of communal agreement is reached. A good example of this problem is given by Harry Collins, one of the countertraditional sociologists of science, in his discussion of the apparent failure to replicate early experiments thought to have detected gravity waves.[15]

4

Scientists, then, continually hover on the brink of minute and massive distrust of their own and their colleagues' or competitors' observations. And more than this, it is now clear that there are certain inherent limitations in what scientific procedures can actually determine about the natural world.

The best known of these is the uncertainty principle formulated in 1927 by the German Nobel laureate Werner Heisenberg. The principle states that it is impossible to determine precisely and simultaneously the position and velocity of a moving object. Although the principle applies to any moving object, the formulation is such that the uncertainty becomes significant only with subatomic particles. The term *uncertainty* seems to suggest the kind of experimental difficulty just discussed, but what is involved in fact is a problem inherent in the way the experimenter must react with the natural world, a problem that no amount of experimental sophistication can overcome.[16]

Furthermore, much of science depends formally on mathematics (as it does on language), and fundamental questions about the logical validation of certain branches of mathematics raise concern about the final justification of those areas of science that rely on such procedures. I refer, of course, to the proof published in 1931 by the Austrian mathematician Kurt Gödel that the consistency of arithmetic cannot be established by a set of axioms within the system. But the implications of Gödel's proof are far wider than this statement might suggest. In fact, it implies, as the commentators Ernest Nagel and James R. Newman have said, that "no final systematization of many important areas of mathematics is attainable, and no absolutely impeccable guarantee can be given that many significant branches of mathematical thought are entirely free from internal contradiction."[17]

Thus Gödel's proof raises questions about the dependence of science on a mathematics whose own logical base is uncertain. Similar questions have been raised about the logical foundation of science itself. For example, Michael Polanyi has argued that much as a branch of mathematics cannot legitimate itself in terms of a set of fundamental axioms, so a branch of science cannot legitimate itself by reduction of its conceptual apparatus to the fundamental principles of chemistry and physics.[18] In their eagerness to combat vitalism — that belief that assigns special properties to living systems — some scientists have made precisely this claim: that biological sciences ultimately are reducible to principles of chemistry and physics.[19] To clarify this argument, Polanyi makes use of the analogy with a simple machine, which certainly violates no laws of chemistry or physics but whose functioning can hardly be accounted for by them alone.[20] The argument is sometimes put in terms of emergent properties — that as systems become more complex they exhibit forms of behavior that could never have been predicted on the basis of the system components.[21] Thus, new properties of molecular systems emerge out of the properties of the component atoms but are not additive or subtractive results of them. Knowing the molecular properties, one can see how they develop from the properties of atoms, but on the basis of the atomic properties alone, one could never have predicted how the molecules would behave. Similarly, it is suggested that consciousness emerges unpredictably but naturally out of a sufficiently complex nervous system. Presumably someday one may explain consciousness in terms of the working of the nervous system but undoubtedly without being able to show solely from the properties of the separate components of the system that the combination must inevitably lead to consciousness. Such arguments do not challenge the ability of science to ask questions about the natural world; they do, however, suggest limitations on the kind of answers that ultimately can be obtained.

Still another kind of attack on the unbridled claims that scientific methodology furnishes a direct, privileged, objective, and final access to the true conditions of the natural world is made by philosophers and historians of science in the countertradition. Thus, since the work of Popper, it cannot be taken as self-evident that scientific testing of hypotheses unqualifiedly verifies those hypotheses. Scientific experiments will disprove, never prove; only that hypothesis is true that has not yet been disproved. The debate between the most extreme paradigm-relativists, who would give scientific knowledge no truth value at all, and the scientific realists, who would assert that such knowledge is indeed true and of the real world, that debate is likely to remain long unresolved. Nonetheless, it would seem clear that there is a large degree of paradigm dependence in scientific matters — that is to say, that scientific findings are findings only with respect to the context in which they occur. Such a position should come as no real surprise, for it is but a reformulation of the commonplace that scientists, like ordinary folk, tend to find what they are looking for. In the *Origin of Species* Darwin offers several instances of precisely this effect. "I have seen it gravely remarked," he says, "that it was most fortunate that the strawberry began to vary just when gardeners began to attend to this plant."[22] And again, "Authors sometimes argue in a circle when they state that important organs never vary; for these same authors practically rank those parts as important (as some few naturalists have honestly confessed) which do not vary; and, under this point of view, no instance will ever be found of an important part varying; but under any other point of view many instances assuredly can be given."[23]

One need not accede to claims that, since paradigms are incommensurable, all paradigms are equivalent, are within their own terms equally true. After all, scientists do reach consensus, do decide between competing paradigms, do achieve working agreements as to how their own corner of the universe is constituted. Such agreements are provisional — they do not have the truth status of geometric propositions or conclusions deductively arrived at — but one need not assert that they are mere constructs, purely abstract formulations. Indeed, they are rooted in scientific experience (though that experience is itself not unmediated). Experiments work ("the bombs do go off," as one of my humanist friends puts it); and in working, they ensure that only those hypotheses that predict they will work are tenable. In this sense, of course, science always remains in touch with the real. But the favored hypothesis of the moment is not carved in stone to be worshiped by succeeding generations of scientists.

In many more ways than is commonly believed, then, the methodology of science — what the scientist does — is subject to difficulties and constraints of procedural, theoretical, and conceptual nature. To these I would add linguistic constraints. It is a central part of my argument that the entire scientific enterprise is in large measure determined by the language in which it is formulated. In one sense this is simply an extension of the point of Kuhn and Feyerabend to assert that the scientist's work is determined not by the paradigm alone (if one could divorce the paradigm from its language) but by the language-formulation of the paradigm.

Since many who have had no practical experience with scientific work will be somewhat skeptical that the scientists' language shapes what they do, let me quote from Michael Polanyi (himself a working scientist of distinction before he turned his attention largely to philosophical problems):

> An illustration . . . may exhibit [the] dual movement of comprehension in learning a [scientific] language. Think of a medical student attending a course in the X-ray diagnosis of pulmonary diseases. He watches in a darkened room shadowy traces on a fluorescent screen placed against a patient's chest, and hears the radiologist commenting to his assistants, in technical language, on the significant features of these

shadows. At first the student is completely puzzled. For he can see in the X-ray picture of a chest only the shadows of the heart and the ribs, with a few spidery blotches between them. The experts seem to be romancing about figments of their imagination; he can see nothing that they are talking about. Then as he goes on listening for a few weeks, looking carefully at ever new pictures of different cases, a tentative understanding will dawn on him; he will gradually forget about the ribs and begin to see the lungs. And eventually, if he perseveres intelligently, a rich panorama of significant details will be revealed to him: of physiological variations and pathological changes, of scars, of chronic infections and signs of acute disease. He has entered a new world. He still sees only a fraction of what the experts can see, but the pictures are definitely making sense now and so do most of the comments made on them. . . . Thus, at the very moment when he has learned the language of pulmonary radiology, the student will also have learned to understand pulmonary radiograms. The two can only happen together. Both halves of the problem set to us by an unintelligible text, referring to an unintelligible subject, guide our efforts to solve them, and they are solved eventually together by discovering a conception which comprises a joint understanding of both the words and the things.[24]

The point so clearly demonstrated here by Polanyi is that the language of science is an inescapable part of the methodology of science, that the two go together hand in hand, that the language not merely describes what the scientist does but actually helps determine it.

The relationship of the scientific paradigm and its language is a reciprocal one: the language shapes the paradigm, and the paradigm shapes the language. What the words mean is governed by how they are used. The same words have different meanings for scientists operating within different conceptual frameworks. The atom of Lucretius is not the atom of Dalton; the atom of Dalton is not the atom of Rutherford; and the atom of Rutherford is not that of Bohr. Even at the same moment in time, the physicist's atom is not the chemist's atom or the biologist's. What scientists mean when they talk is of course determined by what they say, but one cannot understand what they say without knowing what they mean. This is why learning a science and learning the current language of that science go hand in hand. This is also why scientists are so uninterested in the historical documents of their sciences; those documents are written in languages the scientists no longer speak.

5

This argument has rendered moot any challenge to the third of the basic assumptions implied in a representation theory of scientific discourse, namely, that having come to know the natural world through their work, scientists now translate that knowledge into language-representations. In fact, everything in their conceptual formulation of the real world, as in their methodological approach to that world, is already organized by means of language. Scientists cannot finally turn to language to transcribe what their language has already wrought.

To be sure, at some stage in scientists' work a writing down (or writing up) occurs; they prepare, finally, written documents, scientific papers or reports, which—can one still say it?—"represent" their findings. Yet the specific language in such a paper does not arise de novo when scientists come to write; much of it is already present in posse in everything they think about their work, and indeed some of it will exist in esse, on paper, in the form of notes, notebook entries, drafts, and so on. Indeed, as historian Frederic L. Holmes has found in his studies of Lavoisier's notebooks and preliminary manuscript drafts, the preparation of such notes and drafts itself influences scientists' thinking about their research programs and helps shape their course.[25]

But can one consider such a document, in any sense of the word, a *representation*? Yes, if by representation one means "a specific formulation of what the scientists in question *conceive* they have discovered in their work." Insomuch as the scientists' world is conceivable to them only within their own conceptual framework, it follows that any representation of the real world must be contingent upon that context. The mirror that scientists hold up to nature is the mirror their science has devised. One must not think that the real world of the scientist exists "out there," like Dr. Johnson's stone, waiting to be kicked to make its presence felt or sitting to have its portrait painted by the scientist's words.

But why should one wish to retain for scientific discourse any sense of representation at all? Simply because the scientist does not work in a void. I do not argue that scientific discourse is relevant only to itself. Polanyi's student does not learn just the language of pulmonary radiology; he learns the science of pulmonary radiology. In pointing out that the two interpenetrate, Polanyi does not claim that pulmonary radiology does not exist, that there is only its language. Similarly, although I insist that scientists' papers (formulated in writing) do not stand over and against their work (accomplished as nonwriting), I do not claim that their work does not exist, that only the papers are what matters. To say that the work is itself conceived in language does not make that work go away. The scientists have done something; they have results — understood in language — and when they write the paper, they report that something, represent those results in a specific formulation, a coded message, a series of signs, which (they hope) conveys their view of what they have accomplished to someone else who shares their language as well as their sense of what that language conveys.

Traditional science, then, has a view of the representational character of its discourse that must be challenged. Such representation, I argue, is not, as the traditional view would hold, a verbal image of an external, pre-existent real but rather a conventionalized formulation of a contextualized, conceptualized "real," a re-presentation of a concept, not a representation of a real. Such a formulation seems very far from the representation theory of conventional literary discourse with its emphasis on mimesis, the mirroring by literature of the world. To the important question of the comparison of scientific and literary representation I will return, but first we must see more precisely how this altered version of scientific representation accords with the actual writings of scientists in their work.

6

Much of this discussion of scientific representation has focused on the importance to their enterprise of scientists' recording of their activity.[26] Let us first consider, then, the following brief, not untypical account of a routine experimental operation gleaned from a scientific paper. (The paper is one of which I was coauthor in my years as a chemist.) The procedure described is the final step (chemically a dehydrogenation) in the synthesis of a chemical compound presumed to be identical with one obtained by degradation of a natural alkaloid, atisine. The purpose of the work is to verify that presumption.

> A sample of the . . . material [obtained in the previous step] (262 mg) was treated with 100 mg of 10% palladium-on-carbon [catalyst] at 225–235° for 45 minutes. After cooling, the material was taken up in hot ligroin [solvent], filtered to remove catalyst, and concentrated. On standing there was obtained 121 mg (55% of theoretical) of crystals, m.p. 74.5–82.5°. Recrystallization from ligroin gave an analytical sample, m.p. 83.5–85°. A mixture with an authentic sample from the de-

hydrogenation of atisine showed m.p. 83.5–85°. The infrared and ultraviolet absorption spectra were identical with those of the material from atisine.[27]

Although this passage is likely to read to the uninitiated like pure technical jargon at best, its meaning is rather easily teased out. What is described are (1) the catalytic dehydrogenation step, (2) the isolation and purification of the synthetic material produced, and (3) the confirmation of the identity of this material with that from atisine by mixture melting point (no change observed) and by comparison of two types of light absorption spectra obtained from the two materials. Also present in the paper for the reader's inspection, but not reproduced here, are one pair of spectra, and analytical data to confirm the elemental composition of the synthetic material and of two so-called derivatives (prepared as a further confirmation of identity).

The lay reader of this passage is likely to be struck by the paucity of methodological detail. How is the material "treated," "taken up," "filtered," "concentrated," and "recrystallized"? How are the melting points obtained? How are the spectra prepared? But, of course, to the chemist these are (or were in my period as a working chemist) routine operations, carried out dozens of times a day and described somewhere, in a handbook perhaps (certainly in student laboratory manuals), but hardly appropriately presented in a scientific paper.

The traditional version of scientific representation would label this a "true" representation of what I actually did in S. William Pelletier's laboratory — more of a blueprint, perhaps, or a schematic drawing than a photograph, but nonetheless a kind of one-for-one, step-by-step, verbal simulation of the actions I had carried out. In this view, what we have are two distinct things, the work actually done and the account of it in the scientific paper, a kind of mirror image of the real thing existing separately and independently of it. But that judgment must be qualified. Indeed, both sides of the equation, the representation and the represented, are alike embedded in preexisting concepts and linguistic formulations. The laboratory activities, themselves not unproblematic, and the account of those activities are both determined in some measure by the intellectual framework in which they reside.

Let us first note evidence of the kind of generally unspoken experimental uncertainty that always plagues science. Most notable, here, is the fact that the experimental procedure itself led to only 55 percent of the desired product. As it happens, this is not an unexpected outcome of a chemical procedure that has not been carefully worked out to yield an optimal result. But it does leave the question of the remaining material. What happened to it? The chemist will immediately think of likely possibilities, unchanged starting material perhaps and side products such as might result from partial dehydrogenation. But if other products may result, how does the chemist know the main product is the desired one? In this case, the product obtained from the natural material had already been all but certainly identified, so that there was no real need to repeat this work on the fully synthetic material if the two were shown by other means to be identical. To the chemist this slight equivocation is not a serious concern.

The identification here depends largely on the melting point evidence, and I can still remember, some thirty years later, the kinds of uncertainties involved in taking melting points — variations induced by change in the rate of heating, difficulties involved with softening of crystals before true melting, unsureness over the moment of initial appearance of liquid or the final disappearance of crystals. Standardization of technique goes a very long way toward overcoming all these problems, and I remember also the efforts we made in the laboratory to ensure standard, repeatable results and the resulting confidence we felt in our work. I have no reason now to suppose that changing standards of scientific performance would call those results into question. I mention these matters only because they are an inescapable part of science and one that the rhetoric of science traditionally suppresses.

The central problem in this scientific effort is the confirmation of identity of two materials, one derived from a natural product, the other fully synthetic. Everything depends upon what one thinks will provide that confirmation. In this case what is taken to be suitable evidence is varied: analytical data, coincidence of spectra, and apparent identity of derivatives, besides the all-important melting point evidence. Unspecified assumptions go something like this: crystalline compounds identified as pure usually have specific, sharp melting points; mixtures of such compounds typically have broad melting ranges, often lower than the narrower melting points of the pure materials. Thus, if two samples of crystalline material, each with the same sharp melting point, are mixed and the melting point of the mixture remains sharp and undepressed, the two materials are assumed, as in the present case, to be the same. But it is only in the context of such assumptions that the work performed in the laboratory constitutes a confirmation of identity of the two materials.

The work here also exists in a larger context. ("Context" may avoid the philosophical baggage associated with "paradigm" or "framework.") This larger context includes the notion of complete identification of natural materials by two distinct routes, analytic and synthetic; both are considered necessary if identification is to be achieved. Thus Newton is at great pains in the *Opticks* to confirm the identity of white light as a mixture of colored lights not only by splitting (analyzing) white light into its component colored "rays" but also by recombining (synthesizing) the separate, colored rays to reproduce white light.[28] In our work, we were concerned not with the natural material itself, atisine, but with a degradation product from it; ultimately the work on atisine would be complete only when the structure of atisine itself had been confirmed both by degradation and by synthesis (and again one must apply the standards of verification of identity to the two materials).

Further, this work must be situated in the context of an ongoing program of chemical identification and synthesis of biological materials, part of the long story of the assault of chemistry on vitalism. To the chemist the watershed event in this struggle is often taken to be the synthesis in 1828 by Friedrich Wöhler of urea, a substance previously thought to be producible only by the action of a living organism. This landmark event must be somewhat qualified, however, because Wöhler had prepared his urea from ammonia and cyanic acid, then derived from organic substances.[29] The first unqualified synthesis of a purely organic substance from entirely inorganic sources is more precisely said to be that of acetic acid in 1844. Today chemists are convinced that there is no substance in any living organism which in principle they could not produce from scratch in the laboratory (although some substances might be so enormously complex that nothing could justify the years of work that would be involved).

For the organic chemist, the connotations of "synthetic" and "natural" are not the same as those for the layman. The chemist may well prefer to work with the synthetic version of a given material, rather than one from a natural source, because the synthetic material lies more fully under control; it can be reproduced by standard procedures and obtained in conditions of verifiable purity. For the organic chemist the sobriquet "synthetic" may be an accolade—it sings of the skill and capability of the scientist— not an opprobrium. To the ordinary person, "synthetic" may imply cheap and shoddy, may stand for the substitute rather than the real thing.

Organic chemists are likely to be puzzled by those who prefer natural vitamins to synthetic ones. To them the character of the material is determined by its chemical identity; the natural and synthetic materials are in fact precisely the same. (They are aware that minute impurities, possibly different impurities owing to the variations in methods of preparation, may be present, but this thought they will in all likelihood suppress.) They are constantly troubled by talk of chemical additives and chemical poisons, when they know that every substance is, in fact, chemical. The natural materials of the world are as chemical as the additives added to them. Nor do they equate "chemical" with "poisonous," for some substances of purely natural origin are more poisonous than any the chemist has developed.

Typically, working organic chemists do not conduct their experiments at the level of individual molecules, but their thinking about the materials they work with in macromolecular amounts is largely in terms of the underlying molecular structure. The crystals whose melting points they determine are present to the senses as they are manipulated, but they are likely to seem the mere gross embodiment of the particular molecular species they represent. The molecular identity exists as a kind of Platonic Idea behind the physical material. It is this molecular Idea that to the chemist determines the essential nature of the material. It is not the physical form that is the essence of things — grinding crystals into a powder or melting them does not change their chemical identity. Nor is it the origin — the vitamin C from the chemist's test tube is the same as the vitamin C extracted from rose hips. The purer the chemist's compounds are, the more likely they are to be in the form of beautifully shaped crystals or limpidly clear liquids, and the more they seem to be the embodiment of the molecular Ideas. To the chemist the smelly tinctures and brown powders of the back-to-nature folk are too impure, too variable in content, too contaminated, to be taken seriously.

One need not suppose that the chemist who reads the short account of the synthesis of the atisine product consciously thinks any such thoughts as laid out here. But surely that account does not make sense in any other context. The procedural description represents (depicts) a real, a valid procedure only to someone who shares this particular notion of what the chemistry of natural products is all about. Neither the laboratory manipulations nor the brief, shorthand account of them can have any meaning outside of some such context. Further, I would urge, without attempting to establish the point, that accounts of scientific procedures always have this quality, that the account represents the procedure only within the conceptual world in which both are situated.

7

The physical descriptions scientists include in their writing are more likely on the face of things to seem to be representations than are the accounts of the experimental procedures. But if the revised version of representation theory is correct, descriptive representation is subject to the same kind of unspoken contextual qualification as procedural representation.

To test this judgment, let us examine a brief excerpt from an early paper by the Nobel Prize-winning geneticist H. J. Muller. The paper reports and describes a newly discovered mutant fruit fly, along with evidence that locates the mutated gene on a chromosome on which such mutations had not previously been found. Here is the description of the physical manifestation, the "character," of the mutation as it appears in the affected flies:

> The new character is a recessive wing and leg abnormality, the wings being held out from the body but bent backwards near the base, and the metatarsal joint of the legs being frequently greatly shortened and thickened. The wing is also apt to be curved, with the dorsal surface convex, and shortened. The character varies somewhat, but there is very rarely any difficulty in distinguishing it from the normal form, unless the flies have been raised in very dry bottles. Drought therefore hinders the manifestation of this character, as it may also, and to a greater degree, in some way hinder the development of the character "abnormal abdomen," a case reported by Morgan.[30]

It is easy enough to read this as representation pure and simple, to see it as simply holding a mirror up to nature. To be sure there are some technical terms, *dorsal* and *metatarsal*, and one must read *recessive* and *character* in the geneticists' sense, but on the whole this is remarkably jargon-free writing—one can almost visualize the wings "held out from the body but bent backwards near the base."

Yet the scientist's role as observer here is completely suppressed. Muller does not tell us how things seem to him, how they look to him, but how they *are*. Further, the uncertainties in his observations, though not hidden, are quite glossed over. "Frequently" and "apt" first hint at the problem, and then he confesses that "the character *varies* somewhat." But, he adds at once, "There is *very rarely* any difficulty distinguishing it from the normal form" (and again a qualification) "unless the flies have been raised in very dry bottles." Yet, again, however, he is reassuring: an analogous situation has previously been reported by Muller's teacher, the founder of

American genetics, Thomas Hunt Morgan. In Muller's work, being able to identify the presence or absence of the "character" is all important because the evidence for locating the mutation on a particular chromosome depends on the distribution during mating experiments of this character with respect to others already known to be caused by mutations on particular chromosomes. I do not here suggest, of course, that Muller's work is scientifically suspect, merely that the rhetoric of representation masks an observational situation that is somewhat less clear-cut than meets the inattentive or uninformed eye.

Further, it must be noted that Muller's description is situated in its own conceptual context as complex as that of Bill Pelletier's and my work with the degradation product from atisine. First, there is the peculiar nature of the geneticist's notion of characters, bundles of physical traits that seem always to appear more or less together, though with varying overall expression and differing emphasis on the particular manifestations (in Muller's "bent wing" character, leg versus wing abnormalities). The features that constitute a character must be read against a background of ever-varying physical traits that characterize the normal state, in reality a kind of blurred and imprecise range, of the physical makeup of the populations of the organism. The situation much resembles that of the physician's "syndrome," a collection of variably expressed symptoms that must stand out and stand together against the equally variable normal state of the human organism. One can easily picture the young geneticist gradually learning to perceive the various normal traits exemplified in a heterogeneous collection of fruit flies and then perceiving various specific characters against this background, much as Polanyi describes the education of the pulmonary radiologist.

The character to the geneticist is the mark in the organism of the state of a particular gene, normal or, in various ways, mutant. Such thinking must inevitably invoke the name of Gregor Mendel and the thought of his experiments with pea plants, reported in the 1860s. What Mendel perceived in his experiments was to provide the key insight for genetics when that science came into being some forty years later, namely, the particulate nature of inheritance. In this view, distinct traits, characters — in Mendel's case, tallness or dwarfness in the plant, yellow or green color in the peas — appear, disappear, and reappear in successive generations according to fixed laws without merging or melioration. Mendel, at least as the folklore of classical genetics would have it, was the first person to look at a living organism and see its form as the summing up of a number of discrete decisions, the realization of a set of alternate impulses, or — to be anachronistic — the setting of a number of switches at positions labeled "on" or "off," "tall" or "dwarf," "yellow" or "green."

Molecular biologists now characterize a gene biochemically as a portion of a strand of DNA, but to the geneticist, certainly the geneticist of Muller's day, the gene is another Platonic Idea, an analogue of the chemist's molecule. The geneticist distinguishes between the genotype, the inherited map of development the organism carries in its genes, and the phenotype, the manifestation or the working out of the genotypic set of directions into the finished product of the living organism. The geneticist looks at the organism and reads as well as possible what is phenotypically significant, what stands out from the ever-changing background as traits, or characters, and then infers the nature of the underlying genotype. The chemist *looks at* the substances in the test tubes but *sees* the molecules they represent. The geneticist *looks at* living organisms — fruitflies, conveniently, for generations of geneticists — but *sees* the interplay of genes.

As molecular biology has developed over the past few decades, it has in some cases traced in exquisite detail the chemical pathways that lead from the genes, the nucleic acid bound up in the chromosomes of the cells, through the enzymes and other proteins they direct the cells to make, into the kinds of gross bodily changes into which the geneticist reads characters. But even when the early geneticists like Muller could only infer that some such pathways must exist, they operated on the assumption that each character was the mark of a simple gene in a particular state — a state that changed when the gene mutated. The biochemist's equivalent of this thinking is the so-called one gene–one enzyme hypothesis, the idea that each gene determines the structure of a particular enzyme or other protein, and that functioning of that protein, wherever it occurs in the organism, makes manifest the state of the gene. Although the geneticist studies the organism for the genetic characters it displays and the molecular biologist examines cellular components and determines the patterns of bases within nucleic acids, the two processes are conceptually comparable.

Thus, the character Professor Muller sees in his mutant fruit flies and describes (represents) in his paper is present in the fruit flies only to someone who "knows" that such characters can be perceived to begin with. The idea of characters, and indeed the language that speaks of characters, is as much a part of what Muller sees as it is of his description. Thus, again, if there is representation in the discourse it is representation only within a self-defined context; outside the context there can be no representation.

And the case here, I argue, again without demonstration, is typical. Scientists must always learn to see what it is they describe, and their descriptions can represent what is seen only within the context of that learned experience.

8

When they examine the real world, scientists draw inferences about it that take several forms. The most interesting of these from the standpoint of representation theory are the models scientists construct, the mathematical, physical, graphic, or verbal simulations of whatever it is the scientist is studying. Thus, engineers make mathematical and graphical models of how liquids or gases flow around obstacles; chemists make physical models of how atoms and molecules are constructed; and psychologists construct verbal models of how people behave under particular circumstances. Models always represent translations of some sort; the model is in one medium, form, or size, and the thing modeled is in another medium, form, or size. Thus, physical structures are reduced to mathematical ones, three-dimensional structures to two-dimensional ones, minute structures or enormously large structures to conveniently sized ones. The model fully reflects only some features of the original, the size ratio of its parts to one another, for example; but it can be manipulated in ways the original cannot, thereby giving information that is (more or less) applicable to the original and unobtainable otherwise. Although the model is often not literally a picture of the thing modeled, it would seem difficult to imagine a clearer instance of scientific representation at work than one finds in model building.

That judgment, however, cannot be allowed to stand precisely as is. There are a number of detailed philosophic and linguistic analyses of the roles of models in science (exemplary are Max Black's *Models and Metaphors* and Mary Hesse's *Models and Analogies in Science*; James Bono offers a recent review and discussion),[31] but science provides its own critique. To begin with, a model can never exactly duplicate, mirror, the original (or it wouldn't be a model), just as looking at a map is not the equivalent of a trip through the countryside. Thus, in a wooden ball-and-stick model of a molecule, the wooden balls are far less easily deformed than atoms, and the sticks are more rigid than interatomic bonds. One can use softer balls and employ springs in place of sticks, but the deformability of the balls will not be the exact equivalent of that of atoms, nor the flexibility of the springs precisely that of bonds. In a sense these are merely technical problems; by solving them with more and more success, one can make the model come closer and closer to the original. But in the final analysis some deviation will always be present, and not having full access to the original, one can never be sure how much.

One can, of course, explain the deviation, put into words one's sense of how well or how badly the model fits the original. In fact, even without the problem of deviation, one is likely to have to explain which aspects of the model are to be taken as corresponding to the original and which are not. Thus, if the wooden balls are colored, one is not to assume they represent colors of atoms, though by an arbitrary code they may indicate which elemental species the atoms are to be taken as belonging to. Therefore, even though the model may not be a linguistic one — may be a physical structure, a drawing, or a set of mathematical equations — it will function as a model only by virtue of an attendant enabling structure of language.

But that "enabling structure of language" extends into the original as well as the model. There is no a priori original "out there," known independently of the conceptual framework utilized in modeling it. The very notions of atomic dimensions and atomic bonds are comprehensible only in terms of the way scientists have come to study molecular structures. They don't "know" any "real" atoms, independently of how they study atoms and how they talk about them. The notion of an ultimate original and a contrived model, a true object and a fabricated image, must give way to a view in which both the original and the model are seen to have elements of the construct about them. The original is a concept; what is being modeled is itself a model, an image of reality — indeed, the scientist's world is all model.

To test this view of scientific modeling, let us briefly examine another paper by Muller. This paper, which defends a particular model of the arrangement of genes ("factors of heredity"), appears at first sight to contradict nearly all of what has just been said. Entitled, "Are the Factors of Heredity Arranged in a Line?" the paper begins with the following paragraph:

> In the February (1919) number of the *Proceedings of the National Academy of Sciences*, Professor Castle states that he has "shown that the arrangement of the genes in the sex-chromosome of *Drosophila ampelophila* is probably not linear, and a method has been developed for constructing a model of the experimentally determined linkage relationships." This declaration is so widely at variance with the conclu-

sions jointly agreed on by all *Drosophila* workers, that the arguments or assumptions which it involves would seem to call for careful examination. It may be stated at the outset that the principle upon which Professor Castle constructs his models appears exceedingly direct and simple — it is merely to make a figure such that the distances between all the points represented on it are exactly proportional to the frequencies of separation actually found between the respective factors in the most reliable experiments. If this is done, Castle contends, the models will be three-dimensional instead of linear in shape.[32]

In the body of the paper, Muller challenges Castle's model in detail and argues that the proof for the linear model is already established: "The discussion and data given in the original papers supply all the materials necessary for a decision of the matter, at least so far as the germ plasm of *Drosophila* is concerned." He then makes the supplementary point that the genes must be not only arranged in a linear order but physically connected in that fashion. He concludes: "The idea that the genes are bound together in a line, in order of their linkage, by material, solid connections thus remains as the only interpretation which fits the genetic findings."[33]

This seems to present an unambiguous choice between competing models of the genetic material, one of which, it is said, corresponds with (represents) the true situation and one of which does not, just as Galileo asserted against the authority of the church that the Copernican system would seem to be a true model of the solar system whereas the Ptolemaic system would not. The argument is clear-cut and unambiguous, and sixty-five years of subsequent scientific research would probably not reverse the judgment. As early as 1931, subsequent Nobel laureate Barbara McClintock, with Harriet Creighton, showed that in corn the physical changes in the chromosomes during mating experiments correspond to those predicted by the linear arrangement of the genes, as inferred from the kind of evidence used by Muller. And the subsequent isolation and identification of the genetic material as DNA confirms that it is, indeed, "bound together in a line . . . by material, solid connections" (taking as metaphoric, as one must, the assertion that the chemical bonds are "material" and "solid," when they are in fact anything but).

With the scientific judgments one cannot seriously disagree, though one must in other respects qualify the agreement. To begin with, the connection between the model and the original is not simple and must be explained, as I have suggested is usually the case. For the straight line of the model is only metaphorically a straight line in the original (the model, in general, is the scientist's version of the poet's metaphor) just as the "circularity" of the circulation of the blood is only metaphorically a circle. Muller provides a footnote of explanation:

> The fact that the *geometrical* line which represents the linkages of the factors should be taken as straight does not imply that the supposed *physical* line in which the factors lie is straight. So long as the factors lie in any kind of physical line at all, then, if their linkages are determined, in some way, by their distances as measured *along* this line, these linkages should be representable on the basis of a straight geometrical map, inasmuch as all distances taken *along* a curved line must have the same interrelationships as distances in a straight line. Hence the curving of the chromosome filament is a matter entirely aside from the issue here involved, since the separation frequencies of the factors in the supposed filament are not conceived of as dependent upon their direct distances from each other but rather upon their distances along this filament. Thus the filament may, for these purposes, be treated as if it were straight.[34]

What is notable about this explanation is the way in which Muller's conception of the nature of the genetic material influences his formulation of the argument — not merely his choice of model but his view of the original that the model represents. If the model, in Muller's view, is a straight line, the original, the genetic material, is a chromosome filament. But characterizing this material as a "filament" is to give it the character of a model, for whatever the chemical structure would turn out to be, the molecule could only metaphorically be a filament. Indeed, the problematic nature of this filament, in Muller's account, is indicated by the subsequent reference to it as the "supposed filament." In short, the same kind of thinking that conceptualizes the model (the supposed physical line) also conceptualizes the original (the supposed filament).

Our concern is not with any ongoing scientific debate about the validity of the linear model. If, indeed, McClintock's early work helped establish the physical reality of the linear model in certain respects, her subsequent studies, more than those of any other person, have suggested the fluid nature of the genetic material in other respects, with some genes movable almost ad libitum. But, as Muller asserts, for "all *Drosophila* workers" of the 1920s the linear model is surely a better representation of the genetic material than a three-dimensional model would be. (One can make this judgment in the same way that one accepts Galileo's championing of the Copernican over the Ptolemaic representation of the solar system — knowing, however, that Einstein's relativistic representation is better than either in that it accounts for the motion of the perihelion of Mercury, the steady shift of its orbital position closest to the sun.)

What must be challenged is any notion that the model represents a true picture — even, in this case, a kind of schematic diagram — of a reality independent of the framework in which the reality is approached and the model constructed. Muller himself seems to have no such illusion. In his opening he refers to the "conclusions jointly agreed on by all *Drosophila* workers," affirming — in anticipation of the position of the countertraditional sociologists — that what is at stake is the collective judgment of the community of geneticists (with whom Muller identifies himself), that it is they who will adjudicate between the two views and thereby determine wherein lies the "truth." Further, in his concluding sentence, Muller carefully specifies that the linear model is "the only interpretation that fits the genetic findings," not, as one might anticipate, "fits the facts"; nor does he refer at any point to the true structure of the chromosomal material. To say that the model is the only one consonant with the genetic findings is immediately to place the model within the geneticist's world (precisely the qualification I would make), to situate it among the entities geneticists view through their own spectacles, manipulate with their instruments, and describe with their language. It is only within this world that the claim can legitimately be made that the straight-line model *represents* the chromosome filament.

❡

Scientists use models as one way to express the inferences they draw about the natural world, as their work seems to them to reveal it, a way that is particularly easy to characterize as representation. But this is not the only kind of inference scientists draw; there remain the specific, factual judgments scientists make about the particular materials they work with. Are these judgments subject to the same kind of contextual qualification required by other varieties of scientific representation? Surely, yes. Thus, when Bill Pelletier and I conclude that the substance we have synthesized is "identical with an authentic sample from atisine" and add that "the identification of this base provides the first evidence establishing the position of the nitrogen atom in the atisine skeleton,"[35] we are indeed representing something specific we believe true about the atisine molecule, but sensibly so only within the context earlier delineated. Similarly, when

Muller concludes of his *Drosophila* bent-wing mutant that "the gene for bent wings segregates independently of the sex-linked group of genes and of the two hitherto known non-sex-linked groups; accordingly, the genes of *Drosophila* now fall into four divisions, one sex-linked, corresponding to the x-chromosome, and three non-sex-linked, corresponding to the three pairs of autosomes,"[36] he too is producing in his inference a representation, but only of what his work can be taken to signify within the context of *Drosophila* genetics.

Ultimately scientists come to those large generalizations they call laws, exemplified, let us say, by Newton's first law of motion and the second law of thermodynamics. (Knowing the latter is, for C. P. Snow, the litmus test of scientific literacy.)[37] Such laws in representing the general behavior of things reflect a myriad of particular instances, much as the Pythagorean theorem is a general truth about every Euclidean right triangle in a plane (though verification of these two kinds of general truths is very different). One need not quarrel with the notion that the general law *represents* the individual particulars, but one must, nonetheless, extend the qualification of contextuality even to these grand formulations.

Newton's first law — which states, roughly, that a body remains at rest or in constant motion in a straight line unless acted upon by a force — clearly is operative within the Newtonian universe but not within the universe described by Einstein. Its references to "rest" and "motion" must be understood in terms of the rigid, absolute framework of a transcendent time and space (likened here earlier to a proscenium stage), the very existence of which the Einsteinian view denies. No one says, of course, that Newton's law was valid — was a true picture of the universe — until Einstein overthrew it; rather it is said that Newton's law represents a general state of affairs comprehensible within the context of Newtonian science.

The situation is similar, though not so clear-cut, with the second law of thermodynamics, which has not obviously been scientifically superseded, or at least limited in its range of applicability, as has Newton's law. The second law is variously formulated. It states that one cannot operate a heat-cycle engine that produces an equivalent amount of work from the heat absorbed from a body at constant temperature; some energy is inevitably lost in the process. This law has numerous consequences of considerable significance. One is that it disallows the perpetual motion machine. (The second law is what makes scientists reject without even examining them the countless claims of inventors around the world to have produced such devices.) More significantly, however, it asserts that the entropy, the measure of disorder, of the universe must constantly increase, that the universe is drifting inevitably into ultimate chaos, meaninglessness — a notion with profound philosophic consequences.[38]

It is easy to think of instances that seem to violate the second law, such as the spontaneous crystallization of a cooling liquid. Surely the crystalline mass is more highly ordered, more entropy-poor, than the antecedent liquid. But the answer is that in thinking so one has drawn one's boundaries too narrowly: when crystallizing, the liquid gives off heat to its surroundings, which then become correspondingly more entropy-rich. Today, however, it is argued by some that there are natural domains, such as the intellectual and social spheres, in which the second law cannot be made to hold even by the redrawing of boundary lines, that a society can, in effect, increase its store of organized knowledge or its ordered social existence without an attendant and compensatory increase of disorder elsewhere.[39] Most scientists today, however, would probably not accept any such limitation of the universal validity of the second law of thermodynamics, just as a century ago any scientific challenge to Newton's laws would have been unthinkable. But contextually this is of little concern. Within their own contexts both laws are equally representative of the behavior of things. That the context in which the second law is a valid representation happens to be shared by most scientists working today is another matter.

A modern instance of the formulation of a new general law is the promulgation and labeling by Sir Francis Crick of the "central dogma" of molecular biology.[40] (James Watson asserts in *The Double Helix* that the idea essentially was his.)[41] What the central dogma says is that genetic information is maintained in DNA in the nuclei of cells, transcribed into messenger RNA molecules, and then transported outside the cell nucleus where it is translated (via the RNA templates) into protein molecules. The nuclear DNA then is a kind of library stacks, with the messenger RNA molecules acting like library pages, photocopying portions of the DNA texts and carrying them out into the library proper where they are put to work. Once the principle is established of a correspondence between DNA structure and protein structures (those of active enzymes, say), the concept of a genetic code emerges. And, indeed, a few years after the statement of the central dogma, when the genetic code was deciphered, it was found that specific sequences of bases in the DNA molecule cause the incorporation of specific amino acids into corresponding positions in protein molecules. Much of the subsequent development of molecular biology, including the discovery of techniques for gene manipulation, so-called genetic engineering, derives ultimately from the basic notion that the information flow is from DNA to RNA to protein. Hence it is no exaggeration to assert that the central dogma is indeed central to the science of molecular biology.

Equally appropriate, in a different way, is Crick's choice of the term dogma, considering the special character of the molecular biology movement in the 1950s. Clearly the term is intended with some irony — irony that is presumably directed at those vitalists who, often on religious grounds, proclaim the special, sacred character of the living organism, particularly the human being. But materialistic science is not without its own religious overtones. The very idea of "natural laws" seems to presuppose a lawgiver, and the forerunners of the modern scientist often believed they were reading God's will writ in nature just as it was inscribed in God's other book, the Bible. The molecular biologists themselves, who built their professional lives around the central dogma, behaved much like the religious true believers they were likely to revile. They had their own set of beliefs, most notably that the complex laws of biology could be reduced to a few simple molecular interactions. The movement even had its John the Baptist in the person of Erwin Schrödinger, of quantum mechanics fame, whose book *What Is Life?* first called to public attention the messiah of the new movement, Max Delbrück.[42] A physicist turned virologist, Delbrück had, in fact, taken up the genetic information problem in the expectation that it would reveal some entirely new type of natural law.[43] What the ingenuity of the molecular biologists and the power of their reductive method revealed, however, was that the old laws of nature, abetted by the central dogma and the genetic code, were enough to explain how stored genetic information could be translated into physiological systems by way of active proteins. Still, as it swept on to one scientific triumph after another, molecular biology acquired something of the air of a crusade. United in their unrelenting pursuit of mechanistic truth, its members marched ahead waving their banner, with its emblem of the double helix, proclaiming their motto of the central dogma and shouting that they had discovered the secret of life.

In retrospect, the molecular biology crusade looks somewhat quixotic. This is not to denigrate the scientific accomplishments of the molecular biologists but merely to note some of the sobering concomitants of those accomplishments and to question some of the more grandiose philosophical claims. To begin with there is that troubling stepchild of molecular biology, genetic engineering. (One cannot quite avoid the obvious allusion to Frankenstein's monster.) That human beings can now intervene directly to alter their own genetic makeup surely poses humankind its greatest potential threat since the development of the atomic bomb. (Is it some final irony that mechanistic molecular biologists in their antivitalistic crusade should themselves acquire the power long attributed to the gods?) But more than this, biologists proper have now stepped forward to remind us all that, vitalism aside, there is more to life than the movements of molecules in cells.[44] Biology has its own domain, its own scientific problems, and discovers its own laws, which are not the laws of chemistry or physics. Growth, development, and behavior may in time find molecular explanations, as genetics now has, but those explanations will not even touch on those aspects of the problems that are of biological importance. The central dogma, the double helix, and the genetic code are not the secret of life; they are only the chemistry of genetics.

Even the central dogma itself is now, alas, not absolute truth. Like all scientific laws it achieves its generality by idealizing. So the central dogma too has its exceptions. Many viruses, including viruses of interest because of their role in carcinogenesis and AIDS or their utilization in genetic engineering, circumvent the central dogma by carrying their genetic information as RNA and passing that information on to DNA, thereby reversing the direction of transmission the central dogma posits. It now even seems that many organisms, by various contrivances, employ this same reverse pathway to switch genetic information, thereby causing major physical changes and shortcutting the Darwinian mode of evolutionary alteration. Thus, the central dogma is only a simple scientific law after all, true enough in the domain in which it was enunciated, explaining the facts it was intended to explain, but failing as transcendent truth. And the molecular biologists who proclaimed it are not prophets but merely great scientists, like Newton or Clausius (usually credited with first enunciating the second law of thermodynamics). Like them, the molecular biologists have found a "truth" in nature, but a "truth" that is embedded in their science and that takes on a different appearance when that science turns a corner and views the "truth" from a new perspective.

10

As these examples of scientific discourse have shown, they may be characterized as representational, although one must strongly qualify one's sense of what such representation must entail. To do so, one challenges the notions that what is represented is, in an absolute sense, both real and known, and that the act of representation is a simple matter of image making or replication. To say that in their discourse scientists represent the world they are studying can only mean representation of the world as the scientists conceive it, within their own scientific frame of reference, and only as it is revealed to them through their methodology (itself constrained and interpreted within their frame of reference). Further, it must mean that that representation is presented by the conventionalized practices of scientific discourse. If, then, scientists in their writing hold a mirror up to nature, that mirror is perforce an imperfect one.

The judgment that scientific discourse is in this fashion representational does not entail (as literary critics have largely insisted and scientists largely agreed) the further judgment that it is exclusively or even chiefly so. What else scientific writing might or might not be, we will consider in subsequent chapters. First, however, we must compare the scientific uses of representation, properly understood, with the literary uses.

To begin with, the current eclipse of representation theory in literary critical circles, noted above, does not imply that the notion that the literary artist *represents* is entirely passé. To begin with, the modernist and postmodernist literary voices are not the only ones heard in the twentieth century. Much premodernist literature is still read and not only in academia, and a realist movement of sorts has persisted throughout the century. Also, the postmodern literature that is emerging contains its own strain of neo-realism.[45] But even modernist literature itself could not entirely abandon representation as one of its functions: everything that passes for literature comes to us as experience. Life comes to us an experience. If the one does not relate to the other, what, one might ask, is the point of it?

Furthermore, though it may deemphasize representation as a function of literature, not all modern criticism would insist that representation is not one of the things that literature does.[46] For example, the critical formulation of Roman Jakobson situates literature among other varieties of discourse by singling out from among six "universal" functions of language, one, the "poetic" function, as distinctive of literature, but Jakobson's formulation does not deny to literature the other functions, including what he calls the "referential."[47] Much twentieth century criticism, however, sees little point in focusing on the representational aspects of literary language. That is not to say that it denies that such aspects exist altogether; rather, it is a matter of not remarking what is unremarkable, of taking for granted what is part of the given background.

But what does our analysis of scientific representation reveal about how the two modes of representation, scientific and literary, compare? To begin with, as already noted, traditional scientists are not likely to see their variety of representation as illusionistic, as the poets or the novelists are likely to see theirs. Nor, indeed, are scientists likely to see their writings as fictive, nor as meliorative or realistic, as, variously, their literary counterparts have seen theirs.

As to illusionism, the traditional scientist conceives scientific writing to be merely read, not experienced, not participated in as a lived event. To be sure, one must perceive the kind of responsive chord the scientist's language will evoke in its true readers, the few specialists who can share and understand the original experience. The cryptic phrases of scientists ("the material was taken up in hot ligroin"; "the wings being held out from the body but bent backward near the base") tell more of their real experience to their fellow practitioners than outsiders can ever infer. It is true that scientific writing will be at its least illusionistic when it comes to drawing inferences and enunciating general laws, but literature, too, creates the least illusion when it is most general — Dr. Johnson (the poet should not "number the streaks on the tulip")[48] notwithstanding. Still, as our examination shows, there is a significant difference here. The representations of scientists do not attempt to re-create the world of sensory experience itself. Scientists *will* take the trouble to "number the streaks on the tulip" ("121 mg of crystals . . . , m. p. 74.5–82.5°"), but they will not seek to — as Dr. Johnson goes on to advise the poet — depict "such prominent and striking features as recall the original to every mind."[49] It is the poet's task to provide what Eliot calls the "objective correlative,"[50] that telling detail that conveys the heart of the poet's experience, that makes the readers seem to experience it themselves. But it is the scientists' job to give the readers the blueprint by which they could actually construct a similar experience for themselves.

Although much of literature is fictive — "made up," in childhood parlance — at the same time much of what passes for fiction is autobiographical. Writers, it is commonly said, almost invariably write out of their own experience. In addition, whole genres — the essay, biography — deliberately eschew fictionality without stepping beyond the pale of literature. Hence, one can hardly use fictiveness as a defining character of literary representation. Nor, on the other hand, in spite of the traditional view, can one quite expunge from scientific writing the "taint" of fictiveness, for, if nothing else, scientists frequently minimize or deemphasize the uncertainties and imprecision that cloud their methods. I will return to this controversial assertion when I point out that the scientist's paper does not even pretend to be a true account of everything that has transpired in the laboratory: what scientists do is select from their experience what they are to report. This is, of course, not unlike what poets do when they come to make their poems. But, again, if the distinction must be blurred, it cannot be abandoned. However much scientists might shape their experience for their presentations there are limits beyond which they do not go (short of chicanery). The events they report are (assuming their honesty) never simply created to make their point, as the poet's poetized events may be. And all literature, even the literature of fact — the "factual novel" — proclaims some mark of fictiveness, of contrivance, of artifice, which every scientific report, however formalized and schematicized, denies.

Even when literature indulges its fictive bent, however, it seeks to say something of some general significance. Though it would no longer adopt the Aristotelian formula of representing the general and the probable or heed the neoclassical call to represent the ideal, yet literature cannot finally disdain to make its particulars signify beyond themselves. Science, too, traditionally or counter-traditionally viewed, aims at the general. Its laws, as we have seen, are avowedly so. And those laws indeed describe probabilities. Even the bizarre indeterminacies of quantum mechanics are probabilistic, predicting what is likely to happen (without really explaining how or why it happens). Traditional science would, as I have noted, deny that it seeks to represent the ideal rather than the true. Scientific laws, however, like the ideal gas laws, always represent how things would go if only the world were a simpler, cleaner, "better" place. Nobody really expects our cluttered, chaotic, messy world to follow the ideal laws of science, any more than one would expect it to follow the formal strictures of the neoclassical drama. In this respect, scientific and literary representation are indeed comparable. But, as we have observed, the scientific law is expressed in abstract terms, whereas the larger truths that literature finds are exemplified in specific and telling instances. If literature's favored mode of expression is the Hegelian "concrete universal,"[51] then science's must be the "abstract universal," the formalized statement of the general truth.

Even as it generalizes, however, literature aims to be, in some sense at least, realistic, true to life. If, in retrospect, certain literary periods seem more prone to idealization than to realistic representation, it is unlikely that the notion of being "faithful to life" is ever entirely abandoned. Even the art of the French neoclassical stage, often taken to be the high point of neoclassical artificiality, was viewed by its audience, according to Erich

Auerbach, as "not only masterly and overpoweringly effective but also reasonable, in accord with common sense, natural, and probable."[52] Yet realistic literary representations are achieved only by means of conventions, social conventions that govern our notions of what the world itself is really like and artistic conventions that determine how it is to be realistically portrayed — conventions in both cases that are, as we have seen, periodically changing ones.

Science, however, in the traditional view, disdains to seem realistic because it is simply true. Its views of the world are thought to be not matters of convention but, again, of truth; and its modes of representation are supposed to be not guided by convention but determined solely by the facts to be recorded. Such judgments the countertradition would challenge. Indeed, the conclusion that the findings of science are context-dependent is surely the counterpart of saying that literary representation is dependent on social convention. What the scientist does and finds in the world, like what the poet does and finds, is determined in large part by (changing) anticipations and expectations. As to the scientist's modes of representation, the patterns of discourse employed, these, too, like the poet's, are (as we have seen, and contra tradition) conventional and presumably matters of changing convention.

The scientist's primary mode of representation, modelmaking, has been likened — here and frequently elsewhere — to the poet's use of metaphor. In both cases a presumed reality, too tenuous, too complex, too strange to be represented directly is presented as something else: "love" is a "rose"; an "atom" is a "miniature solar system." The scientists' activity of modeling, which purports to produce simply a more convenient or more understandable likeness of the inconvenient and incomprehensible world extends into the very act of conceiving that world. All the scientists' attempts to make the world comprehensible must be via models; there is no other way to bring the world into mind. What is represented can be only represented, not known by some direct perception. The poet too employs metaphors, not as decoration, not as fancy ways of saying something simple, but because there is no other way of telling what is seen. To delineate the ineffable, the poet and the scientist alike can only metaphorize. But in their discourse, the poets, certainly the novelists, do something other than make models of what they perceive: they seek to clothe it as experience, as felt experience. Scientists, however, do not; they create their own alternate version of the world, one they can bring into mind as they cannot the real world beyond. The scientist's vision of the world comes to us as model, as metaphor; the poet's, the novelist's, as experience. Thus, both represent, but they do so in very different ways. The representation of the poet is illusionistic, experiential, and realistic, though fictive; that of the scientist is diagrammatic, generalized, even idealized, though (by its own measure) scrupulously true.

Literary tradition, even as it has variously applied or not applied representation theory to literary discourse, has with singular force applied that theory to the discourse of science. That attribution I do not challenge, though we must, I believe, markedly alter our sense of what scientific representation can mean — just as we have redifferentiated the modes of scientific and literary representation. Thus representation in science is not the simple mirroring that it is so often supposed to be. In effect, the original and the mirror image blur into one another, and indeed, it is only through the image that one "knows" the original. Nor does one "know" either independently of the enabling conventions that permit one to conceive of them.

Finally, both scientists and poets, as part of what they do, represent the world as they currently conceive it, within the context of their experience. Both come to know life in a special way — the scientist through scientific judgment and a knowledge of past science, the poet through poetic sensibility and a command of past poetry. Both, in their writings, with whatever difficulty and in their own different ways, mirror what it is they see in life. The scientist builds a model of it; the poet creates a fictive experience with it. This is what makes science; this is what makes poetry.

CHAPTER THREE

Writing without Expression

THE PROMETHEAN THEFT OF FIRE HAS BECOME A FAMILIAR SYMBOL FOR the scientific endeavor — the wresting of the secrets of nature from the gods and conveying them to humankind to ease its lot. But the traditional image of the scientist-as-writer, an image common both within science and without, is, in contrast, a peculiarly humble and constricted one. Gone are the creativity and daring of the Titan. In their place is the self-effacing toil of the amanuensis, for, unlike poets, who are free to create the world anew as they write of it, scientists must be totally circumspect, must expunge every trace of their own personalities from their work, as they record only what is there. The scientist must view the world through some impersonal ocular device, the spectacles of objectivity, rather than through the eyes of a person. The scientist must weigh the world not in a hand but in a balance; must measure it not with a stride but with a calipers. The Promethean scientist may uncover the secrets of the gods but must whisper them — like someone with an artificial larynx — in a voice devoid of emotion so as not, as the Fiesers put it for their fellow chemists, to "divert attention from the story we are trying to tell." Above all, scientists dare not run naked through the streets shrieking "Eureka!" or they will, as the Fiesers say, "violat[e] principles of good usage."[1]

This view of the discourse of the scientist cannot be allowed to stand. Rather, the scientist-writer must be untrammeled and encouraged to express individuality. This aspect of my argument will receive little support even from the countertraditionalists, especially the new sociologists, who emphasize the communal nature of the production of scientific knowledge. In their view it is not the expressivity of the individual scientist to which one must direct attention but the social organizations, the collaborative groups that represent institutional science, for ultimately it is they who determine even the substantive content of science.

Nonetheless, the authorial status of scientific discourse has undergone considerable sociological examination and linguistic attention that have fleshed out Bloomfield's linguistic analysis without departing from his central acceptance of the self-presentation of the scientific author as a nonpresence in the text. The textual features that operate to produce this effect of depersonalization — the codified descriptions, the passive constructions, the avoidance of first-person pronouns (other than the generalized *we*) — have frequently been noted and their force attended to. As Gyorgy Markus has recently summed up the conclusion of this body of analysis, "Due to all these indicated characteristics the 'inscribed author' [the 'implied author' of the literary critic] of the natural scientific text appears as an anonymous performer of methodologically certified, strictly regulated activities and a detached observer of their results — without any further personal identifying marks beyond possession of the required professional competence."[2]

One must not accept at face value this self-presentation of the depersonalized scientist-author. Markus, for example, adds that "the independence of the experimental report from its author's personality is to a large extent *fictitious* in the sense that no two scientists performing the same experiment (according to the accepted criteria of 'sameness,' since literal replication of experiments is in principle impossible) will write it up in an identical way. What is more, the differences between the various 'expositions' will reflect not only inessential personal idiosyncrasies, but can have far-reaching cognitive effects."[3] It is precisely this area of concern we will explore.

If the depersonalized author is something of a fiction, it is also to a degree unnatural, a practice that has been learned in several senses: learned by all individual contemporary scientists as they are trained in the current practice and presentation of their work, and learned by science as a body as its discourse has evolved over the centuries of its employment. The present linguistic strictures, which themselves imply the nonauthor the reader infers, have gradually emerged in a historical process that, as Markus has observed, is much in need of being charted. One has only to glance at the scientific classics of earlier generations to perceive the vivid presentations of authorial self and authorial feeling ("But, damme, there are no pores [in the cardiac septum]," says William Harvey in evident exasperation with the blindness of his predecessors.)[4] Such exclamations modern science would entirely eschew.

It may seem quixotic, in arguing for the kinship of scientific and literary language, to speak for the expressivity of scientific discourse even as contemporary literary critics take such little note of expressivity in their analyses of literary texts. But the histories of science and literature in this regard are not the same. In the past, literature has made a considerable point of proclaiming its own expressivity[5] (indeed, marking itself off from scientific discourse in this respect), and if contemporary criticism tacitly chooses to ignore this aspect of literary art,[6] it cannot quite succeed in effacing it altogether. Science, on the other hand, since the founding of the Royal Society at least, has made a shibboleth of denying the expressivity of its discourse, even when it exercised considerably more expressive freedom in practice than does the science of today. It is in order to capture for scientific discourse its full range of expressive potentiality that these judgments must be altered. If one is to accord to scientific discourse — as nearly as the case will allow — precisely the range of potential attributes commonly assigned to literary discourse, one must uncover for science that quality of expressivity it has too long kept veiled.

With this end in mind, I must broaden the conclusion earlier arrived at — namely, that the language of any given piece of scientific writing is dependent on its context, with reference, then, to scientific context. The sense of "context" must now be taken to include personal context. There is no such thing as an impersonal person — even a scientist — and, consequently, no such thing as purely objective discourse.

2

Expression theory, certainly in its romantic manifestation, makes a twofold assertion about language: that it is individually expressive, the expression of a unique, self-representing voice;[7] and that it is expressive of idea and emotion, giving voice to thoughts and to feelings of a deeply human kind.[8] On both grounds the traditional literary critics and scientists alike would declare scientific discourse nonexpressive. The scientific voice, they would assert, speaks not individually but anonymously, not with feeling but as void of affect. Let us consider these propositions separately.

It is the chief thrust of the Bloomfieldian view of scientific language, which one may take as paradigmatic of the traditional stance, that it is a communal, not an individual, matter:

> As, by convention and training, the participants in scientific discourse learn consistently to ignore all private factors of meaning, the lexical, grammatical, and stylistic features of their informal discourse become indifferent: each scientist responds to each discourse only with the relevant operations or their linguistic substitutes. Thus, half-a-dozen differently worded treatises, say on elementary mechanics, will produce the same result, so far as science is concerned. In this uniformity the differences between languages (as English, French, German), far-reaching and deep-seated as they are, constitute merely a part of the communicative dross. We say that scientific discourse is *translatable*, and mean by this that not only the difference between languages but, within each language, the difference between operationally equivalent wordings has no scientific effect.[9]

It is widely argued, with Bloomfield, that the "lexical, grammatical, and stylistic features" of scientific discourse are so modified from those of ordinary language as to give scientific discourse its special power, its objective certainty. These claims — and, of course, the view they represent — may be attacked from the perspective of science itself.

To begin with, one may smile at Bloomfield's view of the informal exchanges of scientists at their work, that they "ignore all private factors" and respond "only with the relevant operations or their linguistic substitutes." Can Bloomfield ever have stepped into a scientific laboratory and listened to the give-and-take, the verbal sparring, the "private factors," many of them, at least, relevant to the work and not only highly expressive of individual opinion but evocative of equally individual response?[10] But it is the view that such individual differences do not matter, that in spite of them the discourse is scientifically comprehensible in a neutral, public, mutually shared way, that we must address. By the very nature of language, this view is impossible; everyone's experience with, hence understanding of, language is different, as Bloomfield obviously recognizes. In another sentence — "In the terminology of physics, the most advanced branch of science, one can see how far this stripping [of superstitious connotation] has been carried and surmise how much farther it still must go"[11] — Bloomfield reveals that his "descriptive" account is really normative. He tells us that scientific discourse is what he believes it ought to be and what he infers it aims to be, not how, in fact, he finds it.

Further, Bloomfield's claim of the "translatability" of scientific language, though certainly widely shared, hardly bears close scrutiny. It is commonly said, especially by boosters of science, that its language is international and is mutually comprehensible around the world. But, of course, the facts are otherwise. The need for scientific translation is an evident indication, a need many scientists obviate by learning a second language explicitly for international scientific communication. For years German operated as a kind of universal scientific language; now, for much of the world, English does so. Nor, even with scientific languages, is translation simply a lexical matter, plugging in the right word from a matching word list, as shown by the difficulties attendant on computer translation. Bloomfield, as a linguist, knows these things. His argument is that such differences, including those in connotations, do not matter for scientific purposes. But can this be the case? For a simple counterexample, take the names for certain of the standard chemical elements. In German these were built up from vernacular roots, in English from classical roots — thus, *Wasserstoff*, "hydrogen"; *Sauerstoff*, "oxygen." As it happens oxygen was given its name by Lavoisier (*oxygène*, roughly "acid maker") on the mistaken notion that it was an essential ingredient of acids. In English, the *oxy-* root has for all practical purposes lost any connection with acidity; it is used only to indicate the presence of oxygen. But in German the word for acid is *Säure*, and the spurious connection of oxygen, Sauerstoff, with acids is constantly maintained; it is as though in English one always said "acidogen" for "oxygen." German chemists, of course, are not fooled by its name into thinking that oxygen behaves differently than it does, and — this is Bloomfield's point — both German- and English-speaking chemists have the same substance in mind when they speak of "Sauerstoff" and "oxygen." But surely, the associations, the connotations, the idea of the kind of thing one is dealing with, is different in the two cases.

Bloomfield argues further that even within a language differences in wording between scientific utterances do not signify so long as they are "operationally equivalent." But achieving operational equivalence among different groups of scientific workers is often difficult even when everyone speaks the same language. Every laboratory has its own practice and performs its routine functions in its own way — hence the difficulty in achieving precisely repeatable results from laboratory to laboratory using even a single procedural description, and to expect the variants to be operationally equivalent is highly unrealistic.

Bloomfield, in all these cases, believes or claims to believe that connotation has no scientific significance, that scientific words simply have explicit scientific meanings. Thus, he says, the "superstitious" connotations of number words like "seven" or "thirteen" are stripped from their meaning in scientific discourse. But what is one to make of the deliberate decision by subatomic physicists to designate a classification scheme for subatomic particles as the "Eightfold Way" in explicit reference to a Buddhist doctrine of the route to enlightenment? Here, the "superstitious" connotation is thrust upon us by the scientists who employ it for their own purpose — namely, to emphasize the fundamental nature of their formulation. Similarly, it is often said that when ordinary words like *force* or *pressure* are used scientifically, they are given precise meanings and shed (or are stripped of) their ordinary connotations. But if so, why were those particular words chosen in the first place? If force and pressure as used scientifically did not mean something comparable to what the words ordinarily indicate, they would not have been selected to bear the more precise scientific meanings. In fact, that such words do carry connotations causes problems even for scientists. A case in point is the attribution of the word *spin* to an aspect of the behavior of subatomic particles, which is in some respects analogous to the spinning of, say, a top: for instance, the spin state of the particle can be in one of only two forms (like clockwise and counterclockwise). Even physicists, however, sometimes forget the real sense of *spin* and carelessly speak as though such particles really were spinning, rotating about an axis. In naming the properties of subatomic particles, their discoverers have occasionally sought terms less likely to cause confusion. Thus, some such particles are said to possess *charm*. Obviously there is some playful irony at work here. But is the irony directed at those who think the word *spin* does not carry any sense of spin, or those who think it does?

One cannot expect the language of science to constitute a single, unified, mutually comprehensible body of discourse because its conceptual bases are not monolithic but multifarious. Science may be divided rather superficially into national and institutional groupings, each with its own language; it is fractured fundamentally into different disciplines, each with its own operating procedures, conceptual schemes, and, yes, language. Even within the science of physics, the world of quantum mechanics looks and sounds nothing like the world of ordinary mechanics. The two are, of course, not in conflict, but they deal with different bodies of experience that are comprehensible in different ways, each following its own pattern and rules of behavior. Even within a discipline, as Kuhn and Feyerabend argue, scientists may work under separate paradigms, and conceive everything they do in diverse terms.

More than this, individual scientists themselves have their own ways of thinking, their own notions of the kinds of things they want to look for in nature. Recently historians of science have come to recognize in the works of individual scientists certain common themes; Gerald Holton, the leader in this movement, prefers the Greek term *thema*. Holton, in his studies, sees scientists as committed, often unconsciously, to one of certain pairs or triads of contrasting themata — such as atomicity versus continuity, analysis versus synthesis, or constancy versus evolution versus catastrophic change — which occur again and again, like leitmotivs, in their work.[12] Sometimes such thematic differences are the distinguishing features of opposed paradigms, but often they simply mark the differences between the work of individual scientists operating within a particular paradigm.

It is a commonplace in the world of science that individual scientists, especially those who break new ground, exhibit certain characteristic styles in their work. Sometimes such differences are easily analyzable in terms of allegiance to particular paradigms or themata, but often it is a more subtle or elusive matter, a case of finding unusual or unexpected relations, for instance. "Everything they do," such scientists' colleagues say, "bears their stamp." Surprisingly often, too, such matters of scientific style are described in aesthetic terms. It has become almost a cliché that research projects that other scientists find intellectually satisfying are called "beautiful" or even "elegant." One account of a recent Nobel laureate's work ends with this reference to a key experiment: " 'It was such a beautiful and elegant experiment,' said experimentalist Jack Sandweiss of Yale, 'that it was the equivalent of listening to Rudolf Serkin play Beethoven.' "[13]

It is also beginning to be recognized, though still tentatively, that there is a connection (perhaps a loose or tenuous, but certainly complex) between scientists' personalities and life experiences and their scientific styles. Holton explicitly perceives such connections in his studies of themata.[14] Although only a little has been done so far to work out the precise details of how the person and the life shape the science, that the connections are there is becoming increasingly clear. Let me give some relevant excerpts from a recent account of Nobelists Frederick Sanger and Walter Gilbert, both honored for their work on the sequencing of DNA. Although in this account the respective personalities and scientific styles are simply juxtaposed, it is all but impossible not to read a causal connection between the two:

Sanger and Gilbert are about as different as two scientists can be, and they came upon their sequencing methods by entirely different paths. Sanger is quiet, modest, self-effacing; Gilbert is much more flamboyant. Ted Friedman of the University of California at San Diego, who spent a sabbatical year with Sanger, says, "If you talk to Sanger and do not know who he is, you would think he is the lab caretaker. If you allow him to, he will melt into the woodwork. . . .

Sanger's method evolved gradually from more than one line of attack on the problem.[15]

But as to Gilbert:

In contrast to Sanger, Gilbert did not deliberately set out to sequence DNA. A highly visible, active scientist who runs a large laboratory, Gilbert has worked on a wide variety of problems in the past 20 years. . . . He is also chairman of the board and cochairman of the board of directors of the gene splicing firm Biogen.

Gilbert, working with Allan Maxam, who is now at Harvard Medical School's Sidney Farber Cancer Institute, came upon a DNA sequencing technique almost by chance.[16]

It is, of course, not surprising that scientific style should reflect to a degree the scientist's personality, just as literary writing reflects the writer's personality (at least as it is perceived through the mask of the persona). But, generally, when scientists speak of their colleagues' "style," they are not referring to their writing because they do not consider it even a partial determinant of the scientific style. To them, the writing is only the transparent window through which the scientist's working style is, as it were, revealed. It is my contention, of course, that the verbal formulation of scientists' ideas is part and parcel of what they do from the beginning, that they have no work — hence can have no style — apart from the language in which the work, and the style are enunciated.

To be sure, one must acknowledge some divagation from the monolithic, traditional view that the language is not a component of scientific style. Several fragments from a review by Stephen Jay Gould (himself hardly a typical scientist) of a book about the life and work of Barbara McClintock will make the point:

She never did all she could to promote her chances in the admittedly tough battle for acceptance and understanding of transposable elements [in genes]. She planned a minor campaign, writing an introductory paper and presenting a seminar to key people at Cold

Spring Harbor. But when these initial forays met with little response and general incomprehension she folded her tents. With her usual fortitude and self-reliance (though not, of course, without bitter disappointment), and using her own version of the immemorial phrase "bugger them," she pressed on in her own way, knowing that she was right and that the rest of the world would eventually catch up. She published most of her subsequent work in the annual reports of her laboratory, surely an inauspicious place to launch a scientific revolution. I have read her main papers and they are, to put it mildly, tough sledding. With their unrelenting passive voice, and their compression of complex reasoning and experience into single paragraphs, they are marvels of their genre but not models of optimal communication.

Keller [the author of the book under review] argues, I think correctly, that . . . a primary explanation for McClintock's years as *vox clamantis in deserto* [is] her unconventional style of scientific thinking. . . .

First, and more general, McClintock does not follow the style of logical and sequential thinking often taken as a canonical mode of reasoning in science. She works by a kind of global, intuitive insight. . . . This procedure makes scientists suspicious and has often led colleagues to label her as a "mystic" in the pejorative, not appreciative, sense. . . .

Second, and more specifically but more importantly, McClintock practices a style of biology quite foreign to the norms of molecular biology and genetics (and often denigrated, sometimes explicitly, by leaders in these professions — though less so now than before, as appreciation and recognition mount). Keller captures this style in her well-chosen title — "A Feeling for the Organism."[17]

It is easy to see McClintock's scientific papers, which are such "tough sledding," as reflecting the "fortitude and self-reliance" of this scientist, whose work was so long neglected (indeed, "denigrated"), and their "compression of reasoning and experience into single paragraphs" as related to her thinking in terms of "global, intuitive insight." Although the connections are not explicitly made here, it is almost unavoidable that we sense the relation between McClintock the person who does not "promote her chances," McClintock the scientist of "unconventional" style, and McClintock the writer of such "inauspiciously" placed annual reports, with their "unrelenting passive voice." Indeed, it is inevitable that the connections exist because, as the biography by Evelyn Fox Keller goes far to attest, because the three McClintocks are in fact one.

3

In Gould's account of McClintock's writings, those writings seem to convey her all-prevailing "feeling for the organism" (the corn plants with which she works) almost in spite of themselves. That they manage to do so serves to raise the second of our major concerns — namely, that scientists' writings, like the poets', are expressive not only of the individual but of both idea and emotion. Keller's title beautifully manages to convey both aspects of what is expressed, the emotional and the ideational. Thus, *feeling for* suggests "emotional investment in," but it also conveys "having intimate knowledge about," as in "He has a real feeling for cabinetmaking." And both meanings are clearly intended by Keller: she tells us not only of McClintock's emotional involvement with her corn plants but of her almost intuitive skill in handling them.[18]

One of the more striking features of McClintock's story is the way she brings her own ideas into realization in her experiments. An even more arresting account of this phenomenon is given by June Goodfield in *An Imagined World*. As the title suggests, this story of the life of a scientist, pseudonymously named "Anna Brito," reveals how her initial inner conceptions are, through the complex procedures of science, brought finally to fruition as "discoveries." As Anna Brito says, "Normally [the scientist] is alone with uncertain ideas, or one idea, and that is wonderful; it is exciting. One can almost anticipate the form of the future data. Then vroom! it comes, or it does not come. That's the excitement."[19] And, Goodfield insists, the uniqueness of the scientist in conceiving and realizing the discovery is important. "Individuality in science," she tells Anna, "surfaces strikingly in [an] act of courage. . . . If you want to make your own pattern of science and have your own 'crazy' view of your field accepted, you can do it. But since you'll be bucking the collective trend, your colleagues will not always appreciate your efforts."[20]

Surely one should distrust one common stereotype of scientists, namely, that they are unemotional and unfeeling, that they shut themselves off from life to work in the cold, sterile laboratory. Rather, one must suppose that scientists come in all shades and colors of emotionality, gregariousness, and extroversion. But people who have not associated personally with them may not recognize the degree to which their work gives scientists of many emotional stripes a special feeling, a kind of joy, not daily, perhaps, but when things go especially right, when results begin to appear. Scientists often remark at how lucky they are to be able to spend their lives doing what gives them so much pleasure. Even otherwise cold and unfeeling scientists may be transformed when they enter their laboratories — as may more ordinary ones. While scientists move with a sure touch through the familiar world of their research, they may display a kind of power and strength they do not exhibit elsewhere. Even speaking about their work may make the most inarticulate scientists highly persuasive.

Perhaps the most important element here is that most scientists, certainly all great scientists, possess something comparable to McClintock's "feeling for the organism." Good scientists, I believe, develop this intense feeling for, this intimate awareness of, the objects they study, whether they are McClintock's corn plants, Muller's fruit flies, or the chemist's crystals. It is this kind of intense awareness that Polanyi calls "tacit knowing," and though he likens it to a kind of extension of the self,[21] it might equally well be considered an exploration of the "other"; the scientist comes to know this object intimately, exploring its limits and changes, its extensions and diminutions, its vagaries and constancies. Spouses of scientists are often aware and, sometimes with good reason, jealous of this special feeling, this "love," of their spouses for what they study. Goodfield's Anna Brito describes the process from her perspective: "Here is a cell. It has been going around all the time, and nobody has taken any notice of it. Suddenly you fall in love with it. Why? You, the scientist, don't know you're falling in love, but suddenly you become attracted to that cell. . . . Then you are going to have to go through an active process in relation to it, and this leads to discovery."[22]

This area of object relations, explored so extensively by D. W. Winnicott and others, has, as far as the scientist is concerned, another dimension in addition to the kind of attraction just described. Not only are scientists drawn to their scientific object; they seek to gain mastery over it. It is the aim of the exploration of the object to understand and ultimately to control or dominate it. Keller, in a second book, *Reflections on Gender and Science*, has characterized this impetus more fully and has labeled it as "aggression," an "aggressive force . . . [that] must make its . . . appearance in the relation between the scientist and his object, that is, between science and nature."[23] Although one may not fully agree with this characterization, it is easy to see an urge for dominance over their scientific objects expressed in the feelings of many scientists about their work.

Protocol, convention, the habits of the profession, call for scientists to suppress such feelings when they write or at least to avoid their overt expression in the writing. But they are so much part and parcel of the scientists' shared world, so much part of the common experience they bring to bear when they read, that the slightest clue is likely to invoke them. Thus, the vividness of Muller's description of the "bent-wing" character in his fruit flies must be much more vivid to the scientist who also works intimately with fruit flies and daily scrutinizes hundreds of them searching for precisely such characters! I believe that this kind of heightened feeling for the objects under scrutiny is a kind of substratum, underlying all scientific discourse.

Another aspect of the feeling that scientists have for their work is the sense that they are uncovering the fundamental laws of nature. Einstein recorded that one of the things that impelled him to become a scientist was his sense of wonder at the behavior of a magnetic compass showed him by his father.[24] The compass seemed to respond inexorably to an unseen force, something hidden that dictated its response. Most scientists believe that the laws they are perceiving have a kind of absolute validity, like the truths of geometry, transferred from the abstract world into the real one. Further, it is often said, these laws themselves have a simplicity, elegance, which adds to the aesthetic enjoyment of the scientific enterprise. It is not surprising, considering this, that Sandweiss compares a scientist's work to "playing Beethoven."

Every scientific endeavor, even though it may not lead to the formulation of general laws of nature, asserts in its own way something new about how the world works. Every paper claims to light at least one small candle against the dark, to add one small pearl, hauled up from the deep and prized from the oyster, to the world's precious store of knowledge. The reason, other than ego (and the promise of material and immaterial reward), that scientists fret so about priority is that the be-all and end-all of science is to say something new, to claim something about the world that has not yet been claimed. Although this feeling, the pride, the satisfaction, the joy in discovery, is not often made manifest, it is implicit in the assertion of novelty that every scientific paper, however modestly, makes. Thus, Bill Pelletier and I begin the abstract of our paper on the atisine degradation product as follows: "A key degradation product obtained from atisine by selenium dehydrogenation is the $C_{16}H_{15}N$ base of Jacobs and Craig. This compound has now been identified . . . by an unambiguous synthesis." And the abstract concludes: "The identification of this base provides the first evidence establishing the position of the nitrogen atom in the atisine skeleton."[25]

It is not my purpose to anatomize or fully characterize the ideas and feelings that scientists bring to their work and inevitably express in their writings. Rather, it is to suggest that such ideas and feelings do exist, are expressed, and must be taken into account in any serious consideration of scientific discourse. They are, to revert to the terms of the earlier part of this discussion, made manifest in the scientist's style — the writing as well as the working style, since the two, I hold, are one.

4

One's sense of how life works is compounded in large measure from one's own experiences, and one commonly calls up those experiences to test — to validate or confute — the inferences one draws about the workings of the world. Thus, for me, and presumably for many of those who were organic chemists in the 1950s, to speak of scientific style is immediately to evoke one name — that of R. B. (for Robert Burns) Woodward of Harvard University. One of the best-known American practitioners of our specialty, in fact one of a handful of top American chemists of any variety, Woodward, to no one's surprise, received the Nobel Prize in chemistry in 1965. Woodward's forte was not chiefly the determination of structure of natural substances (though he did that superlatively well) but the chemical synthesis of such substances. This latter activity he performed with such flair that every organic chemist of our generation could recognize at sight the Woodward touch.

I know nothing of Woodward's private life, did not work with him, and cannot speak of him as a person. But I heard him lecture on several occasions and can give some account of the public persona. One I remember most vividly (though what I remember is probably a composite of the various occasions): it took place at a summer research conference in rural New England, one of dozens of such conferences that allow kindred scientists at different institutions to come together in a quiet and neutral setting to inform one another about their work in progress. Woodward's talk, as I recall, had the announced title, "Recent Advances in the Chemistry of Natural Products"; he preferred, it was said, a generic title so that he could, at the last moment, pick the one project of many that seemed nearest to fruition and the most likely to make a striking presentation. It was understood that he would not attend the whole conference but would appear the day of his paper, mingle dutifully, make his presentation, and depart. And so it transpired.

Woodward was not, as I remember, tall, nor was he quite corpulent, but he had the kind of stolid dignity I associate, rightly or wrongly, with Henry James. He was somewhat dapper without being well dressed. Whereas everyone else wore sports clothes, Woodward came in a blue blazer and badly rumpled trousers. He was famed for always wearing a pale blue tie. At the conference, he was largely closeted with a select few of his intimates and emerged only for his address. His voice was not loud, his accent was Bostonian, and he spoke with a dry, rather ironic condescension, addressing a group of his scientific peers as though they were rather slow-witted undergraduates. Like every chemist speaking of complex molecules, he made use of slides, and at one point, referring to a familiar structural representation carried over from previous slides, he remarked drily, "Some of you may recall this substance from the previous slide."

The reader who has had and not enjoyed a course in organic chemistry will find it difficult to believe that the typical Woodward talk had considerable dramatic interest, at least for its intended audience. The affair was handled with some theatrical skill. His slides were beautifully prepared, with great portions of the molecular structures highlighted in color, and when he drew diagrams on a blackboard he employed colored chalk brought along especially for the presentation. And he generated considerable suspense as he worked his way through the particular project he was describing, emphasizing the difficulties and delaying the final triumph.

As was usual with Woodward, his topic was the synthesis of a natural substance; I believe that at the time I am referring to it was vitamin B_{12}. The substance chosen was always of great interest pharmacologically because of its biological activity and chemically because of its complex structure, which seemed to place impassable roadblocks in the way of synthesis. (Synthesis promised generally to make the compound more readily available and to permit the preparation of closely related substances, which might have properties of even greater value than those of the natural substance.) With Woodward, however, the game was not just to synthesize the substance by any means he happened to hit upon but to devise a rational synthesis based upon the latest theoretical understanding of how chemical compounds behave when they react. Woodward belonged preeminently to the then new camp of *scientific* synthetic organic chemists who sought to operate on the basis of theoretical understanding of chemistry, as opposed to the older, pejoratively labeled, "cookbook" school, who saw their calling more as an art than a science, a skill to be acquired by years of laboratory practice rather than a body of knowledge gained in the library and worked out on the blackboard. To the cookbook school the game of chemical synthesis was to get the substance needed by hook or crook; to Woodward and his school the synthetic product was valuable largely as the victory flag marking the triumph of the scientific method.

With his position at Harvard, his reputation for brilliance, his access to large sums of support money, and his numerous contacts throughout the academic and industrial research establishment, Woodward had no dearth of graduate and postgraduate research assistants. His laboratories were reported to constitute a virtual factory, and his detractors claimed that for every research project he undertook, he assigned different groups of students and collaborators to explore a variety of alternate schemes. Whichever succeeded, or succeeded first, was labeled the "rational" approach, the "scientific" method, and given the Woodward seal.

In any case, the Woodward presentation invariably followed a common plan: laying out the importance of the goal; specifying the extreme difficulty of achieving it; proposing a novel method for overcoming the difficulties, based on the latest chemical theories; describing the employment of the method in the laboratory, against all odds; and finally, announcing the ultimate success of the method. The whole affair was skillfully orchestrated and invariably produced a round of applause.

Woodward's published papers usually follow the same pattern and proclaim the same theme: the triumph of chemical theory in achieving difficult, important, and useful goals. They are of necessity less caustic and less self-consciously theatrical than the oral presentations. But they carry the stamp of the Woodward style, a rather ornate portentousness, which unkind critics see as pomposity. Editors of scientific journals sometimes loosen their strictures against personal expressiveness on the part of their authors, and the more eminent the author, the greater the loosening is likely to be (one can only wish the practice were more general). Certainly, R. B. Woodward was permitted to be "expressive" in a way, one suspects, an unknown organic chemist would not have been.

To apprehend the Woodward style, let us examine part of a major paper, one reporting the first total synthesis of naturally occurring steroids. The synthesis was achieved during the first flush of interest in cortisone, aroused much attention among scientists and the public alike; it is specifically referred to in Woodward's Nobel citation. The paper is entitled "The Total Synthesis of Steroids." The introduction follows:

> The extensive and brilliant researches of Windaus and Wieland on
> the earliest known steroids, the members of the cholesterol and cholic

acid groups, led to the proposal of the correct structures for those substances in 1932. Interest in the total synthesis of steroids has been widespread since that time, and has received added impetus as the recognition of the great importance of steroids in medicine and in animal physiology has grown. The attack on the problem has been marked by certain signal successes. The first bastion fell with the synthesis of equilenin by Bachmann, Cole and Wilds in 1939. Almost a decade later, the more difficult problem presented by the synthesis of oestrone was first surmounted by Anner and Miescher. These advances were consolidated by the achievement of independent syntheses of both aromatic steroidal hormones by Johnson and his associates.

There remained the task of the synthesis of naturally occurring steroids, such as the sterols proper and the androgenic and progestational hormones, which contain the complete hydroaromatic tetracyclic nucleus, whose presence is characteristic of the vast majority of steroidal substances. A particularly challenging objective was provided by the emergence of the rare 11-oxygenated cortical steroids as powerful agents in the treatment of disease. In this communication we describe the achievement of each of these goals, by methods of particular applicability to the cortical group.

Every approach to the synthesis of steroids has been complicated by the presence in these substances of a number of asymmetric carbon atoms. Inevitably the resulting stereochemical problem has become ever more serious as the more remote objectives have been brought under attack. Thus, the presence in cholestanol of nine such centers makes possible the existence of five hundred and twelve stereoisomers of that structure. Some comfort might be taken in the fact that the steric course of interconversions *within the steroid group* often is subject to control, or in any event is well understood. None the less the stereochemical aspect of the synthetic problem is still formidable, and in these circumstances we considered it advisable, in so far as it was possible, to introduce successive asymmetric carbon atoms in a stereochemically controlled fashion.[26]

Although these words speak for themselves, a few comments may be in order. To begin with, the title is not without interest. "The Total Synthesis of Steroids" is at once simple and global (I hesitate to say "grand"). It is in sharp contrast to the titles of most chemical papers, which are highly specific; the two-part title is common, announcing a general topic and then the specific achievement, as, say, "The Synthesis of Diterpene Alkaloids: Preparation of. . . ." But Woodward's title is the kind that might appear on a multivolume set of works reviewing decades of work in scores of laboratories around the world. It promises to say all that has to be said on the synthesis of steroids. In fact, the title is pretty close to the mark. Woodward's approach not only produces the first synthetic nonaromatic, naturally occurring steroid but leads for the first time to the synthesis of all major classes of steroids of interest — the cholesterol group, androgenic and progestational hormones, and the cortical hormones. One might quarrel with the use of the definite article — surely this is only "a" total synthesis of steroids — but the monumentality of the rubric as it stands is in itself a triumph.

Nonchemist readers presumably will not understand exactly why the asymmetric carbon atoms are a problem (the various atoms attached to them must be oriented spatially in a particular way, something that is very difficult to achieve), but they will accept that it is a problem. And they will recognize that the problem grows with the number of such carbon atoms; each new such carbon added, in fact, does not simply add to the possibilities but multiplies them. The result of having nine asymmetric carbons, as the paper indicates, is that 512 versions of the molecular structure are possible, only one of which will be identical with the natural steroid structure the chemist is trying to duplicate. Achieving the correct one out of 512 possibilities is precisely the problem.

How successful one finds Woodward's extended battle metaphor in his introduction is a matter of taste, but it is hardly standard usage for chemical articles. "Attack," "bastion [falling]," "advances . . . consolidated," "challenging objective," "approach," "brought under attack," "formidable" — the heightened rhetoric is obvious, as is the assumed life-and-death nature of the struggle for scientific accomplishment. Here is explicit expression of what I have earlier described as the scientist's urge to achieve dominance over his scientific object — indeed, employment of the very terminology of the "aggression" Keller calls attention to. In the paper that follows there is a virtual accelerando of successive "triumphs" recounted, as problem after problem is solved, obstacle after obstacle overcome, and objective after objective reached. What is not evident to the nonchemist, of course, is the chemical ingenuity, the dependence on exact chemical science, by which each triumphant success is achieved (or, to be precise, reported to be achieved). It is perfectly obvious, of course, that the rhetorical effect is consciously achieved, but that does not mean that it is inappropriate or ineffective. My point is simply to indicate what is so clearly the case: that there is a particular style manifest here as well as a degree of feeling (directed toward dominance), and that these are integrated into the explicit scientific content — that the language is, in short, expressive.

But my singling out certain aspects of the language as carrying a considerable portion of the expressive burden should not be construed as implying that those aspects of the language are mere ornamentation, certain rhetorical flourishes added to an otherwise bald and scientific account. Rather one must presume that this is the language in which the Woodwardian style — the scientific style, if one can still make that distinction — is conceived. The bastions that fall before Woodwardian guns are scientific bastions, not purely verbal ones. One can hardly doubt that Woodward himself saw objectives and planned campaigns to reach them. Indeed, the training of every organic chemist includes devising hypothetical synthetic routes to complex molecular structures. It is inherent in each such chemist's cultural makeup that he or she will respond to the expressions of accomplishment in Woodward's account; this is what organic chemists try to achieve, though few proceed with Woodward's persistence, his brilliance, his flair, his style.

One cannot, to be sure, rule out here the suggestion of self-dramatization, cannot refute any claim of deliberate coloring of Woodward's own accomplishments to further his reputation. But nothing compels one to this view. What one reads has all the marks of the expression of genuine emotions; one need not accuse Woodward of contrivance. Scientifically, practically, the work is important; it is appropriate that the doer should feel, and show, pride in the accomplishment. Furthermore, the effort to promote a particular kind of chemical research is not unpraiseworthy. There can be little doubt that the scientific school of synthetic chemists saw themselves as engaged in a laudable struggle to wrest their science from the stranglehold of a reactionary cookbook school. That this struggle was also their key to professional success — to winning grants, achieving publication, furthering careers — need not impugn their motives.

As it happened, the success of the Woodwardian enterprise, scientific and otherwise, fostered a crop of Woodward epigones. Some of these sought to emulate Woodward in all things, including the more superficial aspects of his writing style. The following passage, which one must take to be merely an unfortunate lapse in the writing of an accomplished scientist, is the opening of a paper entitled "Stereochemical Implications in Sesquiterpene Biogenesis." (The sesquiterpenes belong to the general class of terpenes, natural substances not unlike steroids, and biogenesis is the process of natural as opposed to chemical synthesis.)

The domain of terpene biogenesis, which was for too long a haven for undisciplined speculation, has been brilliantly codified and extended in recent years by the Swiss group of Ruzicka, first in an original and authoritative presentation of the entire field in 1953, and then in the elegant conception of triterpene and steroid biogenesis which must rank as a model of the critical approach to this speculative realm which is made possible by the application of modern reaction theory and the stereochemical limits implicit in it. An attempt is made here to apply this approach to sesquiterpene biogenesis, extending the ideas of Ruzicka and Barton on the involvement of large rings in order to incorporate stereochemical features.[27]

Whatever one may think of the naturalness (or lack of it) in Woodward's style, this passage must read like a parody. The battlefield metaphor has become merely a geographical one. And surely the metaphor is forced, if not mixed. (Are the connotations of haven quite compatible with those of domain and realm? Can one codify havens or domains?) Further, Woodward's simple praise of the work of his predecessors ("extensive and brilliant") has become so hyperbolic as almost to suggest hypocrisy or sycophancy ("brilliantly codified and extended," "an original and authoritative presentation," an "elegant conception," "a model of the critical approach"). The Fiesers, incidentally, warn their fellow chemists against "appraisal of another investigator, favorable or otherwise, for such appraisal is presumptive and hence in bad taste."[28]

This example is enough to make one regret any thought that editors of scientific journals might be more tolerant of personal idiosyncrasies of style. But, of course, one must distinguish successful self-expression from imitation and must encourage expression that carries important associations with the work itself while opposing mere decoration. Even here the fulsome language must not cause us to overlook the fact that this paper, too, applauds the extension of scientific methodologies to a field where the writer believes they were not previously operable.

This is, to be sure, one of the more troubling areas of stylistics — the precise dividing line between expressive language and stylistic ornamentation. But it is certainly no solution to this problem to pretend that some forms of language — namely, scientific ones — can or should have no expressive dimension at all. Attempting to enforce that "solution" merely encourages the production of a kind of language that expresses still, as all language must, but in a narrow register, and only for those few readers who are able to call up their own affective associations on the most meager of verbal cues by virtue of the closest possible identity of experience with that of the writer. In other words, scientists whose expressive use of language is artificially constrained, as is so often the case, can express their emotional responses to their scientific work only to those closest colleagues in their field, who are able virtually to intuit those feelings. For every Woodward paper, with a style that expresses obviously and to many, there are a thousand accounts of chemical research that are hardly permitted to express anything at all and only to a very few. But there is nothing inherent in the scientific enterprise that demands that this should be the case (rather, in fact, the contrary, as the next chapter will suggest).

5

It is not news even to traditionalists that scientists express ideas in their writings (though such traditionalists may be reluctant to acknowledge the degree to which those ideas themselves help to determine the facts that are also presented), but there is no stronger stricture in the traditional prescription for scientific writing than that it not convey emotion. In challenging that shibboleth, I would point at once to one obvious exception, that of Charles Darwin in the *Origin of Species.* So much has been said about Darwin as a writer that I hesitate to add even a small measure to that volume, but the example is admirably suitable — he expresses his feelings clearly in his work, particularly his "feeling for the organism."

Darwin's theory of evolution is often excoriated by those with vitalist persuasions as unnatural, mechanical, relying on the workings of chance; yet virtually everything that Darwin wrote is suffused with his identification with the natural world. Nothing could be less unnatural than Darwin's love of nature. One of the things that make the *Origin* such pleasurable reading is Darwin's persistent personification. His personifications, particularly his anthropomorphism of nature itself, have been the subject of commentary since Hyman.[29] Recently Beer has suggested that the personifications serve the tactical purpose of covertly bringing man into a work whose strategy demands that he be absent (Darwin wishing to defer the overt situating of man within his evolutionary scheme).[30] Especially indicative of affect, however, is not the personification of natural forces but that of other species.

Now it is easy enough to anthropomorphize other mammals — dog and cat owners do it all the time — but Darwin extends the process to every organism he encounters. Especially striking is his personifications of plants and insects. In a few memorable phrases he describes a dwarfed Scotch fir, repeatedly browsed down by cattle, and with twenty-six rings of growth, showing that it had, "during many years, tried to raise its head above the stems of the heath, and had failed."[31]

Of special interest in this regard is a passage that occurs when Darwin is presenting his demonstration that instincts are conceivably modifiable by natural selection just as are physical traits. One of the examples he uses to illustrate the general point is the instinct of ants of certain species to enslave those of other species. (His argumentative strategy is to show that gradations of the instinctive behavior exist at present, the simpler of which could be comparable to stages through which the more fully developed instincts could have passed as they evolved.) Some of the slave ants are strictly "household slaves"; they carry out such domestic chores as caring for the larvae and pupae. Others work outside the nest "marching along" with their masters in search of food and other materials. All the slaves clearly "feel quite at home." When the nest is attacked, the slaves "like their masters are much agitated and defend the nest." In extreme cases, the masters are completely dependent on the slaves for maintaining the domestic economy. Darwin describes another naturalist, Pierre Huber, who set up thirty such ants "without a slave, but with plenty of the food which they like best, and with their own larvae and pupae to stimulate them to work, [but] they did nothing; they could not even feed themselves, and many perished of hunger. Huber then introduced a single slave (*F. fusca*), and she instantly set to work, fed and saved the survivors; made some cells and tended the larvae, and put all to rights" (pp. 398–99).

This memorable slave ant, like an English Victorian household servant looking after her improvident and otherwise helpless masters, is typical of the ants reared in slavery, but the situation is quite otherwise when the slave-making masters set out to "conquer" otherwise independent colonies and reduce them to slavery. Now one encounters true warfare: one group of slavers Darwin observes approaches "an independent community of the slave-species (*F. fusca*)"; they were "vigorously repulsed," he says, "sometimes as many as three of these ants clinging to the legs of the [much larger] slave-making *F. sanguinea*. The latter ruthlessly killed their small opponents." After the unsuccessful attempt Darwin plays a prank on the slavers: "I then dug up a small parcel of the pupae of *F. fusca* from another nest, and put them down on a bare spot near the place of combat; they were eagerly seized and carried off by the tyrants, who perhaps fancied that, after all, they had been victorious in their late combat" (pp. 399–400).

But *F. fusca* was not always successful in repelling *F. sanguinea*:

> One evening I visited [a] community of *F. sanguinea*, and found a number of these ants returning home and entering their nests, carrying the dead bodies of *F. fusca* (showing that it was not a migration) and numerous pupae. I traced a long file of ants burthened with booty, for about forty yards back, to a very thick clump of heath, whence I saw the last individual of *F. sanguinea* emerge, carrying a pupa; but I was not able to find the desolated nest in the thick heath. The nest, however, must have been close at hand, for two or three individuals of *F. fusca* were rushing about in the greatest agitation, and one was perched motionless with its own pupa in its mouth on the top of a spray of heath, an image of despair, over its ravaged home. (pp. 400–401)

The pathos of the final tableau is unmistakable even out of context. It comes as a fitting conclusion to several pages of vivid personification. What the reader does not expect, after these extended passages of personification and the final vision of Darwin's tragic victim, are the words that immediately follow: "Such are the facts."

Clearly Darwin wishes his reader to view the material he has presented as evidence ("the facts") to support his argument. Indeed, the *Origin* is stuffed with supporting detail of every kind, quotations from authorities, experiments carried out, and, like this material, Darwin's own encounters with nature. The last, as Hyman remarks, have the air of "personal testimony: I was there, I saw it, this happened to me."[32] The personification serves to intensify the immediacy of such accounts.

From external evidence, one can determine that the effects of such passages are deliberate, that the passages themselves have been worked up to convey them. Darwin's observations of the slave-making ants are first described somewhat lightheartedly in the postscript of a letter to his friend Hooker: "I have had some fun here watching a slave-making ant; for I could not help doubting the wonderful stories, but I have now seen a defeated marauding party, and . . . a migration from one nest to another of the slave-makers, carrying their slaves in their mouths!"[33] And indeed, the phrase "an image of despair" is added in the second edition of the *Origin*, obviously to heighten the effect. This is Darwin the writer at work, aiding Darwin the scientist in making his scientific point. One will surely agree with Beer that these personifications serve the purpose of making the personified creatures man's kin and thereby of casting man into the net of evolution. But one must also observe that they do so with considerable power, forcing the reader to feel, for instance, the despair of the ant over its ravaged home. The reader indeed naturally assumes that the felt emotion coincides with Darwin's own. But one must not confuse Darwin with the persona the text creates. One must, rather, perceive a Darwin-writer who has employed this strategy for his own larger ends. Included in those ends, presumably, is the creation of the effect of a shared experience with the reader. One of the valuable lessons the new sociologists of science teach us is the importance of the communal experience in validating the findings of science and the role of scientific writing in creating that experience. Surely that is what Darwin is about here.

Significantly, however, the means he has chosen to his end are much like those the poets choose to bring their private epiphanies into shared experience with the reader. A study has documented the specific influence of Wordsworth on Darwin,[34] and one can here see something of a common structure with Wordsworth's creation of a poem as an emotional experience "recollected in tranquility." Darwin, like Wordsworth, has his direct experience with nature and then at some later time re-creates that experience in his writing, which becomes the vehicle of the shared experience with the reader. Darwin's own original experience — which his readers can never really know any more than they can the poet's — must be an instance of that "feeling for the organism," the "love" of the scientist for the scientific object. ("Here is an [ant]. . . . Suddenly you fall in love with it.")

Much of the time, lay readers are unable to share the experiences of scientists re-created in their writing (though their colleagues can). It is one of Darwin's great virtues as a writer that through his books we are all able to know something of what his experience with the natural world must have been like.

6

But, it may be objected, Charles Darwin, the nineteenth-century gentleman-naturalist, is a far cry from the highly specialized, coldly rational scientists of today; it is only to be expected that his writings would be *expressive* in a way theirs would not. Let us turn then to the writings of a contemporary scientist.

As a test case we may use the writings of Barbara McClintock, described as such "tough sledding," with their "unrelenting passive voice" and their "compression of complex reasoning and experience into single paragraphs." We will begin, however, not with one of the "inauspiciously" placed yearbook reports but with her Nobel acceptance speech, delivered in December 1983. Here is the opening paragraph:

> There are "shocks" that a genome must face repeatedly, and for which it is prepared to respond in a programmed manner. Examples are the "heat shock" responses in eukaryotic organisms and the "sos" responses in bacteria. Each of these initiates a highly programmed sequence of events within the cell that serves to cushion the effects of the shock. Some sensing mechanism must be present in these instances to alert the cell to imminent danger, and to set in motion the orderly sequence of events that will mitigate this danger. But there are also responses of genomes to unanticipated challenges that are not so precisely programmed. The genome is unprepared for these shocks. Nevertheless, they are sensed, and the genome responds in a discernible but initially unforeseen manner.[35]

This is a remarkable passage, notable for its frank indulgence both of personification and of teleology. Not only is the genome given human characteristics — it "faces" shocks, "senses" events — but its behavior shows deliberate purposefulness; it seeks to fulfill its own ends — it "responds." Of course, the genome, the cell's collection of genes, is not itself a living entity, certainly not a conscious one; it can have no awareness, no purpose, no ends. Yet the personification and the teleology are not errors of thought here, but matters of usage, ways of simplifying complex biological situations. Biologists commonly speak like this because they cannot help observing that organisms, cells, even subcellular structures do behave as though they know what they are doing, do act as though they can perceive and work to accomplish their own particular ends. Biologists well know that organisms act in these ways not because they elect to do so; rather, natural selection has chosen them because they are programmed to perform such acts under such circumstances. (It is the great contribution of Darwin to biology to have shown how adaptation, the best evidence of design in nature, could come about without a deliberate designer.) Biologists, of course, do not have to explain that they understand this every time they speak or write to one another; it is easier merely to say that organisms, even cellular structures, "sense" things and act "in order to" achieve particular goals, even when one knows otherwise.

But what is significant about McClintock's remarks is that it is the genome that is given conscious, purposeful behavior. It is true that the genetic material of the genome carries the information that permits the manufacture of all the substances of the cell, true that the expression of that information, variously as needed, determines the behavior of the cell; yet it is more typical to conceive of the cell itself as the living entity, to personify it, to see it as the purposeful being that draws on the information carried in the genome and employs that information for its own larger ends. But McClintock's thinking is different. It is the genome, not the cell, that "faces" shocks, the genome that "senses," that is "prepared" for some shocks, and though "unprepared" for others, nonetheless "responds." Here the genome is not simply a component of a living system, not even a parasite of that system, but its living center, its site of consciousness, its initiator of all activity. In McClintock's world, the genome is the brain of the cellular body.

One of the genome's responses to shock is to reorganize its own material — "to restructure itself in order to overcome a threat to its survival" (p. 793). But in restructuring itself, the genome makes its altered state felt chiefly in the next generation of cells (or those even further down the line). What is important, then, is the continuity of the genome from generation to generation. The genome does not just direct the cell; it transcends it. The genome dominates the cell to ensure its survival to dominate the lives of successor cells (even when it must reconstitute itself to do so). But McClintock's corn plants — unlike, say, bacteria — are multicellular organisms, not single-celled ones, and here the role of the genome is more complex. The remarkable state of affairs is that each such organism begins life as a single cell, which under the guidance of the genome undergoes a dizzying sequence of cell divisions and cell differentiations until the adult organism, with its myriad of diverse cell types, is finally reached. In the adult, the genome with one hand directs maintenance operations, replacing single cells as needed, while readying the organism for its reproductive mode, which ultimately will lead to new "seed" cells, with their own genomes, ready to undergo the same dizzying process once again.

The trick of thought in all this is to single out the genome as the active element, the agency that employs the whole system for its own end, the production of more genomes. As the old scientific joke puts it, "A chicken is just an egg's way of producing another egg." All organisms, then, are really devices employed by the genome to extend its sway. We human beings, with all our complex civilization, are simply a contrivance of the human genome to further its domination of the earth. Already, in fact, that genome has exploited humankind to get itself briefly to the moon; in some decades it will permanently infect that location and move on to Mars; in a century it will be mobilizing for an assault on the stars. There is no end to the ambitions of the genome.

In all this story, it remains something of a puzzlement that the adult organism contains cells of so many different types, all of which stem from one parent cell with a single genome, yet, it is the genome that determines the character of the cell. Obviously things must happen during development: parts of the genome may be "expressed" in some cells, other parts "expressed" in others; genes, in short, may be turned on in some cells, off in others. But, conceivably, the genome itself might become modified along the way, fundamentally altered so that it directs one cell to do one thing, another to do something else. It is one of the staggering implications of McClintock's work that this process indeed seems to occur.

In her address McClintock describes atypical plants with variegated leaves, sectors of which appear as "mirror images" of one another accordingly as they have more or fewer green streaks against a white background. "After observing many such twin sectors, I concluded that regulation of patterns of gene expression in these instances was associated with an event occurring at mitosis [cell division] in which one daughter cell had gained something that the other cell had lost" (p. 793). That something proved to be what she calls a "transposable element," and much of McClintock's work deals with how such elements work to transform the genome. The transformations she studies are (in her terms) "responses" to "shocks," unusual circumstances, because this is what makes the transformation apparent. But it is entirely possible that transposable elements participate in the processes of "normal" development as well.

In McClintock's address the genome itself, without losing its essential identity, becomes plastic: it "reorganizes," "restructures" itself; it "ruptures"; pieces of it form "bridges," move from one location to another (p. 798). Clearly this is a long way from the old picture of the genome as a "filament" or even as a "string" of gene "beads" and is expressive of McClintock's thinking about the transformable character of the genome. Genomic transformations, as it happens, have other important biological implications. They may, it now begins to seem, be involved in processes by which new species sometimes form from old ones by a shortcutting of the Darwinian path of evolution by natural selection of repeated minute variations. Thus if a genome undergoes a wholesale restructuring, a new species may arise, as it were, at a single bound.

The reader need not be nudged at this point to perceive that Mc-

Clintock's language is highly expressive, a far cry from the traditionalists' ideal of the objective, dispassionate, coded transmission of the automaton scientist. What McClintock does in this address is characterize the genome as a living entity in such a way that her readers choose to share its fate and fortunes. It is McClintock's language that induces one to respond strongly to the ideas and feelings she expresses here. The real question, however, is whether or not her regular scientific papers — such "tough sledding" for the reader — share to any degree the expressivity we have found in the Nobel address.

The forewarning that McClintock's scientific papers are not easy reading is largely correct. Certainly one does not find them as overtly expressive of the feelings that motivate her work as is the Nobel address. Yet, even here, the language is expressive for those who are prepared to read it. Let us look briefly at one of the "inauspicious" yearbook reports, written some thirty-five years before the Nobel address.

There are overtly expressive elements: a cluster of newly arising mutable genetic elements is a "burst"; atypical kernels of corn are "aberrant," even "exceptional"; an extra-heavy effect is a "double dose"; the genetic material still undergoes "rupture," "fusion," "bridging." But there are significant changes. Only latent are the personification, the teleology: "shocks" are now only "events"; "responses" merely "consequences." Here, at somewhat greater length, is her then-current hypothesis for the behavior of transposable elements:

> A normal, wild-type locus may be totally or partially inhibited in action by the insertion of a foreign piece of chromatin adjacent to it. Total or partial release from inhibition will occur when this foreign chromatin is removed or altered in organization. The insertion, removal, or change in organization of the foreign chromatin occurs because this chromatin becomes adhesive in certain somatic cells at very precise times in the development of a tissue. The adhesiveness causes a rupturing of the chromosome at the adhered positions during the subsequent mitotic cycle, which results in removal, transposition, or alteration in constitution of the chromatin materials involved. The chromatin primarily concerned in these events is heterochromatin. Its behavior as revealed in this study of the origin and expression of mutable loci may reflect one aspect of its normal behavior in the development of an organism.[36]

Here there is no reference to *genome*; the operative word now is *chromatin*: *genome* is an abstract term for the total collection of genes; *chromatin*, a cytological term for cellular material that stains a certain way. In a sense the terms are, or may be construed as, equivalent. The material that stains in such a way as to be identified as chromatin turns out to be, indeed, the genetic material, nucleic acid; this, in turn, is the material substance that corresponds to the genes. But there is a world of difference: *chromatin* is operational; *genome* conceptual. Still, the centrality of the chromatin to the thinking here is obvious. And its behavior, its character, is comparable to that of the *genome* of the Nobel address. The material is adhesive; it has, as already noted, the same kind of plasticity, and its implications for the biology of the organism are as apparent.

Behind the writing, in each case, clearly lies a focus of attention on a single, identifiable entity (chromatin or genome) around which everything else revolves, on which everything else depends. And that substance is perceived very much in the same way, as active, flexible, and self-conserving. The differences in mode and intensity of expression have obvious sources. For one thing half a lifetime of scientific work and thought lies between them; for another, so does a remarkable difference in circumstances. The author of the earlier paper was, we have already heard, a scientist whose views were essentially rejected or ignored, who was working doggedly nonetheless and publishing "inauspiciously" merely in the yearbook of her institution, presumably more for the record than to reach a responsive audience. The author of the address was a scientist at the height of public acceptance of her ideas, speaking to a wide and general audience, on the most auspicious of all occasions for a scientist: she knows her words will be heard by notables and will be made available to whatever members of the scientific and broader intellectual community should care to attend to them. It is not surprising that one should find the language on the two occasions different; it would be surprising, in fact, if one found anything similar at all.

The secret of McClintock's scientific success — her "feeling for the organism," the corn plant — is particularly evident in her descriptions of corn kernels and seedlings, as well as the cytological details of chromosome structure and behavior. But the dominant feature in her thinking is really something else: out of all the buzzing activities of the cell, out of the complex patterns of cell division and differentiation, McClintock has the ability to tease out one element, the genome, and single-mindedly focus on it, not merely as the center of interest but also as the initiating element in the biological processes themselves.

In a sense this is the Platonizing abstraction of science so often perceived, the ability to conceive of the general at work in the particular; it is a mode of thought, a particular mind-set, but it is also manner of expression. And in McClintock's work that expression is or can be warmer, more engaged, than the phrase "Platonizing abstraction" might imply. There is a conception here of the genome as a particular kind of thing, an organizing element, plastic and alterable, yet always maintaining its identity, struggling to perpetuate itself, to extend its domain, in the face of whatever shocks to its system chance events will provide. There is also feeling here: a sense of kinship, of identification with that genome in its tenacious struggle to prevail over every adversity. How overtly that conception and that feeling are expressed in the writing, how explicitly that genome emerges as a responding being, depends on the circumstances, but the same sense of the nature of things motivates the expression in either case. And it is this sense of the nature of things that makes McClintock the scientist, and the writer, that she is.

7

It is not, I believe, quixotic to argue that scientific language can be — indeed, must be — expressive in an age when literary criticism is markedly uninterested in the expressivity of the literary text. Even in a time in which critics have decried authorial intention as a mark of validation of a critical reading, they have not denied that literary language can be in some measure expressive, as has so categorically been said about scientific language.

I do not maintain that all scientific language is highly expressive or that all scientific language is equally expressive. What I argue is that scientific language can be expressive, in the several senses of the term employed — that is, expressive of the individual self and expressive of ideas and of powerful feelings. It is perfectly true that the writing in most scientific journals today shows little individuality of expression and overtly demonstrates little genuine emotion. But there is surely a residue of both, and the closer the reader is to the science under discussion, the more important that residue becomes. Scientists who know well the workers in their particular field will know precisely who wrote a given paper, whether or not the name appears on it, and they will know equally well what the author's feelings are about the work reported. That scientists would be more expressive in their writing if given a free rein, I do not doubt (biologists today are no less feeling individuals than was Charles Darwin), if the dead hand and deaf ear of official editorial science were lifted from the page or attuned to the sound of the human voice. It is not an inherent part of the scientific method that people cease to be people when they become scientists.

I have not established — nor could one in such a short space — that the ranges of literary and scientific expressivity are essentially the same. I can only suggest that, given the opportunity, the scientist can be expressive in much the same way and to much the same degree of much the same spectrum of ideas and emotions as the poet. At the same time, however, I vigorously deny that traditional assessment in both literary and scientific camps that one, if not *the*, discriminating feature between literary language and scientific language is that the former is expressive and the latter is not. Not every poet is a wild flame, burning out a life to illumine the world. And not every scientist is a self-effacing scrivener, perched on a high stool and endlessly, unfeelingly, copying what is written in the great book of nature. Both the poet and the scientist have their own individual experiences with life, and both try to express as well as they can what those experiences mean to them.

CHAPTER FOUR

The Rhetoric of Science

N TURNING TO EVOCATION THEORY, WHICH ASCRIBES THE VALUE OF the literary work to the effect it produces on the reader, I shall attack at once the notion that scientific writing per se is produced without such rhetorical intent. Since the argument is inductive, one may presume — only in part facetiously — that a single counterexample will suffice to disallow it. The rhetorical patterning of the *Origin of Species* provides such a counterexample.

The book is laid out according to the pattern of a classical oration, complete with exordium, narration, exposition, partition, confirmation, refutation, digression, and peroration. The opening paragraphs of the introduction serve as an exordium: they remind the reader that the author is Darwin of the *Beagle* (his account of the voyage had been something of a best-seller), and they label his topic with a borrowed phrase as "that mystery of mysteries" (though Darwin was likely privately to refer to it more prosaically as the "species question").[1] They seek to establish respect for Darwin's labors, "five years' work [before] I allowed myself to speculate"; for his deliberation, "I give [these personal details] to show that I have not been hasty in coming to a decision"; and for his ethical behavior with respect to Alfred Russel Wallace, "Sir C. Lyell and Dr. Hooker . . . honored me by thinking it advisable to publish, with Mr. Wallace's excellent memoir, some brief extracts from my manuscripts." And they call for the reader's sympathy,

"As my health is far from strong, I have been urged to publish this abstract [the *Origin*]."[2]

At the same time, these and the next few paragraphs may be said to constitute the narration, since they relate how Darwin came to the problem, worked on it, and devised his solution. Next, in several more paragraphs, comes the exposition. Here, Darwin lays down the problem, averring that though it is "quite conceivable" that a naturalist after reviewing various bodies of facts might conclude that species had in fact evolved from other species, nonetheless such a conclusion would be "unsatisfactory" unless a means could be found to account for how such changes could have occurred (pp. 72–73). Next, in the partition, a chapter-by-chapter precis of the book, Darwin sets out his argument that it is natural selection that provides that means (pp. 73–75).

The body of the book falls into three large sections, each consisting of some four or five chapters. In the first of these sections, the confirmation, Darwin presents the detailed working out of his argument that natural selection operates on minutely variant individuals by way of the "struggle for existence" to produce ultimately new species (pp. 77–320). Then, in the next few chapters, the refutation, he replies to various objections to the theory, that it could not account for the production of organs of great complexity, like the eye, and so on (pp. 321–520). Finally, in a digression (which Cicero allows but rather disapproves of),[3] Darwin draws new support for his theory by showing how successfully it accounts for the distribution of beings in time (as revealed by geology) and in space (as shown by geography), as well as for a number of puzzling biological facts, such as the existence of vestigial organs (pp. 521–718). The argument in the confirmation is largely argument from efficient cause; in the digression, from consequences.

The last chapter opens with a recapitulation of the entire argument and then moves into an affecting peroration in which Darwin considers some of the implications of his theory (pp. 719–59). This culminates in the final paragraph which elaborates Darwin's famed metaphor of the "tangled bank," a symbol for the complex interrelations he observes among the community of living creatures. The last, highly charged sentence, invoking both Newton and the Creator, proclaims the "grandeur of this view of life."

It is easy to see why Darwin would have made use of such a pattern for his work, which he himself describes as "one long argument" (p. 719). And one need not document that Darwin in his typical nineteenth-century education would have been exposed to abundant examples from classical authors employing the pattern and indeed would have had training in the use of it, for, even if one were to believe that Darwin had simply hit upon the form as an effective way to present an argument, one could not view the argument as other than rhetorical. Like all argument, it clearly aims to persuade, and it makes no move that does not have the reader in mind.

The point here is not, of course, that one example alone demonstrates that rhetoric as such plays an important part in all scientific discourse (especially when the example is from the nineteenth century and is hardly a typical scientific document even of its day), but rather that one cannot categorically rule out rhetorical considerations from the study of scientific discourse simply because that discourse is scientific. Yet that judgment has traditionally been made by both the literary and the scientific communities as they mark off literary from scientific language.

It is worth noting if only in passing that, unlike the previous critical theories we have examined, evocation theory retains something of a potent force in the modern critical world. Opinion may be divided between those who assert that it is the text that "constructs" the reader and those who claim that it is the reader who "constructs" the text, but in either case interest remains centered on the interaction of text and reader. Significantly for our argument, contemporary evocationist critics are unlikely to exempt scientific texts from their judgments that all texts carry their inherent rhetoric with them or that readers construe all the texts they encounter.

Within the scientific countertradition as well, this view of scientific rhetoric prevails. When paradigms conflict, the paradigm-relativists say, the choices between them cannot be made on scientific grounds, so they must be made on what are essentially rhetorical ones. And, the constructivists assert, when scientific communities grapple within their own ranks to achieve consensus, to construct their agreed-upon versions of the truth, they must do so, again, by way of rhetoric.[4] (A philosophical argument to this end is presented by Walter Weimer in "Science as a Rhetorical Transaction,"[5] and the sociological position is stated in Michael Overington's "The Scientific Community as Audience: Toward a Rhetorical Analysis of Science.")[6] Without fully endorsing the countertraditional positions, however, I argue that rhetorical considerations are, and should be, an important part of most, if not all, scientific discourse.

2

Although it can never quite succeed in its aim, the stylistic straitjacket imposed on scientist-writers as they report their work in official scientific channels is, I have said, intended to restrain their most expressive gestures. This style of scientific discourse, which has evolved over several centuries as institutional science has sought to regulate its enterprise, may well be construed as an official rhetoric of science — a rhetoric, moreover, that presents itself as no rhetoric at all, indeed as its very antithesis.

The more obvious marks of this style, this rhetoric, have often been noted.[7] To begin with, the language is generally what English teachers label "agentless prose"; that is, there are no doers of the actions reported, and in fact, the actions themselves often disappear. Verbs are cast in the passive voice — "20 ml of sulfuric acid was added to the solution"; or they are converted into substantives — "the addition of 20 ml of sulfuric acid was completed." Comparable with this nominalization of verbs, the scientific style also frequently mandates the reification of quality. Thus scientists dealing with thick, sticky liquids concern themselves with a property they call "viscosity." And to cite but one more characteristic of the scientific style, scientists make a habit of piling up modifiers — "the Smith-Jones colorimetric iron impurity determination method."

Some of these stylistic markings are frequently justified as being singularly appropriate to the scientific enterprise. In particular, agentless prose is cited as reflecting the objectivity and impersonality of science. As one technical writing text remarks: "Much technical writing is concerned with the description of work so objective that the reader does not care who did it. The reader is interested solely in the work itself and is not interested in the agency or agent involved."[8] Attention is less often directed at the reification of quality, but stacked modifiers receive their share of attention from English teachers, who invariably deplore them. They seem, however, to be tacitly ignored by technical editors, who often do not insist even on the punctuation that would make their inner relationships clearer: hyphens within unit modifiers, commas between adjectives that modify coordinately. What is needed, of course, is a careful rhetorical analysis of the particular style of scientific language (an analysis the countertradition has already begun). Ultimately, such an analysis would reveal more precisely the ranges of the scientific style and consider in detail the various effects it achieves.

Short of such a detailed analysis, several points can be made at once. First, the language of science is learned; it is not simply a natural mode of expression adopted spontaneously by each working scientist. The ephebe in any science, like Polanyi's fledgling pulmonary radiologist, learns the language of science from a mentor along with and indistinguishably from learning the subject matter. Then, upon entering the profession, the young scientist encounters the whole editorial apparatus of science, which considers and approves or rejects proposals, grant applications, and papers submitted for publication, all of which must conform to the expectations of those reviewing them in terms of rhetoric as well as protocol. What is so often said descriptively about the language of science — that it is clear, unambiguous, objective, and impersonal — is really intended prescriptively. The young scientist — indeed the working scientist at any stage of career, Nobel laureates perhaps excepted — is told that the language used must bear the marks of clarity, precision, objectivity, impersonality, and so on if it is to be accepted as scientific language. Scientists make much of the self-correcting nature of the experimental side of their work; they say nothing, indeed are often quite unaware, of the self-policing nature of their rhetoric. (What is rejected is, of course, rejected not as bad rhetoric but as bad science. The offender learns to correct the rhetoric until the science conforms to expectations.)

What is involved here surely *is* rhetoric. The scientist who decides to write "20 ml of sulfuric acid was added to the solution," rather than "I added 20 ml of sulfuric acid to the solution," is making a rhetorical decision. The same action is referred to in either case; the difference is in the effect on the reader. To claim that the language of science is, or should be, objective because science itself is objective is to confuse cause and effect. The apparent objectivity is the result of the decision made about language usage, not the cause of it. But it makes no difference who performs the action, the technical writing text instructs its readers. Perhaps. But when I was a chemist I had laboratory mates whose technique was such that the rest of us would absent ourselves from the laboratory when they added 20 ml of sulfuric acid to anything. Indeed, the repeatability of scientific results, the checking of results in other laboratories, is not so easily accomplished nor so unambiguous as the official rhetoric would suggest. But that is not the point. It is not that scientists misrepresent when, by use of the passive voice, they make the tacit claim that their work is infinitely repeatable, that every scientist who tries to duplicate it will observe precisely the same effects; it is that this methodological claim is made by way of rhetoric. As Wayne Booth has said in another context, "The author cannot choose whether to use rhetorical heightening. His only choice is of the kind of rhetoric he will use."[9] Science has a perfect right to opt for an official rhetoric of objectivity; but merely because that rhetorical choice has become a habitual one, indeed almost surely an unconscious one, one must not believe that it is no longer, nor ever was, a matter of rhetoric but rather a true voice of science, a simple reflection of how science works, the bare record of what science is and does.

Nor must one think that the rhetorical choices the scientist makes are trivial ones, "mere" rhetoric. Much of what one thinks about science — the nonscientist and the scientist alike — is determined by that rhetoric. When science is judged as objective and impersonal, as having privileged access to the truth, it is in part because the rhetoric of science compels one to this view. Preliminary study is already revealing significant effects on the workings of science of the various markings of the scientific style.[10] Even such a seemingly trivial matter as the stacking of modifiers may well function for the profession (as many tricks of specialized language do) as a kind of gatekeeper, separating those who have mastered the jargon and can perceive the intended relationships among the modifiers from those who have not. Others of these scientific markings, such as the nominalization of actions and qualities, seem to be of central importance to the workings of science proper. It seems quite likely that this habit of thought — this concretizing, this reification, of what is otherwise transient and variable — serves to focus the mind in ways that are scientifically rewarding. Thus, there is good reason to suppose that Aristotle's mechanics failed to develop as Galileo's did because Aristotle thought in terms of *bodies* moving, changing, whereas Galileo thought rather of *motion* itself as an abstraction and more precisely discriminated uniform motion (velocity) from ever-increasing motion (acceleration).[11] Without the little trick of nominalization, this step could not have been taken.

But can one speak legitimately of rhetorical effects when one considers how scientists' verbal formulations affect their own thinking? Does not any sense of rhetoric presuppose a listener (or a reader)? To be sure. But scientists, indeed all persons, must respond to their own verbal formulations much as they would to those of anyone else. We are the hearers, the readers, of our own thoughts. The words in which those thoughts are couched have their effects on us much as they would on anyone else. We are then, willy-nilly, the victims of — or simply the responders to — our own rhetoric. Hence it is appropriate to speak of how the linguistic habits of scientists affect their own thinking. The official rhetoric of science determines not merely how outsiders think of the scientific enterprise but how scientists themselves think of it, indeed how they think *in* it.

The official rhetoric of organized science is not the complete story of scientific rhetoric, however. The mere fact that scientists have individual styles that assert themselves to varying degrees against the general backdrop of scientific discourse implies that scientists employ, to a greater or lesser degree, their own personal rhetorics. All scientists undoubtedly evolve their own rhetorical strategy or strategies, which they employ, probably unconsciously, when they communicate their results. As circumstances change, these personal rhetorics variously supplant, supplement, are superimposed on, or lie submerged in the official rhetoric. In a great many cases, because the control over scientific usage is strict and the pressures to conform great (livelihoods depend upon it), the impact of personal rhetorics on the overall body of scientific discourse is small. Yet their influence need not be negligible, and indeed, to ensure the progress of science, I will insist in a moment, they are essential.

In speaking of personal styles as personal rhetorics, one must note that the expressive elements identified in the last chapter, particularly the widespread expressions of dominance and the "feeling for the organism," can equally well be construed as rhetorics. In pairing expression and evocation theories, one realizes that the two cannot be separated, that expression completes its agenda only when it evokes a response. Consistent with that view, then, expressive elements must serve evocational ends. Significantly, Keller observes the same rhetorical elements in her argument on gender and science. Thus, she identifies a "rhetoric of domination, coercion, and mastery" as the prevailing rhetoric of modern science.[12] Along with this rhetoric, however, Keller perceives other, essentially erotic elements, which "persist throughout history only sotto voce, as minor themes made inaudible by a dominant rhetoric."[13] Although one may contest the balance of the two in Keller's argument, what is significant is that she has recognized both elements in the discourse of science and conceives of them in rhetorical terms.

In any discussion of rhetoric one tends to be intentionalist, thinking of rhetoric as the pragmatic, "how-to" side of evocation, even as one acknowledges that the response that is evoked may arise from material that is unconsciously expressed (aggression, perhaps). But if rhetoric seems to center on the rhetor (chiefly the writer in the domain of scientific discourse), it is the reader who receives the emphasis in the most recent version of evocation theory, the reception and reader-response movements.[14] In them, the reader's experiencing of the text becomes the center of interest, and it is to scientist-readers and their experience that we will now turn.

3

Science rarely canonizes venerable texts the way that literature does. Most of the "great books" that have shaped science sit moldering unread on the shelves of ancient libraries. Those that do not, those that still have an audience today — like Harvey's *Circulation of the Blood* — do so in part, I believe, because they belong to a special category to be described shortly and because they have acquired a status as classics in the world beyond science, have in fact entered the canon of significant human documents. Even these books, however, are not read by today's scientists to tell them what they need to know about their science.

It is sometimes claimed that what is valuable in the old works has been winnowed out by science and resides in its fabric of scientific knowledge, which always keeps itself up to date, growing, changing, adding, correcting, as the great enterprise proceeds. In science, this argument goes, it is not documents that are central but knowledge. What the contemporary scientist works with is current scientific knowledge, which has cast off, like the skins of previous molts, the dead documents of the past. In literature, where, as every schoolchild knows (or used to know), the ancient texts are continually being reread and reexperienced, the argument follows naturally enough that it is the readers' responses, continually recurring, that keep the experience of the old texts alive. But if science works by discarding old texts while merely keeping something of their message alive in its own tradition as scientific "knowledge," then it would seem all but impossible to situate the readers' response in any central position in the functioning of scientific discourse. Indeed, the text *as experience* would seem to have been banished from the scene along with the text as document.

But I believe that this argument cannot be maintained. There is no body of knowledge independent of the language that inscribes it in documents or carries it in verbal exchange. Scientists have informal exchanges with other scientists, they attend meetings at which they listen to the reading of formal papers, and they expose themselves to the current published literature in their field. In these various cases, the language perceived evokes its response. In fact, even as they perform their own work scientists respond to the language in which their mind conceives it. One cannot, of course, speak precisely of *reader* response in each of these cases, but there is no fundamental distinction among them — they all involve response to formulated language. Furthermore, the scientific document that has not been read in a hundred years may have entered the fabric of scientific knowledge precisely because it was read at one time and *then* experienced, and the experience of that reading has been sustained by transmission through countless other documents, in their turn read and experienced. Scientific knowledge, therefore, is a continual reexperiencing by scientists of responses to what is said in language; it is, indeed, nothing but the responses of the scientists who participate in the scientific enterprise.

As a corollary of the above, the new sociologists aver that in a very real sense scientific knowledge does not exist until it is transmitted, that scientific information is valueless until it is exchanged, that scientific writings have no function until they are read. It is the experience of reading scientific documents that confers on those documents their scientific validity; until that experience occurs, the document is worthless to science.

The story has frequently been told of Alfred Russel Wallace's sending of his paper outlining the theory of evolution by natural selection to Charles Darwin, who had, ironically enough, been working privately for some twenty years developing precisely the same idea. Also well known is the outcome (which Darwin himself describes in the opening of the *Origin*): that Wallace's paper was read along with some extracts of material by Darwin at a meeting of the Linnaean Society, with subsequent side-by-side publication in the society's *Journal*. The theory jointly announced, however, is now universally known as Darwin's theory. This puzzling fact is usually explained on the basis that the scientific community generally has accepted the evidence for Darwin's priority in devising the theory and awarded him the palm. (One recent writer contends that Darwin and his friends engaged in a conspiracy to defraud Wallace of his rightful credit.)[15] Significantly, however, Darwin, who had vast amounts of research material already at hand, proceeded within a year to write a masterwork, the *Origin of Species*, laying out the case for natural selection in rhetorically compelling terms. Wallace, on the other hand, did not write his book on evolutionary theory for some thirty years, until after Darwin's death (and he titled his book *Darwinism*). Thus the chief statement of the case is Darwin's, and it is the collective readers' responses to the *Origin*, many would argue, that have made Darwinism *Darwinism* and not *Darwin-Wallaceism*.

An even clearer example is given by the fate of Gregor Mendel's paper reporting his experiments with pea plants and laying the foundation of genetics. Again the story is often told: Mendel published two papers in the late 1860s, one of them reporting the pea experiments, and they appear to have been almost completely ignored for some thirty years, until their rediscovery was announced virtually simultaneously by three scientists doing similar work. And thus, in the folk tradition of science, was the modern science of genetics born.[16]

Traditional explanations for the apparent neglect are several: that the key paper was difficult and mathematical, that it was published in an obscure journal, and that Mendel himself was an unknown figure, working outside the biological establishment.[17] Certain revisionist historians, however, have rendered these explanations more or less moot by arguing that Mendel's work was not unknown before its rediscovery, noting some dozen or so citations in the intervening years.[18] Others have suggested that the rediscoverers had not, as they claimed, independently reconfirmed Mendel's findings before they learned of his paper but had come upon them earlier and been influenced by them in their own research programs.[19] The two positions, of course, are not compatible, for if the paper had not been forgotten by the biological community the rediscoverers could hardly have claimed initial ignorance of it. (Historical debunkers have also claimed that Mendel's results were simply too good to be true and that he must have cooked them a bit to make his case more strongly, though that is not germane to this argument.)[20]

The most recent countertraditionalists have undertaken still another reinterpretation of the Mendel story. To begin with, they put Mendel squarely in the ranks of traditional hybridizers, his predecessors and contemporaries. Thus Robert Olby argues that Mendel himself, though conceiving of segregating traits, never thought in terms of paired, particulate, responsible factors (genes).[21] The most thoroughgoing new sociological analysis is that of Augustine Brannigan, whose position is that Mendel's work when it was done was simply Kuhnian normal science, carried out within the paradigm of traditional hybridization studies.[22] Mendel's research, in this view, was not unknown or forgotten but known and accepted by the biological community as he himself intended it, as simply one more contribution to hybridization science.

What happened in 1900, in Brannigan's analysis, is that a dispute in priority over the rediscovery of the laws of segregation, and the importance of those laws to the turn-of-the-century argument over the mechanism of evolution, led to the canonization of Mendel as the real discoverer and the inscription of the discovery of his laws as a major event that laid the basis for the newborn science of genetics. Mendel's work then becomes a discovery after the fact by particular social actions. Indeed, it is Brannigan's general sociological argument, expressed in *The Social Basis of Scientific Discoveries*, that discovery is always a post hoc process, a social procedure that results in the communal labeling of an earlier event as a discovery.[23] As difficult as it is to shake off our conditioned response that Mendel's discovery, presumably like all discoveries, came at the time the discoverer did his work, Brannigan's is an attractive argument. The Mendel story seems to be a classic instance of the paradigm constructing its own history, plucking its ancestral discoverer out of the past to legitimize its enterprise.

Yet Brannigan's reader may not be quite convinced by his argument that Mendel saw and understood his work precisely as it was known and understood by his contemporaries. Mendel's work clearly was not regarded by his contemporaries as important. Those citations of Mendel's paper that have come to light seem very much pro forma, and it seems reasonable to conclude that Mendel's results were not a part of the working knowledge of most biologists for the thirty years of their neglect. As historian Michael MacRoberts has recently concluded, Mendel's paper was "not known at the informal level. . . . It was barely 'known' at the formal level."[24] This is not, of course, a compelling argument against Brannigan's characterization of Mendel's work as, in its own day, normal science. It is the fate of most contributions to normal science to go virtually unread and uncited; they raise their small voices once and are not heard from again.

And Brannigan is certainly right in his observation that Mendel's paper does not overtly announce a major discovery. As MacRoberts points out, Mendel did not subsequently embark on a major campaign to win converts. He was "not in close contact with any of the scientific elite except Nageli." He did not follow up his one publication "by flooding the literature with rewrites of it as scientists commonly do." And he did not "barnstorm the scientific meetings of Europe."[25] Brannigan interprets Mendel's behavior as indicating that he himself saw his work only in the context of contemporary hybridization research and did not conceive of it as a major advance. But in his paper Mendel highlights several of his key findings by italicizing them and explicitly states that his approach "seems to be the one correct way of finally reaching the solution to a question whose significance for the evolutionary history of organic forms must not be underestimated."[26] I would argue that what is at work here is essentially a rhetorical failure, that Mendel understands quite well the significance of what he has done (given the context of the biology of his day), states it once modestly, and then retires from the stage. In short, he applies the rhetoric of normal science to describe what is scientifically revolutionary.

Scientists always face something of a dilemma in communicating their results. There is, on the one hand, the deep involvement, the pride of discovery, and the urge to find adherents to their ideas. As Ziman remarks, the scientist is "desperately keen to *persuade* his readers or audience" (emphasis in the original). This is so because of the element of novelty, when the scientist has the task of "changing a preconceived notion, demonstrating an unexpected contradiction, or announcing an unexpected observation." At the same time, the official style calls for enormous restraint, with its insistence on the relentless passive and its demand for obsessive modesty. Even within such restraints, of course, the official style can have its own rhetorical power. "By a psychological inversion," Ziman observes, "this rhetorical motive is best served by a very plain and modest style."[27] Under ordinary circumstances, then, when what is novel represents a relatively small departure from what is anticipated, the official style functions well, as it is intended to do.

The case of Mendel, however, suggests that when a significant departure from what is expected is to be conveyed, when a major change in thinking is to be brought about, then a significantly different rhetoric is called for. Major shifts in paradigm cannot be achieved with the ordinary rhetoric of science. The modest persona that speaks to us in Mendel's paper is not the voice of the revolutionary. That voice was to come with the rediscoverers. DeVries, for example wrote not one, but three, papers announcing his "rediscovery,"[28] and Bateson, not one of the rediscoverers but an early advocate of Mendelism, took the true revolutionary line, asserting that from the moment of rediscovery of Mendel's laws "in all the great problems of biology a new era began."[29]

One may ponder also the example of Barbara McClintock. The highly expressive language in the Nobel address is suitable, I now argue, for the revolutionary rhetoric her revolution in biological thinking called for. But this rhetoric was barely suggested in the early papers when McClintock remained as *vox clamantis in deserto*. One may well perceive a relationship between the early lack of recognition and the degree of rhetorical timidity.

It is, then, the normal science of Thomas Kuhn, which proceeds in terms of small incremental advances under an umbrella paradigm, that would seem to be the appropriate domain for the standard rhetoric of science. And it is Kuhn's periodic scientific revolutions, the frantic scrambles for shelter under new umbrella paradigms as the old ones begin increasingly to leak, that warrant a more telling, revolutionary rhetoric. The standard rhetoric capitalizes on the paradigm it operates under, takes advantage of the shared commitment of the community of readers to the paradigm to make its discourse meaningful. But to achieve a scientific revolution the scientist-writer must not merely abandon one paradigm and shift allegiance to a new one but also carry along those scientist-readers who have a lifelong commitment and decades of professional activity invested in the old paradigm. It is this task that calls for a rhetoric of a new and different order.

4

One can, however, and perhaps should put the argument in something other than strictly Kuhnian terms. One need only make the natural assumption that there will be a spectrum of possibilities in the degrees of deviation from expectations of any given scientific advance: a great many routine, incremental additions to knowledge; some less frequent discoveries of new relations and the like, occasioning varying degrees of surprise and necessitating varying amounts of adjustment of general views; and, very seldom, those truly astonishing changes — like the Copernican conversion — that cause the rethinking of major presuppositions. If such is the case, there would seem to be a need for a corresponding variety of scientific rhetorics, or a flexible scientific rhetoric, adaptable to situations involving varying degrees of departure of the material from expected scientific norms. We have already evidence for such a view.

It is hard to imagine anything more routine in its science or its scientific rhetoric than Bill Pelletier's and my paper on atisine. We wrote for our fellow alkaloid chemists, our results were precisely to be expected, and we employed the kind of verbal shorthand used by our community to convey such results. With Muller's paper on the linear model for the genetic material, the situation is somewhat different. Here one of the partisans of an old paradigm (the linear model) is fending off an attack by the proponent of a new paradigm (the three-dimensional model) and his sharper, somewhat combative tone ("this declaration is so widely at variance with the conclusions jointly agreed upon";[30] "the discussion and data given in the original papers supply all the material necessary for a decision of the matter")[31] surely reflects that fact. Woodward's highly personal, explicit rhetoric of aggression, also a departure from the scientific standard, is related to the promotion of what was conceived to be a new way of doing organic chemistry. With Darwin and the *Origin* one is clearly in the area where it is appropriate to speak of scientific revolution, and it is plain that Darwin's whole approach in the *Origin* is anything but routine scientific rhetoric. His persistent personification of plants and animals, and his laying out of the book on the plan of a classical oration — neither of these is surprising if the book is intended as an exercise in persuasion; both are hardly appropriate for routine scientific reportage. Darwin knew (he agonizes over it in letters)[32] that what he was proposing was radically new to science and to the public, that it overturned a great many fundamental notions of science and religion, and that it was likely to stir up a whirlwind of public controversy. It is hardly surprising that he called upon whatever rhetorical powers he could command to make his argument effective. Thus, these examples, chosen for other purposes, serve to illustrate the thesis that there is a spectrum of scientific rhetorics, ranging from the routine to the revolutionary.

Of that small body of scientific works that have acquired a classic status and are still read long after the occasions that called them forth, I would now suggest that these are revolutionary works that, unlike Mendel's paper, but like Darwin's *Origin*, found the rhetoric that made them effective documents, that caused them to evoke the reader response that their time demanded and that today's interested reader can still supply.

These views of a "standard" and a "revolutionary" rhetoric of science, or of a spectrum of scientific rhetorics, are much at variance with science's traditional view of its own language, and with the official rhetoric itself. In such a view it is unseemly, "unscientific," for scientists to become advocates. They are expected to be objective, disinterested, and uninvolved, and their language is supposed to reflect that attitude. Of necessity, of course, scientists are subjective, interested, and involved; and it is only by employing the official rhetoric that they can appear not to be so. The studied silence of science on the subject of its alternate rhetorics must not blind us to the fact that such rhetorics can serve a useful purpose.

The countertraditionalists have made much of the notion of competing paradigms and their battle for the allegiance of the scientific community. Under such circumstances, Kuhn and Feyerabend argue, the usual standards of scientific judgment cannot come into play; decisions cannot simply be made between competing paradigms because they are so different that they refer to different bodies of experience. Then, they say, scientists must resort to extraordinary methods to win allegiance to their particular paradigm—in my terms, they must call upon a revolutionary rhetoric. For example, much of what Feyerabend (in his *Against Method*) classifies as antimethodic ("anything goes") or anarchic in Galileo's *Dialogue on the Two Chief World Systems* I would call rhetoric. In Feyerabend's terms, Galileo is violating the so-called scientific method; to me he is employing a revolutionary rhetoric.

In any case, it is appropriate, indeed essential, for scientists to seek to win their readers' assent. Scientists work in communities, as the counter-tradition reminds us, and their standing in the community is determined by the degree of acceptance of their work. It is natural that they should hope to convince their fellow workers of the validity of their ideas. Much of the time this is handled efficiently and effectively by employing the standard rhetoric of science. But it is the same impulse — that their work should evoke a community response, should come into existence as part of the ongoing scientific dialogue — that impels scientists from time to time to utilize other, more striking rhetorics, in order to win acceptance for views that depart in some measure from the accepted norm. It is far more appropriate that one study when and where and how this happens than that one should pretend, with the traditionalists, that it never happens at all.

5

A striking aspect of the rhetoric of Galileo in the *Dialogue* is the way in which Salviati, the spokesman for the "new science," employs a combination of demonstrations, analogies, and what are now termed "thought experiments" to make his various points. And just as Salviati by this means brings his fellow interlocutors, Sagredo and Simplicio, into his discussion as participants, so Galileo engages the reader in his presentation.

One remarkable thing about these demonstrations is the varying degrees to which they call on the reader's imagination. Some of them are presented as literal experiments performed by the interlocutors. To show that the surface of the moon could not actually be as polished as a mirror, Salviati has first a flat mirror, then a convex one, brought forth, and the three participants compare the appearance of each with that of the rough wall next to them.[33] Other demonstrations are simply described by Salviati but not performed; in the conversation, an imaginary ball is rolled down an inclined plane (pp. 23–24), unheard cannons are shot (pp. 126–27), unseen birds fly from trees (pp. 183–86), and make-believe players roll hoops (pp. 157–61). Readers are expected to know from experience how these events occur or readily accept their happening when Salviati describes them. In one famous instance, however, Salviati (Galileo) does not play fair, and Simplicio (the readers, too, of course) is deceived. The ball dropped from the top of the mast of a moving ship does not, as Salviati at first claims, strike the deck at some distance from the foot of the mast (pp. 126, 141, 143–45). Readers thus are led to associate the "wrong" theory with the false experience, so that when they learn the true experience, they accept the "right" theory along with it.

From a literary perspective the most interesting of Salviati's arguments are the full-blown analogies, which, in some detail, bring the readers' experience to bear to illustrate a situation they would otherwise find unbelievable. The best known of these is Salviati's account of the interior cabin of a ship in which everything occurs — fish swim in a bowl, items fall to the floor, and so on — in precisely the same fashion whether the ship is moving (at constant velocity in a straight line) or is still (pp. 186–88). This is, of course, to demonstrate by analogy that one cannot tell if the earth is in motion by the events that occur on earth.

More interesting from the scientific point of view, however, are the thought experiments, experiments that the reader can well imagine and confidently predict the outcome of, even though the experiments could not in fact ever be carried out. Thus, Salviati asks his friends to picture the line that would be drawn in space by a man sitting in a cabin in a moving ship writing a letter. To the observer the line drawn would be virtually a straight line caused by the movement of the ship, with the movements of the man's hand creating minor deviations in it. But to the man, the motions of his hand, not the motion of the ship — the actual writing on the page, not the line drawn in space — are all that can be perceived (pp. 171–73). The point again is that living on earth one perceives as motion only the comparative displacements of objects, while the motion of the whole earth goes unobserved.

In the presumed live demonstrations, when mirrors are really brought forth, the events have the quality of real experience; they seem to occur as one reads. But even the hypothetical demonstrations, the analogies, and the thought experiments share in this illusionary effect because they are discussed — stated, perceived, understood — by the interlocutors, who seem really to be present. Yet the accepted view of scientific writing denies to it any illusionistic quality whatever (reserving that effect for literary language). Scientific discourse, in this view, describes; it does not mimic (it tells rather than shows). But that clearly is not the case here. In the *Dialogue* the interlocutors jointly experience, and the reader shares that experience, or, more precisely, the reader experiences what the interlocutors seem to experience. Given only this one example, three and a half centuries old, one need not suppose that contemporary scientific papers will create similar illusionary effects. But even this rather ancient example demonstrates that one cannot dogmatically assert that scientific writing by its very nature can never exert such effects, or that if it is to be truly scientific, it should never do so. One need not hold that the reader's response, the reader's experience of reading, is invariably the simulation of real experience; nonetheless one is free to insist, as I do here, that the reader's experience is the true test of the text. However it is experienced, the text becomes experience only when it *is* experienced.

6

A more recent example of a revolutionary rhetoric — some three hundred years later — and one that does not indulge in the device of interlocutors is found in the major papers of Albert Einstein. To appreciate the rhetoric of these papers, one needs to know something of the circumstances under which they appeared. The year 1905 was, it has often been said, the annus mirabilis of Einstein (like the year 1665 for Newton, when he invented the calculus, discovered the law of gravity, and determined that white light was compounded of the various colored lights of the spectrum). Then twenty-five years old, a fresh Ph.D. graduate of the University of Zurich, and unable to find a suitable academic post, Einstein was working as a patent examiner in Berne. Nonetheless, in that year he published five papers in physics journals, three of them of major importance — a paper describing the special theory of relativity, a paper on Brownian motion, and one establishing the photon theory of light. At first the papers produced some puzzlement, in part because they were not written within the official rhetoric of science, but not for long. The biographical facts tell the whole story: four years later Einstein was a professor at Zurich and in another four years, almost unbelievably, he was director of the Kaiser Wilhelm Institute in Berlin, then the leading center for physics in the world. In eight more years he received the Nobel Prize, largely for work reported in the first papers.

What was puzzling about Einstein's papers? Leopold Infeld says of the first relativity paper, "On the Electrodynamics of Moving Bodies": "The title sounds modest, yet as we read it we notice almost immediately that it is different from other papers. There are no references; no authorities are quoted, and the few footnotes are of an explanatory character. The style is simple, and a great part of this article can be followed without advanced technical knowledge. But its full understanding requires a maturity of mind and taste that is more rare and precious than pedantic knowledge."[34] Although these remarks may not be precisely true of all the 1905 papers, they are certainly applicable to the three major ones. Further, the three are alike in adopting essentially the same rhetorical strategy. As Gerald Holton, who has made a detailed study of Einstein's papers, says of them,

> One . . . finds that the style of the three papers is essentially the same and reveals what is typical of Einstein's work at that time. Each begins with the statement of formal asymmetries or other incongruities of a predominantly aesthetic nature (rather than, for example, a puzzle posed by unexplained experimental facts), then proposes a principle — preferably one of the generality of, say, the Second Law of Thermodynamics, to cite Einstein's repeated analogy — which removes the asymmetries as one of the deduced consequences, and at the end produces one or more experimentally verifiable predictions.[35]

Although neither of these commentators employs the word *rhetoric*, they are surely suggesting that Einstein has not employed the official rhetoric of science: he has not buttressed his work with a panoply of citations, placing it in the matrix of other related work; he has not effaced his own identity as an independent thinker; he has not made empirical results, as opposed to conceptual thought, the springboard of his work, but only the test of it; and he is willing to force the reader to rethink commonly held assumptions when his theory gives him a compelling reason for doing so. In all these respects his rhetoric is revolutionary.

As to the special relativity paper, "Electrodynamics of Moving Bodies," several clues to its understanding are offered by a little book of Einstein's intended for the general reader, *Relativity: The Special and the General Theory*. The rhetorical strategy involved in each text is the same: to begin with a seemingly insoluble conflict and then with the aid of a new theory, the theory of relativity, solve the problem in a most unexpected way, which itself involves a fundamental rethinking of our concepts of what the universe is like.

The "Electrodynamics" paper begins with a problem: "It is known that Maxwell's electrodynamics — as usually understood at the present time — when applied to moving bodies, leads to asymmetries which do not appear to be inherent in the phenomena." Then after detailing these "asymmetries," Einstein complicates the problem and shows us two seemingly inviolable principles in conflict:

> Examples of this sort, together with the unsuccessful attempts to discover any motion of the earth relatively to the "light medium," suggest that the phenomena of electrodynamics as well as of mechanics

possess no properties corresponding to the idea of absolute rest. They suggest rather that ... the same laws of electrodynamics and optics will be valid for all frames of reference for which the equations of mechanics hold good. We will raise this conjecture (the purport of which will hereafter be called the "Principle of Relativity") to the status of a postulate, and also introduce another postulate, which is only apparently irreconcilable with the former, namely, that light is always propagated in empty space with a definite velocity c which is independent of the state of motion of the emitting body. These two postulates suffice for the attainment of a simple and consistent theory of the electrodynamics of moving bodies.[36]

There are obvious features that make this hardly "physics talk," including an absence of jargon and a discursive manner, and although the conflict between the two key postulates is not overdramatized — the reader learns at once that the two are only "apparently" irreconcilable — nevertheless, considerable suspense is maintained: the reader is given no notion of how the reconciliation is to be achieved or how the two "suffice for the attainment of [the] simple and consistent theory."

In spite of the fact that Einstein says that the layman's account, *Relativity*, presents his ideas "in the sequence and connection in which they actually originated,"[37] Holton finds "the sequence given there ... not in accord with the sequence of steps in the 1905 paper itself" (p. 167). Nonetheless, considering the need for presenting the necessary background material for the lay audience of *Relativity*, including even a development of the idea of coordinate systems, I think the two are remarkably alike. There are differences of emphasis, of course. In developing his principle of relativity, Einstein in "Electrodynamics" works almost entirely from the Maxwell equation asymmetries and only alludes to the "failure to discover any motion of the earth relative to the 'light medium'" (p. 37). But in *Relativity* the situation is reversed: he only mentions the "more recent development of electrodynamics and optics" (p. 13) and concentrates instead on a full discussion of the lack of a fixed orientation of space, something the nonmathematical reader is likely to comprehend more readily than the Maxwell equations. Once the necessary background is out of the way in *Relativity*, Einstein proceeds at once to a chapter entitled "The Apparent Incompatibility of the Law of Propagation of Light with the Principle of Relativity" (pp. 17–20), almost precisely the language of "Electrodynamics." Here, however, the conflict, left implied in the scientific paper, is fully dramatized. Through some half-dozen paragraphs the lay reader is led to perceive what the scientist will know at once — why the two principles do indeed conflict. Then, in *Relativity*, comes the key sentence that gives the game away, both in this text, where the strategy is made explicit, and in the other, where it is only left to do its work. "At this juncture," Einstein writes, "the theory of relativity entered the arena" (p. 19). The rhetorical effect is immediate: "arena" at once labels, dramatizes, and situates the conflict. And the "theory of relativity," which rides to the rescue, is precisely that "simple and consistent theory" called for in the comparable spot in "Electrodynamics." (The lay reader must note that the *principle* of relativity, a general statement that physical laws in nature are not to presuppose some fixed orientation in space, is not to be confused with the *theory* of relativity, Einstein's specific formulation of the time-space relations involved with bodies moving with respect to a frame of reference.) The next sentence in *Relativity* explains what the theory does without, again, revealing prematurely how it does so. The reader is now at precisely the same spot in the two versions of the argument: the conflict has been joined, and the possibility of a solution dramatically raised.

Both works then move to the solution of the problem and proceed in exactly the same way. First the reader is asked to join Einstein in analyzing the basic physical concepts of time and space with the aid of clocks and measuring rods and then to accept a new, operational definition of simultaneity:

> If we wish to describe the *motion* of a material point, we give the values of its co-ordinates as functions of the time. Now we must bear carefully in mind that a mathematical description of this kind has no physical meaning unless we are quite clear as to what we understand by "time." We have to take into account that all our judgments in which time plays a part are always judgments of *simultaneous events*. If, for instance, I say, "That train arrives here at 7 o'clock," I mean something like this: "The pointing of the small hand of my watch to 7 and the arrival of the train are simultaneous events." (pp. 38–39)

I trust that my reader will not be too surprised (considering what we have already seen of Einstein's scientific style) to learn that this passage is from the scientific paper, not from the simplified version for the layman.

The secret to resolving the problem comes next in both versions: it is employment of what are called the Lorenz transformations — equations that relate the changes in time and distance that occur in two coordinate systems in relative motion to one another. The scientific paper at this point derives the equations, whereas the layman's version only presents them (relegating the derivation to an appendix). The reader is now given the extremely surprising consequences of the equations: namely, that measurements of both time and distance made within a moving reference frame are not the same as the same measurements performed with respect to a stationary frame.

This idea is the crux of the theory and it is especially hard to grasp. Here Einstein employs thought experiments (like those of Galileo) to especially telling effect. *Relativity* at this point has a separate short chapter, "The Behaviour of Measuring Rods and Clocks in Motion," whose title precisely indicates how Einstein proceeds. He in effect walks his readers through the system with measuring rods and clocks in hand. What the equations show, he demonstrates, is that "the rigid rod is . . . shorter in motion than when at rest, and the more quickly it is moving, the shorter is the rod" (p. 35). Similarly with the clock: "As a consequence of its motion the clock goes more slowly than when at rest" (p. 37). In "Electrodynamics" the comparable section is more rigorous in treatment but depends in just the same way on thought experiments. The treatment of time is especially like that in the layman's version: "If at the points A and B of K [the reference system] there are stationary clocks which, viewed in the stationary system, are synchronous, and if the clock at A is moved with the velocity v along the line AB to B, then on its arrival at R the two clocks no longer synchronize, but the clock moved from A to B lags behind the other which has remained at B by $1/2tv^2/c^2$"(p. 49).

Einstein and his reader have now reached the promised goal: the irreconcilables have been reconciled, and in the process our understanding of time and space has been altered. As "Electrodynamics" puts it, "We have now deduced the requisite laws of the theory of kinematics corresponding to our two principles" (p. 51). To be sure, there is some work yet to be done in both accounts. *Relativity*, among other things, shows how the new theory leads directly to the famous equation $E = mc^2$ (pp. 44–48), which is the subject of a separate scientific paper. (In neither account, incidentally, does the equation occur in quite the form we have come to know it.) But these additional details need not concern us. The significant features earlier pointed to are now complete: the conflict has been presented and resolved in terms of a fundamental new theory of universal applicability — a theory that necessitates a revision of our basic intuitions about time and space, made comprehensible by thought experiments laid out in extremely simple terms for the reader (scientific or otherwise) to grasp.

The rhetorical strategy is a remarkable variation on what Keller has called the dominant rhetoric of modern science — assertion by a (male) science of mastery and control over a (female) nature. Unlike the battlefield metaphors of Woodward, with their bastions taken in the struggle to dominate nature, in Einstein's imagery one sees fateful conflicts within nature (or our interpretation of it), and these are resolved by science, which rides to the rescue and halts the conflict with its pacific theory. (Nature and nature's laws lay mired in fight. Einstein said, Let Relativity be and all is right.) But there is a price to pay. True, the theory gives us a serene and unconflicted world, made peaceable by science, but it is a new and unfamiliar world, a world which defies our common sense, with its clocks and yardsticks changed by motion. It is, in fact, a world that lives in a new scientific paradigm, which it has been the task of Einstein's rhetoric to create.

Holton's remarks about Einstein's major papers of 1905 suggest that the rhetorical strategy at work in the relativity paper is employed in all of them. With the aid of *Relativity*, one can see that the pattern is of even wider occurrence, for, in addition to the first part of *Relativity*, with its close correspondence to "Electrodynamics," there are two other sections, one on the general theory of relativity and one on the cosmological consequences of the theory. Not only does each section of the layman's account have its counterpart in a scientific paper, but the rhetorical strategy employed in each paper (and, more explicitly, in *Relativity*) remains the same: an apparently irreconcilable conflict resolved by a new theory, which drastically alters our commonsense view of the universe.

It is also of interest that each case involves the use of thought experiments. One of these, from *Relativity*, is especially memorable. It is the well-known account of the man in the chest in outer space. Much like Galileo's man in the cabin of the ship who cannot tell if the ship is moving or not, Einstein's man is in a chest with a hook on the top by which the chest is being pulled along at a constant acceleration. The observers outside the chest in their own frame of reference, see what is happening. But how do things look to the man in the chest, from his reference system? He will "come to the conclusion that he and the chest are in a gravitational field which is constant with regard to time" (p. 67). The point, of course, is that the man's view of things and the outside observers' view of them are equally admissible (just as in Galileo's example both motion and nonmotion may explain what is seen); one may have acceleration/no gravity or gravity/no acceleration, as one wishes. The "scientific" discussion of this point, from the comparable scientific paper, is only slightly more abstract: "Does this permit an observer at rest relatively to K' infer that he is on a 'really' accelerated system of reference? The answer is in the negative; for the above-mentioned relation of freely movable masses to K' may be interpreted equally well in the following way. The system of reference K' is unaccelerated, but the space-time territory in question is under the sway of a gravitational field, which generates the accelerated motion of the bodies relatively to K'."[38] Again, it is only by the thought experiment that the idea is made conceivable.

Now we cannot leave Einstein's papers and the little book *Relativity* without noting that there is something peculiar about their tone. It is, of course, difficult to speak of tone in works examined only in translation (and it is pointless to go to the original if one does not know the language as well as a native speaker, since tone is one of the subtlest of language effects). This said, and granted further that the excerpts examined are brief and are from translations by different persons, one cannot but be aware that, even in the scientific papers, this is not the usual voice of science.

The deviation is more apparent in the general account, of course. And in it there are even more obvious examples we have not had occasion to look at. The author speaks directly to the reader: "In your schooldays most of you who read this book made acquaintance with the noble building of Euclid's geometry" (p. 1). Or he includes the reader: "Let us suppose our old friend the railway carriage to be travelling along the rails" (p. 16). At times, he indulges in a kind of playful hyperbole: "I should load my conscience with grave sins against the sacred spirit of lucidity were I to formulate the aims of mechanics in this way" (p. 9). There is no condescension in any of this, but something of the tone of a patient teller of stories to children, an aim to make everything perfectly clear and eminently understandable. In his preface to *Relativity* Einstein says, "I have purposely treated the empirical foundations of the theory in a step-motherly fashion, so that readers unfamiliar with physics may not feel like the wanderer who was unable to see the forest for trees" (p. vi). I take this to mean that in giving appropriate background he will concentrate on the really essential points while not getting lost in detail, but the remark also suggests the tone of great patience one would adopt in speaking to children.

The overall tone of the scientific papers is not, of course, quite the same, but there are passages much closer to this than one might have supposed: "Let us take a system of coordinates in which the equations of Newtonian mechanics hold good. In order to render our presentation more precise and to distinguish this system of coordinates verbally from others which will be introduced hereafter, we call it the 'stationary system'" ("Electrodynamics," p. 38). Again, the tone of the patient expositor, though now the speaker might seem more like a guide through unfamiliar territory. (This remark could equally well be made of sections of *Relativity*.) In one of the scientific papers, "Cosmological Considerations on the General Theory of Relativity," Einstein makes explicit reference to himself as a guide: "In the present paragraph I shall conduct the reader over the road that I have myself travelled, rather a rough and winding road, because otherwise I cannot hope that he will take much interest in the result at the end of the journey."[39]

Clearly this tone represents a significant deviance from the official style of science with its anonymous, agentless prose claiming to tell us simply how things are, not how they seem to be. Instead there is a writer's real voice: an agent has entered the field of discourse to explain what he is doing and why. What he is doing, of course, is changing the reader's notion of the way the world works. And he cannot achieve that revolutionary purpose with the flat assertions of normal science, with the tacit assumption that he and his readers share a common knowledge. Rather he must lead the reader on a voyage of discovery into a new and unexpected land.

In his study of the three 1905 papers, Gerald Holton has undertaken an extensive survey of the Einstein archival material to locate some type of model for their "shape" and "content." Among the early influences on Einstein, as is well known, was Ernst Mach, the physicist-philosopher, whose self-image as "an isolated fighter" appeared in "his books that young Einstein read" (p. 203). Although Holton does not suggest it, conceivably this is the source of the attitude that finds its expression in the "arena" image in *Relativity*. Holton, most surprisingly, does find the major source for the presentation of ideas in "Electrodynamics of Moving Bodies" in the textbooks of August Föppl, a now quite forgotten physicist and writer of basic texts for scientists and engineers. Holton points out that Föppl's *Introduction to Maxwell's Theory of Electricity* contains a section, entitled "The Electrodynamics of Moving Conductors," which begins much as Einstein's "Electrodynamics" paper does:

> The discussion of kinematics, namely of the general theory of motion, usually rests on the axiom that in the relationship of bodies to one another only relative motion is of importance. There can be no recourse to an absolute motion in space since there is absent any means

to find such a motion if there is no reference object at hand from which the motion can be observed and measured. . . . According to both Maxwell's theory and the theory of optics, empty space in actuality does not exist at all. Even the so-called vacuum is filled with a medium, the ether. (p. 209)

The question of the inability to experience completely empty space (without ether) Föppl refers to as "perhaps the most important problem of science of our time" (p. 209). Clearly this is the kind of problem Einstein repeatedly begins with. Föppl next turns to the asymmetry Einstein refers to as so troubling in Maxwell's equations and interestingly, at this point, introduces a thought experiment of the kind so favored by Einstein (p. 209). Although Holton's interest lies largely in the character and sequence of Einstein's argument, for which he finds a possible source in Föppl, one must also see in Föppl's tone something of the patient guide that hovers behind Einstein's voice. Holton, in fact, comments on Föppl's skill as an expositor of basic ideas in words that could equally well be applied to Einstein:

> The foreword of Föppl's *Mechanik*, dated June 1898, tells us something rather revealing about his special talent as a teacher and writer. His students, he confesses, have sometimes complained that he "proceeds too slowly rather than too fast," but he places very special emphasis on laying the foundations carefully. It is almost as if he had a special eye for a reader who might not have the benefit of formal lectures on the subject, and who might even have had holes in his formal background. (p. 207)

What Holton concludes is that Föppl's is "the kind of thinking that would indeed have appealed to Einstein, and that in fact is far closer to the sequence and style of argument of Einstein's 1905 paper than the work of any of the others who are more familiar — far more so than the books on electromagnetism by Maxwell, Helmholtz, Boltzmann, Hertz, or Runge, for example" (p. 210).

Holton presents a convincing case that Einstein's rhetoric (though he does not use the term itself) has a possible antecedent in the writings of Föppl. Since Einstein wrote an introduction to a contemporary edition of Galileo's *Dialogue*, he was undoubtedly familiar with Galileo's text as well,[40] and it is possible that it too had its influence on the rhetoric he employed to make his revolutionary ideas comprehensible. But my object is not really to trace the sources of Einstein's rhetoric, interesting as that is, but to point to its existence. I argue that Einstein in his papers was approaching a body of readers who were not prepared to take his discoveries immediately at face value. An unknown in the world of physics of 1905, Einstein proposed a series of ideas that were virtually incomprehensible in the contemporary language of physics. What he did, what he had to do, was devise his own language, employ his own rhetoric, for making his revolutionary ideas clear. And this *is* rhetoric: it has the reader in mind as it struggles to make the unfamiliar ideas comprehensible. Though one might argue that the thought experiments are an essential part of Einstein's own thinking, nonetheless they are clearly employed in the writings for expository purposes. Everything involved — the pattern of conflict/resolution, the analogies, the tone — serve only one purpose, to propel the reader into the radical new world of Einstein's devising.

7

It is a hallmark of the official rhetoric of science that it denies its own existence, that it claims to be not a rhetoric but a neutral voice, a transparent medium for the recording of scientific facts without distortion. If the prose of science is largely agentless — if no one in science "does" what "is done" — so are the writings of science presumed to be readerless; they are written solely for the record, to become part of the inscribed knowledge of science. The message is codified in an "objective" text. It is not the goal of official scientists to influence the reader; they aim not to persuade but only to demonstrate. And just as they seek to expunge themselves as writers from the scene of discourse, they aim to eliminate the reader from that same scene.

This view of the language of science is inadmissible. The official voice of science is a rhetoric. And although that voice has not yet been fully characterized, its vaunted objectivity is not cause but effect, rhetorical effect. Further, this rhetorical effect, this inevitable concomitant of the chosen voice of science, operates on those who use, as well as those who heed, that voice. Scientists, as do we all, think in their own voice and are affected by its rhetoric.

To be sure, this official rhetoric of science, like all general categories, is something of a fiction. All scientists develop and utilize their own rhetorics, but — and this is the point — many, perhaps most, of these rhetorics are virtually indistinguishable. Scientists can function only within the community of other scientists; hence all must find voices that are acceptable to that community, must adopt the rhetorical strategy that permits them to become part of the community. Much of the time, when scientists sense that what they have to say will violate none of the expectations of the community, they will content themselves with their own versions of the official rhetoric. Often, however, as they perceive that what they are saying is at variance with what is expected, they will — they must, if their rhetoric is to be effective — deviate to some degree from the expected pattern. In rare cases, as scientists find that their work runs counter to a considerable body of strongly held assumptions, a revolutionary rhetoric is called for. Certain writings, which powerfully articulate revolutionary worldviews, become scientific classics, although they may no longer function among the working documents of science.

In accepting such judgment, I believe, science would regain a lost dimension in its language; it would not be abandoning old ground, won with considerable difficulty as science emerged from the mists of superstition. To say that the writings of science are part of its ongoing work only insofar as they are read and attended to is only to make a judgment of its language that science once unabashedly made, in those early days when it sought to find its place among the intellectual systems that rule our lives — witness the powerful rhetoric of Galileo. It is this respect for its own rhetoric I would reclaim for science. This is not asking science to abandon its objectivity, its hard-won differentiation from magic and superstition; it is only asserting that science cannot gain objectivity by the mere appearance of objectivity. If the work of science is sound — and I surely do not challenge that it is — science need not contrive with its language to make it so. For scientists to deal more explicitly with their own involvement in their work, for them to recognize that the aim of their writing is to convince their colleagues of the superiority of their views, these will not weaken the foundations of science. To say that the writings of science become effective only in terms of reader response is not to assert that that response is to nothing, is about nothing. To say, further, with the new sociologists, that the dialogue of science takes place within the community of scientists, that it is composed of the community response to scientific discourse, does not negate the individual scientists who create the discourse or nullify the ideas to which they seek response. Scientists still do their work, but that work becomes science only when it becomes part of the great dialogue that constitutes science.

The official rhetoric of science is itself not without interest. We need to describe it, to characterize it, in considerably more detail. We need to know more of its effects and how it achieves them. If nothing else, we must dispel the traditional myth that it is somehow the only, the "natural," voice of science, that it is in and of itself a neutral mode of discourse, which serves only to convey true meaning with nothing added or subtracted. We must encourage the recognition that this is indeed a voice, a mode of speaking, which evokes its own peculiar response. But more than this, we need also to study the deviationist rhetorics, those personal departures from the official norm, like that of Einstein. We must come to see not only how these rhetorics work but when and why scientists feel called upon to engage in them. Indeed, if scientific work constitutes, not a dichotomy of the normal and the revolutionary but a spectrum of possibilities proceeding from the expected to the truly surprising, we will surely come to see the range of rhetorics earlier described. Every scientific paper, however routine, however conventional, makes its own small claim to novelty or it would not be publishable. No scientific journal accepts contributions that do not in some way further the science. Hence, one must finally argue, every scientific paper announces its own revolution, however minuscule, and its rhetoric ought to reflect that fact.

I would hope that the scientific community, as a functioning entity, would come to recognize that its writing, like all writing, evokes a response — recognize, in fact, that its aim is to evoke a response. Because the scientific community depends on the responses of its members to carry on its endeavors, it is as much, if not more, dependent on reader response than other bodies of discourse. Surely it behooves science to learn more consciously how to employ the rhetorics it so much depends upon. In particular I would suggest that science recognize the need for certain departures from its official rhetoric and loosen the way in which it permits or encourages scientists to communicate with one another.[41] I would not suggest that scientists study the rhetoric of Einstein so that they might copy his style (any more than I favored the imitation of Woodward's style). Rather I would urge scientists to know more about the range of rhetorics that other scientists have employed effectively and to be aware that the official rhetoric is not the only voice open to them when they come to tell other scientists about their work. I would not prescribe particular rhetorics for science, but rather rhetorical awareness and rhetorical freedom. When new ideas come into the scientific marketplace they should come clothed in new voices. And surely new ideas are a more common occurrence in science than the occasional "paradigm shifts," called, after Kuhn, scientific "revolutions." For science to work as it purports to work, it must be an arena (if I may borrow Einstein's metaphor) of contending ideas. But ideas can come only in the form of language, and if they are to compete as language they must be armed with the most effective rhetorics their champions can devise.

CHAPTER FIVE

The Art of Artless Prose

T IS THE TRADITIONAL VIEW OF THE SCIENTIFIC DOCUMENT THAT IT is not itself a construct but simply a record, a kind of tracing of what was done, like the seismographic record that carries the marks of the movement of the earth's crust. But, in fact, just as the seismographic record is not a literal rendering of the movement of the Earth but itself a translation into a new medium, a representation of time by space, so the scientific document bears only a tenuous relationship to the work it purports to describe. Further, that scientific work itself is considerably uncertain and must be interpreted to be meaningful; it can indeed be conceived only within a preexisting scientific framework. And the document, which purports only to describe that activity, must have, as we have seen, its expressive and its rhetorical dimensions. Indeed, this "naive" view of the scientific document as mere record (the "Reconstruction of an Investigation")[1] has been refuted by the countertradition within science itself, which acknowledges that the scientific document is, if not an art object, at least a construct, that its material has been selected and arranged for presentation.[2]

There are scientists in the countertradition who would move even beyond this view. Thus, ecologist Harold Heatwole characterizes science as "one of the dominant art forms of the twentieth century."[3] But the judgment seems exceptional; by and large, scientists within the countertradition also stop short of conferring art-object status on the scientific document. Countertraditional historians, philosophers, and sociologists concur that the scientific document is something other than a bare record of things done, though not, for all that, a work of art. The new sociologists, in particular, focus on the social functioning of scientific discourse, which demands rhetorical effect, not aesthetic appeal.

It is tempting to accept at face value this view of the scientific document as a construct, a crafted, functional entity—not, to be sure, an art object like a piece of literature, but nonetheless something made by design.[4] Presumably, when scientists come to compose their papers (and the verb must be an active one), they proceed not from their scientific activity itself but from a model, a model of what a scientific paper should be—perhaps an actual paper, perhaps a set of prescribed instructions from the journal, perhaps an internal model generated from past readings of scientific papers in the field. In any case, they follow a pattern already set. One leafs through the pages of a scientific journal, and the pattern sanctioned by the traditions of the discipline at once become apparent; often the internal heads from paper to paper are precisely the same: Introduction, Methods, Results, Discussion. Each scientist merely rings a set of changes on the old tune. The primitive potter must know what a pot is like in order to shape a particular version of the Platonic Idea of the pot, one more working out of the Aristotelian "formal cause" of pottishness. So with the scientist; the scientific paper fulfills in its own way the pattern that shapes it. It is in this sense that the scientific paper must be considered to be a construct.

But does anything in this judgment preclude that the scientific document should also be a work of art? Surely not the fact that the scientist-writer proceeds not from the raw scientific investigation itself but from a model of the scientific paper, for that is precisely how the art object is formed. Gombrich tells us that painters conceive their paintings not directly from the perceived real but at second hand, with the real seen, as it were, through other paintings themselves perceived.[5] And the whole theory of literary genres suggests that the literary object, too, is formed in the space already carved out by generic predispositions.[6] In short, the conventionality of the scientist's discourse does not alone preclude its characterization as art.

But the lack of autonomy? Does not art-object theory—at least as the New Criticism presented it to us at midcentury—hold that the literary object is a thing in its own right, an end to itself, while the scientific document is a carrier of message, a means, not an end?[7] Yes, but the line is not so simple to draw as this argument would suggest. For the literary object, too, is always about something: the signifiers always signify (if only other signifiers). That old dictum to the contrary, the poem cannot *be* if it doesn't *mean*. The ambiguities of representation theory — fictiveness versus actuality, trueness-to-life versus truth, illusionism versus exposition — suggest the difficulties. To say that the literary object creates its own self as a thing to be scrutinized, enjoyed, admired is really only intensifying the idea that it says something; it is the nature of signs that signifiers signify, that textures of meaning come into being as the signs are perceived. Indeed, this may be something new that is created, as the art-object critic would insist, a new texture of signification, not merely a message that is transmitted, an idea encoded.[8] But scientists, too, create; the world they signify with their language is a new world to the extent that the science is new. The world the scientist discovers is meaningful only within the framework of the science. The world conceived comes into being only as it is conceived. What the scientist writes is the product of experience in the light of the conceptual scheme in which that experience is enmeshed. Is this not equally true of what the poet writes?

If the argument according to ends — that the poem is, while the scientific paper does — is difficult to maintain, what about the means to the end, the verbal art that the poet may be said to employ, against the mere expository skill (or lack of it) of the scientist? Presumably, the typical art-object critic and the traditional scientist alike would agree, one cannot confuse the two. Yet the sophisticated scientist confesses that a significant portion of the writing task lies in the selection and arrangement of the materials, and such considerations of form are always a concern of the formal critic. The Russian formalists distinguish *story*, what actually happens, from *plot*, the arrangement of the material in the telling.[9] In one study of the relationship of the fully plotted novel to the framed collection of individual tales (like the *Decameron*), Victor Shklovsky identifies *Don Quixote* as an intermediary type, in which the multitude of included elements are held together by the device of the journey.[10] But a metaphoric journey is used by Galileo in the *Dialogue* as a recurring motif to keep the discussants and the reader informed of the progress of the argument. Einstein, we saw, does much the same thing, and the device is also employed by Sigmund Freud in *The Interpretation of Dreams*. But one need not be so specific. Surely it is a commonplace of poetics that the arts of selection and arrangement are among the more fundamental.

And one cannot be too insistent that the typical literary critic will judge the scientific document as entirely lacking in those literary qualities that make literature "literature"; that scientific documents can possess such qualities is implicit, indeed explicit, in the work of literary critics from Stanley Hyman to Gillian Beer who have directed their critical attentions toward scientific works. Thus Hyman working in the New Critical mode considers the works he examines precisely as art objects, characterizing the *Origin*, for example, as "a work of literature, with the structure of tragic drama and the texture of poetry."[11]

But to be specific in investigating the scientist's verbal art, there is to begin with the matter of the musicality of the language of poetry. Surely scientific prose does not utilize the musical resources of language the way that (or to the degree that) poetry does. But then, neither does any other form of writing in prose, including prose fiction. And scientists are not entirely indifferent to the musical effect of language (any more than is any other writer of prose). For an obvious example, consider the phrase "ontogeny recapitulates phylogeny": to be accepted now in any meaningful sense the phrase would have to be so severely qualified that it would have long since been forgotten were it not for the jingling rhyme. And for what reason other than the consonance do scientists prefer to speak of "nature versus nurture" rather than "heredity versus environment"?

One may argue similarly about metaphor and allusion. Superficially, it would seem, scientists as writers of prose do not employ these devices to the degree that poets do. But that does not mean that they are unaware of or indifferent to them or that they deliberately shun them in their writing. Simple metaphors abound in science: the struggle for existence, the planetary electron, and — to be more up-to-date — the greenhouse effect. In a larger sense, however, as we have already seen and has often been said, metaphor, analogy, and the scientific model are all cut from essentially the same bolt of cloth. Every time science employs a model, it makes a metaphor: the blood "circulates" because the heart "pumps" it. Scientific explanation (except of the most obvious and simplistic kind) can never be anything but a metaphor. Surely it is a metaphor to speak of a four-dimensional time-space continuum. Can an atom have a "structure" in anything but a metaphoric sense? Could anyone say literally what a "field" is? So prevalent are metaphors in scientific discourse that virtually everyone who has examined scientific documents from a literary perspective has directed critical attention to them. Thus, to pick but one example, with every literary Darwinist from Hyman to Beer, Darwin's metaphors have been the object of exhaustive scrutiny.[12]

As to allusions, it is claimed that the words of science have been stripped of their connotative aura. But scientific words, like other words, never spring fresh into life; every use of a word is an allusion to other uses. And, as we have seen, scientists are not only not unaware of this function of language, they are perfectly willing to exploit it when it serves their purpose to do so — the eightfold way, for example. And it can hardly be a coincidence that the name for the elusive but all-important *quark* should be drawn from one of the most playful realizations of the modernist literary temper.[13] Such deliberate exploitations of the richness of association of language can hardly be taken to signify scientists' intent to reduce their language to a symbolic calculus.

Even more out of place in scientific discourse, it is argued, are the literary practices of irony, ambiguity, and polysemy. In order to achieve its principal goal of the simple, schematic conveyance of single meaning, scientific language must be univocal. It must not say other than what it means, say unclearly what it means, or say what can mean several different things. This would seem to be a kind of test case for the application of art-object theory to scientific discourse. For the play of language delighted in by the modernist writers and the New Critics alike would seem on these grounds to be proscribed for the scientist-writer. Yet there is, as I have said, the "playfully ironic" choice of the term *charm* for one of the properties of subatomic particles. Indeed, since irony is one of the criteria more frequently employed to characterize literary language and to mark it off from scientific language, I will deal more extensively with the matter of irony in scientific discourse in a moment.

First, however, there is the assertion that scientific discourse is characterized above all by avoidance of ambiguity and multiple meanings, a point strenuously made by, among others, Aldous Huxley in his 1963 essay *Literature and Science.*[14] To begin with, one must at once suspect that the business of achieving single, simple, clear meanings is not easily accomplished, even by scientists, and may not always be the desideratum it would seem to be. Scientists, like other mortals, are not always sure of what they want to say or how to say it; they must speak when their thoughts are still unclear or ill-formed, must occasionally allow for several possibilities in one formulation, or must express the most complex and novel relationships with the most limited of linguistic tools.

Even the great Newton, the putative master of rational thought, was not always unambiguous or precise in his choice of language. One student of his work has identified five ways in which Newton uses the word *hypothesis*, presumably only one of which (but which?) can be intended in the famous formulation, *Hypotheses non fingo.*[15] It appears, in fact, that Newton spent much of his professional life finding verbal strategies for avoiding, without seeming to avoid, the presentation of a mechanical picture of the operation of gravity, a task he found quite impossible. In the *Principia* the chief strategy is the self-imposed prohibition against the "feigning" (framing) of hypotheses: "But hitherto I have not been able to discover the cause of those properties of gravity from phenomena, and I frame no hypotheses; for whatever is not deduced from the phenomena is to be called an hypothesis; and hypotheses, whether metaphysical or physical, whether of occult qualities or mechanical, have no place in experimental philosophy."[16] Presumably, Newton here is making a virtue of necessity and formulating a law of scientific methodology — namely, that hypotheses should not be framed — rather than forthrightly conceding that he cannot explain how gravity could possibly work. Finally, in one of the later revisions of the *Opticks*, the Master yields to considerable pressure and presents a speculation (already made impossible by other arguments presented in the same volume) on the mechanical operation of gravity by way of an assumed ether. The suggestion, like other of Newton's speculations at the end of *Opticks*, is presented craftily not as an assertion but as a negatively phrased query (which commands assent): "Is not [the etherial] Medium much rarer within the dense Bodies of the Sun, Stars, Planets and Comets, than in the empty celestial Spaces between them? And in passing from them to great distances, doth it not grow denser and denser perpetually, and thereby cause the gravity of those great Bodies towards one another, and of their parts towards the Bodies; every Body endeavouring to go from the denser parts of the Medium towards the rarer?"[17] With this obviously unsatisfactory "hypothesis" revealed, one has a good idea why Newton would prefer ambiguity and admit no hypotheses at all into the world of science.

What is important, however, is that Newton's strategy of ambiguity permitted him to proceed with the production of the *Principia* and the ushering in of the Newtonian Age in science. Indeed, the very stricture against the framing of hypotheses has been all-important in setting modern science on its present course. It is the scientist's job, this line of reasoning tells us, to determine the simple regularities in the phenomena of the universe, to uncover the "laws of nature," not to account for them. What may well have been a face-saving device for Newton has become a way of life for modern science. Following his lead, it seeks only formal causes, not efficient ones.

Sometimes Newton's ambiguities result from real antinomies in nature.

Thus, when he is unable to reconcile his detection of periodic effects in light refraction with other evidence suggesting the corporeality of light, he is driven to speak of "fits" of easy transmission and of easy reflection in the light rays. The "fits" are "dispositions" of the ray, but as to what kind of "disposition," Newton says, "I do not here enquire." For those who insist on "hypotheses," however, he suggests that the alternating dispositions are caused by "vibrations" in the medium like "undulations" in water; his "interval of . . . fits" is quite the equivalent of our "wavelength," though our property is ascribed to light itself, not the medium.[18] Modern science, as is well known, faces comparable antinomies in its studies of light and concludes, with equal ambiguity, that a "photon" of light can behave either like a particle or like a wave depending on the circumstances. How else to express the real state of affairs in nature except by verbal ambiguity?

Before examining in greater detail several examples of deliberately ironic usage of language in science, I shall note again that the employment of language, even in a formal and artful way, is not radically different in the two cases, literature and science. Both scientists and poets have one language available to them, all the resources of which they are free to employ, including the artful and the "poetic" dimension. Though the scientist and the poet may not exploit those resources of language in precisely the same way, it is inappropriate to conclude that two separate, quite alien, languages are involved, that the language of a poem works one way, the language of a scientific paper another. Rather, we must conclude, what the poet can do with language, formally or otherwise, the scientist, in a rather different way, can do as well.[19]

2

Galileo precedes his great polemical defense of the Copernican system, the *Dialogue on the Two Chief Systems of the World*, with an obligatory dedication to his patron, Cosimo de Medici. Then come several pages of remarks directed "To the Discerning Reader." These begin as follows:

> Several years ago there was published in Rome a salutary edict which, in order to obviate the dangerous tendencies of our present age, imposed a seasonable silence upon the Pythagorean opinion that the earth moves. There were those who impudently asserted that this decree had its origin not in judicious inquiry, but in passion none too well informed. Complaints were to be heard that advisers who were

totally unskilled at astronomical observations ought not to clip the wings of reflective intellects by means of rash prohibitions.

Upon hearing such carping insolence, my zeal could not be contained. Being thoroughly informed about that prudent determination, I decided to appear openly in the theater of the world as a witness of the sober truth. I was at that time in Rome; I was not only received by the most eminent prelates of that Court, but had their applause; indeed, this decree was not published without some previous notice of it having been given to me. Therefore I propose in the present work to show to foreign nations that as much is understood of this matter in Italy, and particularly in Rome, as transalpine diligence can ever have imagined. Collecting all the reflections that properly concern the Copernican system, I shall make it known that everything was brought before the attention of the Roman censorship, and that there proceed from this clime not only dogmas for the welfare of the soul, but ingenious discoveries for the delight of the mind as well.

To this end I have taken the Copernican side in the discourse, proceeding as with a pure mathematical hypothesis and striving by every artifice to represent it as superior to supposing the earth motionless — not, indeed, absolutely, but as against the arguments of some professed Peripatetics.[20]

The significant feature of these lines is that every statement is to be read as ironic.[21] In fact, the irony is heavily drawn; it is, as it were, underlined. As everyone likely to read Galileo's book well knew, the "salutary edict" that imposed a "seasonable silence" against "dangerous tendencies" was aimed at none other than Galileo for his earlier, open defense of the "Pythagorean opinion." Further, his readers were well able to attribute to Galileo himself the "impudent assertions" and "carping insolence" concerning the instigation of the decree by advisers "totally unskilled at astronomical observations." As to the identity of the "reflective intellects" whose wings were clipped, surely the most prominent was, again, Galileo. At the time of the decree Galileo was indeed in Rome, where he had gone to "appear openly in the theater of the world as a witness of the sober truth" — of the Copernican, not the Ptolemaic, system. It was largely in response to Galileo's public agitation that the decree was thought necessary, and the "previous notice" given to Galileo was, in fact, a private interview with Cardinal Bellarmine, to which Galileo was summoned.[22] During the interview Galileo was admonished not to teach, perhaps not even to refer to, the dangerous Copernican view. (The precise formulation of the admonition was to figure importantly in Galileo's trial before the Inquisition.)[23] And when Galileo now turns to the book he is introducing and says he is taking the Copernican side in the discourse, "proceeding as with a pure mathematical hypothesis and striving by every artifice to represent it as superior," the reader, armed by the earlier irony, knows at once how to read "artifice." The purpose of Galileo's little exercise is not to tell the "discerning reader" how to read the introductory remarks — the original reader could not help but know that — but rather to instruct the reader how to read the *Dialogue* that follows. The introduction is an object lesson in reading: it says, you know the truth — you know what I think — judge by that, not by what I say. For the *Dialogue* itself is larded with ironic disclaimers (particularly at the beginnings and ends of the various sections where, presumably, the censor would be most likely to see them). Coming from Salviati, the Socrates of Galileo's Platonic dialogue, these remarks echo Galileo's disclaimer in the introduction by asserting that the defense of the Copernican view must not be taken to represent his true opinion. At the same time, Salviati's well-drawn arguments for the Copernican side and the statements of support from Sagredo, the supposedly neutral participant, carry enormous conviction. The properly prepared reader has no difficulty separating the ironic from the sincere.

Here is how the system works. Sagredo is speaking in a particularly compelling way:

> Eternal motion and permanent rest are such important events in nature and so very different from each other that only the most diverse consequences can depend on them. . . . And it is impossible that one of two contradictory propositions should not be true and the other false. Now if it is further impossible to adduce in proof of the false proposition anything but fallacies, while the true one may be proved by all manner of conclusive and demonstrative arguments, how could you suppose that whichever one of you approaches me in support of the true proposition would not have me convinced: I should have to be stupid indeed, warped in judgment, thick-witted, and blind to reason, not to distinguish light from darkness, jewels from coals, truth from falsity.

Whatever one thinks of the logic of Sagredo's argument, its intent is perfectly clear, and it is equally clear which position Galileo himself takes to represent "light," "jewels," and "truth." So clear is the purpose at this point that almost at once Galileo has Salviati deliver the following disclaimer:

> Before going further I must tell Sagredo that I act the part of Copernicus in our arguments and wear his mask. As to the internal effects upon me of the arguments which I produce in his favor, I want you to be guided not by what I say when we are in the heat of acting out our play, but after I have put off the costume, for perhaps then you shall find me different from what you saw of me on the stage.[24]

The "discerning reader" has no doubt who is "wearing the mask" (Galileo or Salviati) and where and when and why.

In one narrow sense, of course, Galileo's strategy failed, for after first clearing the censor, the *Dialogue* was abruptly withdrawn and Galileo was brought to his famous trial and ultimate abjuration. Apparently too many of Galileo's readers (including members of the Inquisition) proved to be "discerning." Yet, in a larger sense, the *Dialogue* succeeded. It was smuggled out of Italy, published around Europe, and helped carry the day for the Copernican system. Today the book is recognized as a polemical masterpiece. It is still read, its irony still savored. Had Galileo weakened his argument, or fully concealed it, rather than presenting it powerfully but veiled in irony, the *Dialogue* might have escaped the wrath of the Inquisition, but it would not have ultimately furthered the Copernican cause or become the document that every "discerning reader" of every age reads with pleasure, the type of scientific classic described in the last chapter.

Today we appreciate the *Dialogue* not for what it tells us about the Copernican system and its advantages over the Ptolemaic one but because of our enjoyment in its exploitation of the ironic possibilities of language (along with its other virtues as discourse). But this is not to say that this is now a different work from what it once was, read in a different way. One must not believe that it once served a purely functional purpose, defense of the Copernican system, whereas it now serves a solely artistic one, the pure enjoyment of the ironical mode of the presentation. Whatever artistry the book carries, it must always have carried. The twentieth century did not invent irony or first come to appreciate its artful use. And it is by virtue of its art that the *Dialogue* generated its own "discerning reader" in 1638 as it does today.

3

The circumstances that led to the writing of Galileo's *Dialogue* were special ones (though censorship, overt or covert, is not unknown in the world today), and the work is more argument than it is scientific report.

A second example, which is untroubled by censorship (except for editorial constraints) and is both considerably more modern and more typically a scientific report, comes at once to mind.

In 1953 a very young American scientist and a not-quite-so-young British scientist, both equally unknown, sent off to *Nature* a nine-hundred-word communication. Ten years later the then extremely well-known James Watson and Francis Crick received the Nobel Prize for their work describing the double helix of DNA, as presented in the *Nature* paper. Needless to say, the paper was not accompanied by a note to the "discerning reader," but for those engaged in the new game of molecular biology, none was needed — the text amply revealed its own ironies. For the rest of the world Watson has provided a gloss on the text in the form of *The Double Helix*, which makes explicit what is implicit in the scientific text.

Some of the revealed ironies are of little importance scientifically, but in exposing the competitive workings of the scientific world to a surprised public they accounted for much of the commercial success of *The Double Helix*. It seems that competing scientists are not always kindly disposed toward one another, nor are their relations as serene and untroubled as one had been led to believe. With the aid of Watson's gloss, then, here are some of the revealed ironies of the famous DNA paper.[25]

> From the paper: "A structure for nucleic acid has already been proposed by Pauling and Corey. They kindly made their manuscript available to us in advance of publication."[26]
> From *The Double Helix*: "Two copies . . . were dispatched to Cambridge — one to Sir Lawrence [Bragg, the head of the laboratory], the other to Peter [Linus Pauling's son, then working in the Cambridge lab and apparently not quite in sympathy with his father]. Bragg's response on receiving it was to put it aside. . . . While Sir Lawrence was pondering whether to chance taking Crick's mind off his thesis, Francis and I were poring over the copy Peter brought in after lunch."[27]

> From the paper: "In our opinion, this structure [proposed by Pauling and Corey] is unsatisfactory. . . . We believe that the material which gives the X-ray diagrams is the salt, not the free acid."
> From *The Double Helix*: "Neither of us . . . had the slightest clue to the steps that had led Linus to his blunder [in choosing the acid form]. If a student had made a similar mistake, he would be thought unfit to benefit from Cal Tech's [Pauling's university] chemistry faculty" (p. 103).

From the paper: "Another three-chain structure has also been suggested by Fraser [a competitor]. . . . This structure as described is rather ill-defined, and for this reason we shall not comment on it."

From *The Double Helix*: "His [Fraser's] idea did not seem worth resurrecting only to be quickly buried. However, when Maurice [Wilkins, Fraser's boss and the physicist who shared the Nobel Prize with Watson and Crick] sounded upset at our objection, we added the necessary reference" (p. 109).

Two persons savaged in *The Double Helix* are all but ignored in the paper. Erwin Chargaff, the biochemist who discovered the fixed ratios of bases in DNA and hence provided the clue to the base-pairing feature of the double helix, is referred to only in a footnote. In *The Double Helix* he is notable chiefly for his scorn of and condescension toward Watson and Crick (pp. 86, 87, 137). Rosalind Franklin, the X-ray crystallographer whose X-ray studies of the DNA model made the structure determination possible, is mentioned by name in the paper in a backhanded acknowledgment, along with Wilkins: "We have also been stimulated by a knowledge of the general nature of the unpublished experimental results and ideas of Dr. M. H. F. Wilkins, Dr. R. E. Franklin and their co-workers at King's College, London." In *The Double Helix* she ("Rosy") is presented as a shrew who terrorizes Wilkins, assaults Watson, and despises Crick (pp. 43, 66, 106). (She seems, like many women scientists, to have been forced to fight for her right to do her own work and not have it appropriated by male collaborators.)

Even the paper's bland, formulaic acknowledgment of Watson's fellowship — "One of us (J. D. W.) has been aided by a fellowship from the National Foundation for Infantile Paralysis" — concealed considerable irony for those who knew of the troubles of Watson or any other American postgraduate student seeking financial support while struggling to obtain the kind of scientific reputation that would secure a regular academic appointment. *The Double Helix* reveals Watson's problems with the fellowship board when he moved to Cambridge from the institution he had originally attended as a postgraduate student (pp. 34–36). The book relates that his first fellowship was terminated, but that he was then given a second one of shorter duration. "My real punishment in not following the board's advice and going to Stockholm was a thousand dollars" (p. 74). But this is not quite the end of the story: "Less than a week later, a new letter came from Washington. It was signed by the same man, but not as head of the fellowship board. . . . A meeting was being arranged for which I was asked to give a lecture on the growth of viruses. . . . My first impulse was to write that I could not come because of an unforeseen financial disaster. But on second thought, I was against giving him the satisfaction of thinking he had affected my affairs" (p. 74). The irony of "unforeseen financial disaster," indulged in but never executed — until the publication of *The Double Helix* when the author was beyond the reach of retribution — is, of course, pure spite. (And it is quite typical of the petty vengeances exacted in *The Double Helix*.) The final personal irony here is that when the *Nature* paper appeared, and Watson and Crick were on their way to becoming *the* Watson and Crick, neither had to worry again about seeking financial support for his work.

But the essential ironies in the *Nature* paper are scientific. (The personal ironies may simply help prepare the reader to read properly the scientific ones.) Indeed, the paper uses ironic understatement as its chief rhetorical device. It is irony that is used to establish the biological importance of the work. To be sure, there are the obligatory claims of novelty ("We wish to put forward a radically different structure . . ."; "The novel feature of the structure . . ."), but the situating of the work, its insertion into the heart of biology, is achieved ironically. In the paper, there is none of the exuberance of *The Double Helix*: "Francis winged into the Eagle to tell everyone within hearing distance that we had found the secret of life" (p. 126). The contrast between the two modes of discourse is clear in this excerpt from *The Double Helix*:

> Our Cavendish typist was not on hand, and the brief job was given to my sister. There was no problem persuading her to spend a Saturday afternoon this way, for we told her that she was participating in perhaps the most famous event in biology since Darwin's book. Francis and I stood over her as she typed the nine-hundred-word article that began, "We wish to suggest a structure for the salt of deoxyribose nucleic acid (DNA). This structure has novel features which are of considerable biological interest." (p. 140)

The irony is at once apparent. Ostensibly claiming less ("considerable biological interest"), the language, in fact, claims more. The remark is too understated to be taken at face value. Modesty or a mere matter-of-fact rendering would have put it otherwise: "great biological interest," perhaps. Nor was the effect unstudied (as the personal ironies attest); Watson confesses in *The Double Helix* to have fantasized for some time about the production of just such a paper, and the working over of the successive drafts is reported in the book (pp. 31, 139–40).

Also this particular brand of irony is not limited to the opening statement. Again, from *The Double Helix*: "For a while Francis wanted to expand our note to write at length about the biological implications. But finally he saw the point to a short remark and composed the sentence: 'It has not escaped our notice that the specific pairing we have postulated immediately suggests a possible copying mechanism for the genetic material'" (p. 139). "It has not escaped our notice," indeed. Nor does the inherent irony escape the notice of the discerning reader, whether a member of the community of molecular biologists of 1953 or the lay reader of today suitably armed with the gloss of *The Double Helix*. The significant irony here lies in the "possible copying mechanism" so "immediately" suggested by the base pairing. This airy formulation obviates any detailed exposition of the possible mechanism, which some forty years of intense scientific work have not provided in full (though, in principle, of course, the problem is "solved").

Precisely this same device operates in the opening statements' reference to the "considerable biological interest" of the "novel features" of the DNA structure. The ironic understatement not only heightens the claims of importance but frees the authors from the obligation of relating precisely what the "biological interest" is in those "novel features." The reader is free to generate whatever solutions to whatever biological problems the structure suggests, with the clear implication that all has already been anticipated by the brief remarks in *Nature*.

It must be clear that these essential ironies are not a surface mannerism imposed on an otherwise straight scientific text; they are an integral part of the scientific presentation and serve to situate the argument in its scientific context. The point is that this paper in *Nature* (it is titled "Molecular Structure of Nucleic Acids: A Structure for Deoxyribose Nucleic Acid") is interesting to read *as writing*. This is a stimulating document, both because it is important scientifically and because it exploits its linguistic medium effectively (the two are not unrelated). This is not something now read into the document, which its original readers would have been quite unaware of. Rather, the original scientific audience was perfectly aware that there was something significant in the manner of the "telling" of the *Nature* paper. One commentator says of the "copying mechanism" sentence that it "has been called one of the most coy statements in the literature of science."[28] The word *coy* is pretty close to the mark here, and even more so is the recognition that the language of the statement is of special interest in its own right.

Does this mean that we are viewing this scientific report as an art object, as the art-object school of criticism views a poem? Essentially, yes. I do not intend to say, obviously, that this document is a poem, but merely that its language is of interest, just as is the language of a poem, *as language*. One does not insist that the "autonomy" claimed for the poem as art object means that the poem is about nothing, that it serves only as pure language devoid of meaning. So one cannot assert that because this scientific report has meaning, it must be devoid of interest as language. Nor need one say that the importance of the scientific message here overshadows any possible interest in the language. (It may or may not contain the "secret of life," depending on one's view.) The death of a well-loved child described in a poem may be a matter of all-consuming interest to the poet, and the reader may share vicariously in those feelings without failing to appreciate the language in which they are expressed. That readers appreciate the writing need not add to or subtract from their empathy with the grieving parent — or their admiration of a major scientific advance. (But it seems to be true of irony that one can enjoy it in art, at least "high" art, less self-consciously than one can the direct expression of emotion — hence, presumably, the tendency of the art-object school to favor the ironic statement.) It is perhaps not out of place here to cite Ishmael's often-quoted dictum: "To produce a mighty book, you must choose a mighty theme." The mightiness of the theme, presumably, does not hinder the enjoyment of the book *as a book*.

4

I have focused on irony as an exemplar of the literary qualities of language because it is said to be one that scientific discourse is least likely to exhibit and because others, such as employment of metaphor, have been so extensively studied. It is precisely such qualities that art-object theory would ascribe to literature and deny to scientific discourse. Another essential element of the theory is its emphasis on the art object *as object*, as a thing in itself, as something of interest for what it does and how it does it. And that too can clearly be said of the Watson-Crick paper. It does not merely report the DNA structure; it reports that structure in a way that is itself interesting. One cannot believe here that the language is unselfconscious, unaware of itself as language. This, of course, is precisely what the traditional scientific view of scientific discourse would say is quite impossible. Even the countertraditional view of scientific language, however, would not suggest that that language could be employed in a way that would carry the interest we see it can carry as language.

This reading of the irony inherent in the *Nature* paper is largely New Critical.[29] But even the "defamiliarization" that is a distinguishing feature of literary language to the Russian formalists is not inapplicable here.[30] A statement noted as the "most coy . . . in the literature of science" must, on the face of it, be "defamiliarized." The Chicago neo-Aristotelian school of art-object criticism, too, would not have found it appropriate to consider the scientific document as an "aesthetic object," would not have examined its "artistic form"[31] — wrongly, I suggest. As part of its analysis of the genre of the scientific paper, this school should include the "manner" of the telling — with that manner not so different after all from that of the more typical literary genres.

The literary critical formalism of the New Criticism and its congeners in the early to middle decades of this century, Russian formalism and neo-Aristotelianism, is no longer with us in an overt way, but to a large degree its mark on critical practice remains. And it is not an empty exercise to assert that the kinds of formal qualities it taught us to see in literary critical texts can be seen equally well in the texts of science when we look for them, contrary to what that same formalism would have led us to expect. That today's literary criticism has its own brands of formalism, I shall note in a later chapter, when I examine other scientific texts to determine the value of such methods in furthering our reading of them.

My argument is not that every scientific paper must operate in the same way as the Watson-Crick paper — ironically, self-consciously — or do so to the same degree, but merely that it can do so, just as it may employ other of the artful modes of language. I assert that it is wrong to close the poetic dimension of linguistic usage to scientific discourse. One may well conclude — though I will not press the point — that far more of the writing of science is of interest as writing than is commonly supposed. In their frequent references to other scientists' "elegant" papers, scientists believe they are strictly praising the work the person has done. Yet they know that work only through the scientific papers, and I would urge that part of the "elegance" lies in the choice of language. (Freud, after all, reportedly nearly received the Nobel Prize for literature — the initial proposal apparently was intended as an insult — and he did indeed receive the Goethe Prize for literature.) Even the ordinary scientist communicating to a few professional peers within the narrowly prescribed confines of the scientific paper may contrive to give pleasure with apt and felicitous language. Let us not deny such a scientist recognition for having done so.Let us, rather, urge that all scientists bring whatever art they can to the fabricating of their verbal discourse, for it is only through that discourse that their science comes to life as science. (Science unknown, as I have said, is no science.) Thus, even the quality of the science *as science* is not independent of the quality of the writing *as writing*.

CHAPTER SIX

The Putative Purity
of Science

GAIN, THAT PLATONIZING TENDENCY IN SCIENCE, THAT HABIT OF
looking at trees and seeing a forest, of inferring general forest laws
and perfect forest functions, irrespective of the blemishes and the
imperfections of the real trees that stand together on the hill: scientists cannot help but extend this mode of thought to their own
enterprise, cannot help but think of science itself as a kind of ideal
function, like the gas law, correct and perfect in itself even though
its realization in the real world may be another matter. It is science
in this ideal sense that claims for its method privileged access to
the truth, and for its discourse freedom from the kind of artifactuality attributed to literary discourse. Scientific discourse is the
rarefied medium of information exchange of ideal science. It cannot be involved with the mythic stories human beings tell themselves to give their lives meaning; it cannot, like those stories, bear
the mark of social, political, or economic forces; nor can it, like
them, be marked by the psychological makeup of its formulators —
for in becoming the votaries of science scientists perforce set aside
their humanity and become only the instruments of science itself.

This picture of an ideal but impersonalized science is — as the
countertradition would attest — a fiction, a myth. There is no science apart from the work of scientists. Science is as science does.
It is schizophrenic to believe in the existence of an ideal science
situated in an abstract space untouched and unmoved by human
concerns. The scientist does not cease to be a human being on

becoming a scientist. Science as an institution does not operate differently from other human institutions. The scientific method is not fundamentally different from other modes of human thought. Nor has science devised a scheme of writing that serves only a referential function and operates otherwise not as language at all. A scientist in employing language cannot strip it of everything that makes it language. In particular, the language of science cannot cease to function as a social artifact because the scientist who wields the instrument of language remains a human being, and it is through that human agency that the language is marked with everything that marks the language of every human being. The scientist who writes is a person, and the world writes through the person, and the writing is the instrument of the world.

Much is made of the gap between the origin of scientific theories and their testing, between the contexts of generation and verification.[1] It is this gap that is presumed to protect science from extraneous influences. However much such influences may affect the scientist in formulating hypotheses, it is claimed, the rigorous testing procedures of science are enough to expunge any trace those influences may have left.

As this argument is usually presented, the opposition is said to be between the contexts of discovery and justification (or verification), with the development of the original idea labeled as "discovery." But the use of *discovery* in this context causes considerable mischief because of its post hoc implication. Thus, Brannigan's argument in *The Social Basis of Scientific Discoveries* is that "scientific discovery" is a social label applied to an event after the fact, as it suits the collective purpose of those making the attribution. Brannigan, however, also asserts that this social basis of applying the judgment "scientific discovery" renders what I would label the "context of generation" — that is, the initial experience that ultimately comes to be labelled a "discovery" — itself social. It is, then, Brannigan's claim that the original development (generation) of scientific ideas is necessarily a social process.[2] It may well be directly so in some cases and indirectly so in others (no one works, after all, in a vacuum), but such generation can hardly be precisely equated with the consensus-achieving activity of canonizing an event as a "discovery." Indeed, "discovery" in this sense follows verification rather than precedes it.

In any case, however, it is the context of verification, with its rigorous testing, that is said to preserve the purity of science. But this presupposes that the testing is not only decisive but itself wholly impersonal, entirely removed from the human sphere. With this, one cannot agree.

The phenomenological nature of scientific experimentation might seem to be decisive. When the experiments proceed as predicted — when the bombs go off — this would seem to prove that the scientists are right, that their theories have passed the test, that their pictures of the world (their models) are true ones. But the theories, the pictures, the explanations, are not unique; the experiments are consistent with what the theories say, but they do not finally prove them to be true. The experiments may proceed unambiguously, but what they mean is not unambiguous. The way of science leads only to conditional truths.

Nor can the testing procedures, by which these conditional truths are so tentatively established, be themselves exempted from the exigencies of the world. The idea of what it is to test a scientific theory — to confirm or refute it — is itself deeply rooted in all the human problematics that blur the picture of the world under which one operates. As the new historians of science have recognized, the paradigm in which the scientists form their ideas also dictates the methods they will employ to test them. The paradigm, the theories, the testing procedures, all originate in the human mind. The scientist generates both ideas and the means for testing them; the paradigm influences one as much as the other. Galileo's rhetoric in the *Dialogue on the Two Chief World Systems* is directed to the end of convincing his readers of the validity of new verification procedures — looking through telescopes, for instance — as much as convincing them of the superiority of the Copernican model. The methods of science are always changing. Today's scientific proof is tomorrow's scientific irrelevancy. Proof is what the scientists of the moment think it is.

Sometimes a distinction is drawn between the private and the public sectors of science rather than between the contexts of generation and verification. Then it is conceded that in their private moments of thinking, working, testing ideas, scientists are fully human, but when they step forth into the public arena, when they publish their ideas, they become public figures, participating in an impersonal dialogue. Out of this grand, depersonalized exchange of views comes the ratification of the individual scientist's ideas, the confirmation of their legitimacy, the bestowal of the imprimatur of "truth."[3] But the scientists who engage in the dialogue, who carry out the ratification, are themselves individuals — often a mere handful of specialists — who in their judgments are as human as are their friends and competitors whose works they are judging. Even were this not the case, however, there is no guarantee of objectivity in collectivity.[4] The collective human enterprise is in its own way subject to social, political, economic,

even psychological, influences. No one believes that the public pronounce-
ments of politicians conform to a new and rigid standard of truth simply
because they are uttered in the public arena. Why should it be thought
otherwise with scientists?

But if the collective nature of the scientific endeavor does not in and of
itself ensure the ultimate objectivity of scientific knowledge, it does nonetheless effectively shape the character of that knowledge. And it does, perforce, identify the scientific document as social artifact. It is the recognition
of that circumstance by the countertradition that marks off its own position
most strongly from that of the tradition. The countertraditionalists no
longer see the scientific document as the bare, unadorned record of what
the scientist has found writ in nature; rather, they see it as an artifact shaped
by the collective activities of scientists and employed by them in their efforts to reach consensus.

In exploring the artifactual character of the language of science, I will
proceed from the claims made with respect to literary language by members of the mythic, the Marxist, and the Freudian schools of criticism, because of their importance.[5] To be more complete (which space would surely
not permit) this chapter would include a section on feminist criticism, with
its view of the literary document as an artifact in the gender power game
that has ensured male dominance in our culture for millennia. Indeed, an
extension of this critique to the discourse of science has already been done
by Keller, among others, in her *Reflections on Gender and Science*, which
makes the argument that myths of male gender identification lie at the
center of the story that science currently tells and has told since its incep-
tion.[6]

The point to be made here, however, is a general one — namely, that the
language of science is not, simply by virtue of its function within science,
sequestered from language generally and freed from the shaping influence
of the society around it. The mythic, the Marxist, and the Freudian view-
points will simply provide a focus for a further brief discussion of the social
artifactuality of scientific discourse.

2

One must not reject out of hand any appeal of mythic formulations
to the scientific mind; indeed, the scientist's view of the scientific enterprise
has its own mythic overtones. The great impersonal god of science is a
myth, but one that obviously has a deep appeal to scientists.[7] As devotees

of science, many scientists demand great sacrifices from themselves and their families or associates in the name of their calling. Others, less scrupulous, justify to themselves and others in the name of that same calling practices they would surely otherwise find unacceptable. One of the fascinations of *The Double Helix* is the way in which the narrative persona blithely ignores the unscrupulous behavior of "young Jim" and "Francis" in their pursuit of the DNA structure.

But the scientist is not only an acolyte serving a jealous god but also a Prometheus, wresting the eternal secrets from the gods and delivering them up to humankind for its well-being.[8] It is the time-honored Baconian justification of science that it will better the lot of humanity, but it is equally time-honored to perceive that the enlightenment that brings that betterment does not come without sacrifice. (It is said that Bacon died of a cold contracted by stuffing a dead chicken with snow to test the preservative powers of freezing.) Woodward's account of the battle to conquer the steroid citadel and bring to a grateful humankind the benefits of synthetic cortisone is simply a recent retelling of the Promethean story. Alternatively, the scientist may undertake an Orphic journey into the underworld of darkness and confusion, only to emerge finally into the "light." Freud invokes this image in the final chapter of *The Interpretation of Dreams* when his path of argument moves down into "darkness" and then upward again with enlightenment.[9]

Keller has a rather different view of the central myth of modern science — namely, that of a masculine science chastely ravaging the body of the female Nature.[10] And then there is that mythic identification of the scientist/subject with the object/nature for which I have employed the shorthand term "feeling for the organism," borrowed via Keller from her biographical subject, scientist Barbara McClintock.

More than the scientist's own role, however, can be conceived in mythic terms. It can be argued that much of the structure of scientific thought is shaped by mythlike formulations. As noted, students of the literature of science are much indebted to Stanley Edgar Hyman's *The Tangled Bank* with its readings, in good part thematic, of Darwin, Marx, Frazer, and Freud. To give but one brief example, Hyman sees in the *Origin of Species* the pattern of a tragic drama:

> In Gilbert Murray's terms, the basic ritual stages of tragedy are *agon* or contest, *sparagmos* or tearing apart, then *anagnorisis* or discovery and *epiphany* or joyous showing forth of the resurrected protagonist.

> Darwin's struggle for existence is clearly Murray's *agon* and *sparagmos*, and his natural selection or survival of the fittest, *anagnorisis* and *epiphany*. For the final exultation that the Greeks felt at the affirmation of Reliving Dionysus, Darwin substitutes a quieter tragic satisfaction.[11]

At the same time Hyman notes that "the archetypal image of the *Origin* is the war of nature,"[12] and he also perceives a scriptural quality to the text, with a deified Mother Nature as the new object of faith.[13] The mythic character of Darwin's texts is also analyzed from a contemporary critical perspective by Gillian Beer in her recent *Darwin's Plots*.[14]

But the most thorough thematic analysis of scientific texts is to be found in the work of physicist and historian of science Gerald Holton. Indeed, if Holton's themata (themes) are not explicitly mythic structures, they are much the same sort of thing — preconceived relations or patterns, conceptual templates that are fitted to the phenomena of the world. Such fundamental ideas as that the foundations of matter must be atomistic or continuous are cultural prejudgments scientists bring to their work, not inferences they derive from it. Scientists can find in the world only what they suspect to be there, and their expectations can be derived only from the cultural formulations, the myths, that have shaped their thought. Holton is clear on this point. At the conclusion of a paper, "Thematic and Stylistic Interdependence," he writes: "I have presented here some speculative considerations on the various ways in which the state of affairs, the folklore and beliefs external to science (in the narrow sense of the word) affect the imagination of the acting scientist." The reason for his interest is also clear: "For without some such support for the imagination, coming to us from beyond the boundaries of science alone, without the help of all the best that has been thought and felt before us, how could we hope that the brief attention we can give to scientific problems during our short lives could even yield anything worthwhile?"[15]

As a physicist, as well as historian of science, Holton is squarely in the countertradition, perfectly willing to grant the influence of external ideas on the discourse of science, though he too will limit the influence to what he calls the "nascent moment," the period of generation of the idea.[16] Since Holton includes in his analysis the public documents of science, however, one cannot help extending his analysis to the context of verification. For the process of verification occurs only via the public discourse of science; and the themata, the myths, that Holton's work shows permeate the substances of that discourse must ultimately affect the outcome of the verification process.

Of all myths, creation myths are the most common; every culture has its example: even the post-Christian West still gives at least part of its allegiance to Genesis. Science, too, has its creation myths.[17] To be sure, the notion of a steady-state universe for a time had its adherents—it has its own kind of appeal to suppose that there was no specific act of creation, that the universe simply is—but currently the steady-state universe is out, and the universe with a specific beginning is in. The currently favored scientific myth of creation is the big-bang theory. Scientists have their own evidence for the big bang, both theoretical and observational; yet surely those scientists who believe in it do so in part because the way has been so well prepared by their culture's myth of a single act of creation by a fecundating God. Indeed, what but the omnipotent finger of the Almighty could ignite a big bang?

For some, both inside and outside the profession, science seems to embody the only myths that offer hope and challenge for the future. Science becomes a golden cornucopia that pours out wonder drugs to cure our ills; it manipulates the genes of plants to achieve a green revolution and feed a starving world; it leads humankind to the edge of space, to help it conquer the final frontier. But science has its dark myths as well as its bright ones. It is the Frankenstein who unleashes the monster of technology on the world; it is the Pandora who unboxes the trouble of pollution to vex us all. In many respects the culture has been "scientized"—whatever one does must be scientific if it is to be valid. In 1964 Jacques Barzun wrote a volume ironically entitled *Science: The Glorious Entertainment*, decrying the trend of the times to view everything through the borrowed spectacles of science.[18] Today, science is even more pervasive in the world, but for a great many people science, even as it rules their lives, doesn't seem to matter very much. They don't understand it, don't know how it works, and, if the truth be known, don't like it very much. It is easy enough to blame this on the increasing specialization of science—it gets harder and harder to understand—but one cannot help suspecting that the official rhetoric of science is partly at fault. In trying to achieve what the countertradition claims finally to be impossible, render their discourse purely objective and impersonal, scientists themselves are obscuring the mythic structures that lie at the heart of their work. Beyond the flackery of "miracle cures" and "final frontiers," what myth does science tell us today that we might truly want to believe? What in science now calls to the heart or sings in the blood?

3

The view that science, even in its substance, is not immune to the pressures of the political and the economic, any more than it is to that of the social, is a major thrust of the countertradition. Initially, sociologists of science concerned themselves with the way in which other institutions, governments, say, influenced science in its institutional capacity, but they held, tacitly at least, that that influence did not penetrate into the *content* of science, that is, into the professional discourse of science. This barrier the countertradition has removed. The new sociologists, especially, have undertaken the study of external (social, political, and economic) influences on particular scientific developments. For example, recently sociologists Barry Barnes and Donald MacKenzie have examined the early twentieth-century dispute over modes of statistical analysis of association of biological variables. One camp, led by Karl Pearson, developed its scientific methodology, Barnes and MacKenzie argue, based on its own interest in eugenics, "at this time an important ideological strand in a body of thought closely associated with the rising professional middle class." The other school, that of George Udney Yule, worked out its research program with no thought to eugenics. "Indeed, it is perhaps the case," Barnes and MacKenzie conclude, "that Yule and his supporters found eugenics and biometry [the methodology of Pearson] uncongenial to their basically conservative social and political views."[19]

The new sociologists have also extended the work of the older sociologists with the institutions of science into its content. It is a major focus of their concern that what comes to be construed as a scientific fact is a matter of consensus-building effort. Even the distinction between the external and internal social forces that shape the nature of scientific activity is blurred, as Bruno Latour demonstrates in *Science in Action*.[20] One cannot effectively separate scientific activity from the social world of which it is a part.

The argument here, however, proceeds not from the perspective of the sociologist or the political or economic historian but from that of the literary critic. And as representative of political and economic criticism, it adopts for discursive purposes the central notions of Marxist criticism. One must note at once that Marxist critiques have long been included in, though they have hardly dominated, the externalist sociological studies of science. Indeed such critiques date from Boris Hessen's classic (though now often challenged) 1931 paper, "The Social and Economic Roots of Newton's *Principia*."[21] But to proceed.

To begin with, let us not be misled by science's traditional response to the Marxist critique that science has a kind of built-in mechanism for insulating itself from political and economic influences, that it will in effect self-destruct in the hands of those who attempt to control it. This is the argument employed by those in the West who take such delight in the Lysenko affair. It is true that by endorsing Lysenkoism, the Soviet government made the mistake of backing a scientific theory that promised to produce results it could not produce. Lysenkoism set itself up to be tested, as all true science must, but it failed the test. (Science that fails tests is discarded; science that passes tests is tested again.) Yet Lysenkoism did not fail *because* the government supported it; the government gave it every chance to succeed. It failed because it was poor science. There is ample evidence that governments can dictate scientific goals and support scientists to achieve those goals: the Manhattan project worked, and the United States put men on the moon. Nor were these projects uniquely successful because of the natural, open society of the West: the Manhattan project was as secret as could conceivably be achieved; the Nazis built the V1 and V2 rockets; the Soviet Union put *Sputnik* into orbit.

Still, the argument is not really over the overt political control of science; it is over the Marxist assertion that the capitalist system of production, operating through the superstructure, determines the content of science as ideology. The point is not that the American government, say, dictates to and politically controls American science (though it may well do so) but that the economic system itself ultimately determines that control. Scientists must have financial support for themselves and their activities; their employers—government, academia, private industry—provide that support and perforce determine the goals of the research. Even pure research is expected to have its ultimate payoff.

One does not need to engage in a Marxist analysis of Western science to perceive that it is organized oligarchically, with the persons who direct the research groups in governmental, industrial, and academic laboratories also heading the scientific organizations that hold meetings and publish journals and sitting on the agency panels that decide what research is to receive federal support and what is not.[22] But this must be so, one is told: scientists succeed by virtue of their work; the best scientists rise to the top because of their scientific success. It is science (the abstract god) that decides, not the individuals who merely seem to make the decisions. Science must be in control of its own destiny (not the politicians); hence, control of science must inevitably go to a certain small group of leading scientists. Perhaps so. But one must recognize the closed, self-perpetuating system for what it is. The same persons accept one another's papers for publication or delivery, honor one another with degrees and prizes, give one another money and opportunity for conducting research, and justify their judgments on the numbers of publications, awards, and grants that have already been given. Indeed, scientists are often judged not so much by the numbers of their own publications as by the frequency of their work's citation by others. The skills that bring success in such a system are not ones normally thought to be attributes of the typical scientist. Most important of all, however, one must perceive that it is the scientific oligarchy that mediates between the political and economic organs and the scientific community. The oligarchs advise government, sit on the government panels, head the governmental scientific bodies; they participate in both the shaping of policy and the implementation of it. They serve industry as well, directing its research, acting as consultants, providing their expertise on demand; they supply the needs of industry from its own labs or in those situated elsewhere, in academia or certain federal agencies. To suggest that this system has somehow insulated science from political or economic concerns is naive if not mendacious.[23]

To distinguish pure from applied science — to assert that the one is the neutral, objective, purified institution, isolated from the hurly-burly of the marketplace, while the other strikes the bargains, makes the compromises, sullies its skirts in the mire of commerce — is to create an artificial distinction and ultimately to beg the question. For even pure research is sold with the old Baconian justification, that the control it gives us over nature will end in improving the lot of humankind; it is only that with pure research the ends are less certain, the gains less predictable, the payoffs more remote.

Though the non-Marxist might wish to use other terms to describe the situation, it is clear that the Western scientific establishment uses the apparatus of the superstructure to exercise its ideological control even over pure science. It determines what scientific research is doable, because it decides what is fundable and what is publishable. Ultimately, it determines what is scientifically thinkable, until the unorthodox idea thrusts its way into the arena, with the force of scientific genius, skillful rhetoric, and iron determination behind it. The pure scientist can sometimes exploit the situation to advantage, or for the advantage of science. When I was an organic chemist, it was standard practice in research proposals to justify the synthesis of new organic compounds on the ground of their potential as anticancer agents, although everyone, including those who evaluated the proposals, knew that the chance of producing useful cancer drugs in this way was virtually nonexistent. The idea, tacitly conspired in by the establishment, was that this was a way to support an enterprise of pure scientific research, developing the skills that might someday provide the ability to produce compounds that would be useful against cancer, when one knew better what those would be. But the ideological decision that this was a useful line of research was still controlling.

To speak of the areas where science intersects with social, political, and economic controls is virtually to catalog the problems of the twentieth century: population growth and strain on the food supply; ready availability of abortion and contraceptive devices; maintenance of life support for the terminally ill; nuclear testing, disposal of nuclear waste, and control of fissionable materials; weapons in space; assurances of drug safety and efficacy; control of food processing and regulation of additives; and on and on. Interestingly enough, the scientific oligarchy in the West (and presumably that in the East) is not a monolith, insofar as these questions are concerned. If there is a scientific culture that favors one side of each question, there is likely to be a counterculture that favors the other. Thus many scientists, some with professional links to the military-industrial complex, hold that industrial pollution is a negligible factor in overall cancer mortality; other scientists, presumably less likely to have such ties, think it is a major source. Similar splits may be adduced for each of the above questions. In many cases the scientific content of the problem is not the real issue: can or should scientists define a precise moment when a fetus becomes a human being? Can or should scientists tell us precisely when a brain-damaged individual has become a "vegetable"? Yet one quickly becomes inured to hearing scientists invoke their scientific expertise to answer such questions. Particularly distressing are the instances of Nobel laureates citing the prestige of the prize in justifying their own views on social issues, even when the scientific aspects of the problem are not remotely related to their area of scientific competence.[24] Scientific-social interaction is thus a two-way street: social, political, and economic considerations impinge on science and in many cases determine the course of scientific research, and science too has its impact in the worlds of social, political, and economic affairs.

If science is ineluctably tied to the social world, its discourse must reflect that fact. Take but one example. Today there are obvious social reasons why it is desirable to stress gender and racial similarities rather than differences. Not surprisingly, perhaps, in this climate, one finds that all research purporting to show racial or gender differences is called into question. (Score one for the counterculturalists.) The argument, however, is not that such research is not socially desirable but that it is *scientifically* suspect (as, presumably it is, though that is not the real reason for rejecting it). There is, to be sure, the scientific scandal that much of the research that seemed to support the heritability of intelligence was faked.[25] But, more important, one now learns, the functioning of the human mind is too complex to be considered under a single variable, like "intelligence," or measured with a single number like "I.Q." Thus, "intelligence" is not a quality that science can legitimately reify and measure as it does, say, viscosity, and not quite incidentally, no group can be deficient in it.[26] The socially undesirable subject is thus banished from the discourse of science — on scientific grounds, not on social ones. The importance of the "scientific" label in a social context is not lost on the anti-evolutionists, who have devised the oxymoron "scientific creationism" to contend that religious dogma ought to be taught in the public schools side by side with scientific hypotheses.

One can indeed develop a neo-Marxist scenario in which various advantaged or disadvantaged social groups replace the traditional Marxist economic classes. Thus, for "proletariat," read "black, female, or gay"; for "bourgeois," read "heterosexual white male." Then, what the heterosexual white male group says to justify its control over the "means of production" is that, "scientifically" speaking, blacks are intellectually inferior, women emotionally unstable, and gays mentally ill. "Pure ideology," the neo-Marxist responds. None of these assertions makes scientific sense: neither intelligence nor emotional stability nor sexual preference can be assessed in any truly scientific way; these are rationalizations used to mask the undiluted exercise of power.

In the final analysis, however, one need not be a Marxist or employ Marxist terminology to become aware that science is not fully insulated from social, political, and economic affairs. Indeed, it may well be that the opprobrium attached to the label "Marxist" is exploited by some in the scientific establishment in the West who prefer, for their own reasons, to maintain that science is so insulated. But surely it is no denigration of science to situate it in the "sublunar sphere" of the Greek philosophers, rather than their "Empyrean realm," to make it a real endeavor of real social beings, and not a rarefied activity of celestial geometers.

4

We turn now from "men's business" to their "bosoms," from social, political, and economic determinism to the matter of psychological influence. The impersonal god of science, the tradition would have it, is served by acolytes who efface their humanity when they don their priestly robes. The true scientist, as a scientist, is as objective, as neutral, as the god who is emulated; when doing science, the scientist becomes a rational creature, no longer a feeling one. The discourse of science reflects that change in status; it too becomes the model of objectivity, neutrality, rationality.

I argue for an opposing view, that the scientist is a whole person, whose personality and experience cannot help but leave their mark on everything done, including the doing of the scientific work and the writing of that work (the exigencies of language force me to make a distinction that I hold not to be real). To this issue the countertradition speaks with a somewhat mixed voice. On the one hand, it is sympathetic to the idea that scientists shape their discourse, at least in part, out of the forces of their personalities. This is almost a direct consequence of Feyerabend's "anything goes" version of scientific argument. Also the ethnographers of *Writing Culture*, questioning the traditional discourse of their discipline, urge the explicit recognition in that discourse of the role of the ethnographer in producing the supposed impersonal portraits of the members of alien cultures. Yet, on the other hand, in its viewing of science as a communal effort rather than an individual one, the countertradition is more likely to see science as the product of social forces rather than psychological ones. Indeed, the new sociologists proceed to search for precisely those social interactions that themselves determine scientific developments. Even the context of generation (in my terminology) becomes for them a social circumstance, not a psychological one. Psychology, too, however, even as it recognizes individual differences, seeks generality and would interest itself less in the idiosyncratic than in the typical behavior of scientists in their endeavors.

As to the official voice of science, there is superficially much to support the claims of objectivity made in its behalf; indeed, it is designed precisely to that purpose (or has survived because it serves that purpose). I will not repeat here the argument to the contrary. Earlier I have noted the occasional overt breaching of the prescribed style and the constant silent transgression of its strictures as the individual personality makes itself known to those who are prepared to read it. Though it does not have a large space to maneuver in, the individual scientist's style serves not only to identify but also to characterize that individual scientist. Scientists who have never met know one another well through their writings. Even our brief exposure to the writings of certain scientists suggests something of their personalities: one cannot miss the calculation of Galileo, the avuncularity of Einstein, the disingenuousness of Watson.

Further, as I have said, the official voice of science constitutes an equally official rhetoric, a rhetoric that seeks to raise its discourse from the region of contention to the realm of truth. The chief weapon of this rhetoric is its agentless prose, whose effect is to desubjectify observation and experience, render them absolute rather than relative, make them simply recordings of the facts. Although this is not the only rhetoric of science, it is worth pausing a moment over, for it is so pervasive and has its own psychological implications. The scientist-writers who are not the subject of their own sentences, who are not the agent of their own actions, who do not even appear on the scene of their own discourse, cannot be the grammatical objects of others' sentences, cannot be the physical object of others' scrutiny, cannot become the psychical object of others' attention. With this rhetoric, scientists make of themselves voyeurs, peeping out at the scenes of life from their hiding place in language. The rhetoric of science is, thus, a rhetoric of concealment, a rhetoric of repression.

One can hardly avoid picturing the personality of the scientist this analysis implies. It comes very close to the stereotyped view of the scientist as the inhibited introvert who retreats to the laboratory to avoid confrontation with other human beings. Interestingly enough, there have been psychological studies that support this picture of the scientist as a loner, maladapted to social interaction.[27] Most people who deal regularly with scientists, however, are likely to conclude that there is no single scientific personality, that there are about as many scientific types as there are scientists. But the official rhetoric of science must have much to do with the prevalence of the stereotype. Even scientists are not immune to the influence. Einstein, thus, gives the motive of worthy votaries in the "temple of science" as "escape from everyday life with its painful crudity and hopeless dreariness, from the fetters of one's own ever shifting desires." (To what degree is this a self-portrait?) "A finely tempered nature longs to escape from personal life into the world of objective perception and thought."[28]

Not fully to endorse this reading of *the* personality of the scientist from the official language of science does not mean, however, the abandonment of the view that the writings of scientists are influenced by who those scientists are. Even the straitjacket of the official style cannot quite keep scientists from expressing themselves when they write.

With respect to the specifically psychoanalytic reading of scientific works, one must begin with an objection often raised against psychoanalysis as a system by many scientists — namely, that psychoanalysis cuts itself off from critical scrutiny by labeling any adverse reaction as "resistance." To criticize psychoanalysis, then, is to offer "resistance," revealing that one opposes the system out of fear of what it will reveal about oneself. Hence, in attacking Freud one is confirming him. (In the same way, Marxism is said to be self-confirming, in that any opposition is evidence of ideological bias, hence of the correctness of the system.) But Freud does not, in fact, seek to ground his system on this argument, though he may offer it in a playful way to confound his critics rhetorically; rather, he holds that it is the therapeutic results that confirm the method.[29] (The patients get better, Freud says, just as the nuclear physicist avers that the bombs go off.) If there is circularity here, it is on the part of the scientists who attempt to conceal every mark of their presence in their discourse and then argue that their discourse is privileged from psychoanalytic examination because it is a special, truly objective, body of language.

One will not settle in a few words whether psychoanalytic readings can help one see scientific documents not as the mere coded representation of scientific data but as the utterances of human beings. But let me note that there have indeed been psychoanalytic readings of scientific works, most notably those of Darwin. (Freud's own *Interpretation of Dreams* is read as a disguised account of his own self-analysis.)[30] Of Darwin, the Freudian view (or *a* Freudian view) is that Darwin's chronic illness was in fact a hysteric symptom resulting from an intense oedipal conflict. This view is derided by Sir Peter Medawar (with heavy-handed irony): "Kempf [the Freudian critic] must, I think, have been first to call attention — obvious though it now seems — to Darwin's intense and continuous preoccupation with matters to do with sex. We need look no further than the titles of his books: the *Origin* itself, of course: *Selection in Relation to Sex; The Effects of Cross- and Self-Fertilization in the Vegetable Kingdom*; and *On the Various Contrivances by Which Orchids Are Fertilized by Insects*."[31]

It is true that one cannot now confirm whether Charles Darwin had feelings of the kind Freudians label oedipal, and one cannot know whether his chronic illness was caused by such feelings. How he felt about his work, when he was or was not able to work, may or may not have been affected by his feelings or by his illness.[32] But it is not absurd, not ridiculous, to consider such connections, to look for evidence that they might exist, in the hope that they will help one better understand both Darwin and the *Origin of Species*. Scientists, too, share in the original sin of being human. It should not be a crime to suggest that their humanity affects their work and the language in which it comes to us and to their fellow scientists.

Specifically, however, does the Freudian system suggest anything of value in reading scientific texts? One of the great mysteries is the generation of scientific ideas; it is the one area of their work about which scientists are largely silent. Although their writing deals explicitly only with the verification of those ideas in the scientific arena, nonetheless one cannot but believe that the precise formulation of the ideas themselves bears in considerable measure the stamp of their origin. And that origin, in turn, must be, in part at least, unconscious. Freud, as the chief architect of our present understanding of the unconscious, presumably will help us to understand something of the unconscious shaping of scientific thought. In *Interpretation of Dreams* Freud describes the various processes by which he believes the dream to be formulated from the unconscious material that seeks expression in it, including such processes as condensation, displacement, and, especially significant for science, symbolization.[33] It is clear, in the Freudian system, that these processes are thought to operate generally, whenever unconscious material makes itself manifest in various forms, including literature and, as I argue, scientific thought.

Science, of course, makes conscious, deliberate use of symbolization to permit mental manipulation of its analogues of physical structures. But science has long recognized that some of the more remarkable symbol manipulations are unconscious. Here is August Kekulé's own account of his discovery of the ring structure of benzene:

> I was sitting, writing at my text-book; but the work did not progress; my thoughts were elsewhere. I turned my chair to the fire and dozed. Again the atoms were gambolling before my eyes. . . . My mental eye, rendered more acute by repeated visions of this kind, could now distinguish larger structures, of manifold conformation: long rows, sometimes more closely fitted together; all twining and twisting in snake-like motion. But look! What was that? One of the snakes had seized hold of its own tail, and the form whirled mockingly before my eyes. As if by a flash of lightning I awoke; and . . . I spent the rest of the night working out the consequences of the hypothesis.

> Let us learn to dream, gentlemen, then we shall find the truth . . .
> but let us beware of publishing our dreams before they have been put
> to the proof by the waking understanding.[34]

Several things are worth remarking in this account. Taken at face value
it reflects much of what is typically said of scientific discovery — namely,
that the role of the unconscious is clearly admitted but is strictly limited
to the context of generation just as it is excluded from the context of verification. ("Let us beware of publishing our dreams before they have been
put to the proof by the waking understanding.") The symbolism is, of
course, ostensibly scientific, but it does not take a Freudian to read the
sexual overtones in the account: "long rows . . . closely fitted together . . .
twining and twisting in snake-like motion. . . . One of the snakes had seized
hold of its own tail."

As it happens, revisionist historians have been hard at work debunking
Kekulé's dream story. ("We believe that we have made a reasonable case
based on circumstantial evidence that Kekulé did not conceive the structure
of benzene in a dream.")[35] Presumably, according to the revisionists, Kekulé's dramatic story of the dream generation of his idea was intended to
preclude any suspicion that he had borrowed essential elements of it from
competitors. As it further happens, however, rehabilitationist historians
have now suggested that the famous dream did indeed occur, though it was
not — as Kekulé himself asserted — a fully formed revelation of the benzene
theory but rather a "condensation nucle[us]" for the theory to form
around.[36] Even if the dream were entirely fictive, however, the vision it
represents is mental; like the fictive representations of the novelist, it is still
grist for the Freudian mill and likely to be indicative of the content of the
unconscious. Furthermore, this is hardly the only instance of the adoption
of phallic symbolism by Kekulé. Earlier he had advocated elongated structural formulae, which had been derided by a competitor as "Kekulé's sausages."[37] Although Kekulé came to use other, more conventional
formulations in time, as one historian soberly remarks, "Kekulé generally
preferred the sausage formulas satirized by Kolbe [the rival]."[38]

A Freudian, given sufficient biographical information about Kekulé and
access to private letters and journals, obviously would make much of this
material and would hope to locate the origin of the symbolism in the apparatus of Kekulé's unconscious. One commentator reports that at the
impressionable age of eighteen, some twenty years before the dream, Kekulé had served as a witness in a trial involving the murder of a countess

who lived nearby. Accompanying the murder was a theft of jewelry, including a ring that consisted of two intertwined metal snakes biting their own tails.[39] Our concern, however, is not with the biographical details that might be thought to account for the symbolization; it is to note that the scientific imagination seizes the clearly Freudian imagery presented by the unconscious and makes use of it in its symbolic resolution of a perplexing chemical problem.

The point must be a more general one, however. Symbolization, even Freudian symbolization, can play a role in science beyond Kekulé's unique vision: certain of the molecular orbitals that today's chemists draw in place of the old chemical bonds have spheroidal, ellipsoidal, toroidal, and elongated shapes — to cite but the first example that comes to mind. More to the general point, however, is to note the frequency with which significantly new ideas come to a scientist not necessarily in symbols but suddenly "out of nowhere" while the scientist is in a hypnagogic or hypnopompic state. The stories have common features: the scientist has been puzzling for some time over a problem that cannot be resolved; then turning away from the problem, dozing, musing, strolling, riding the bus, lying in bed half awake, the scientist suddenly experiences the epiphanic vision, carrying with it both the scientific solution and a sense of blissful release.

This is how Wilhelm Ostwald describes his experience of "seeing" finally how to write his textbook basing physics on energetics. After a long, late-night discussion with friends. he says,

> I . . . slept for a few hours, then suddenly awoke immersed in the same thought and could not go back to sleep. In the earliest morning hours I went from the hotel to the Tiergarten, and there, in the sunshine of a glorious spring morning I experienced a real Pentecoste, an outpouring of the spirit over me . . . . This was the actual birth-hour of energetics. What a year before . . . had confronted me as rather strange . . . now . . . proved to belong to myself, so much so that it was a life-supporting part of my being. . . . At once everything was there, and my glance only had to glide from one place to the other in order to grasp the whole new creation in its perfection.[40]

This example is cited (along with Kekulé's dream) in a remarkable paper, "Dreams and Visions in a Century of Chemistry," presented by chemist Edward Farber at a symposium celebrating the centennial of Kekulé's discovery of the benzene formula. It is Farber's thesis "that dreams and visions deserve to be recognized, without ridicule or pretense, as having an important place, even in modern chemistry." He categorizes the dozen "dreams and visions" he describes as symbolizations, extrapolations, predictions, and universal generalizations. What they have in common is that what is perceived comes from the unconscious. Although the thought comes from within, "it embrace[s] an objective totality," Farber says. "The apparent paradox occurs in all dreams and visions; it is especially great in the universal generalizations." Farber, presumably, is no Freudian, and he establishes no connection between the explicitly Freudian characterization of the unconscious and its role in the chemists' "dreams and visions." He makes it very clear, however, that he sees a connection between the psychological makeup and the nature of the dream: "the psychological conditions would have formed the best basis [for classification] if only the biographical information were available in sufficient depth." Nor does he view the intrusion of the unconscious into the sacred, rational precincts of science as aberrant. Apparently "dreams and visions" are, or should be, part of every scientist's armamentarium: "Dreams and visions are necessary, but they are not sufficient"; also needed are "improved experimental skill and accuracy." But the two are not antithetical: "The complementary nature that exists between visions and experimental skills does not mean that they must be distributed over different personalities; the same man can use one or the other at different times in his work."[41]

Ostwald's comment that what had earlier "confronted" him as "rather strange" now seemed "part of [his] being" points to another area where psychoanalytic thought illuminates scientific practice. That all-important aspect of the scientific genius, "feeling for the organism," is in Freudian terms an aspect of object instincts, one of two fundamental drives, with ego instincts, that govern much of behavior.[42] Of necessity, in Freudian thought, the object instinct is charged with Eros, and indeed there are erotic overtones to the often-obsessive attention that scientists devote to their chosen object. The term *sublimation* comes at once to mind, and it is not inappropriate here. Indeed, Keller in her biography of Barbara McClintock makes almost precisely this judgment about McClintock, though in strikingly different terms. She notes that McClintock had at first done considerable dating in college but had formed no lasting attachments; she quotes McClintock: "There was not that strong necessity for a personal attachment to anybody. I just didn't feel it." Still, the biographer insists, McClintock did not deliberately choose career over marriage. Nonetheless, one sees the emotional decision being made as McClintock describes how the choice came about: "I remember I was doing what I wanted to do [working in the cornfields], and there was absolutely no thought of a career.

I was just having a marvelous time."[43] (Indeed, for a detailed and rather different, though psychoanalytic, account of the role of object relations in the scientist's working life, the reader should consult Keller's *Reflections on Gender and Science*.)[44]

Not every scientist works obsessively, pouring emotional resources into scientific object relations; indeed not every scientist devotes a lifetime to a single, rather narrow range of objects, physical or mental, on which every focus centers. Like everyone else, some scientists are journeymen who work by the clock, shift their attention from object to object as their jobs require, and invest only a minimum of emotional energy in their work. But there is always the possibility of deeper involvement, and one cannot help but believe that those scientists who, like McClintock or Goodfield's Anna, most develop a "feeling for the organism" come to know that organism best and are most able to learn about it something truly new and significant.

The object instinct calls for closer and closer union with the object until a virtual merger of the two is achieved. The self engulfs the object, incorporates it: "it proved to belong to myself, so much so that it was a life-supporting part of my being." In Freudian terms, Eros is opposed to Thanatos, the death drive, the tendency of ego to pull in on itself and sink into a state of minimum excitation — nirvana.[45] Ostwald is a true Freudian in remarking how the object investiture is life-enhancing. It is a remarkable feature of the work of true scientists that they come to know the object of their scrutiny almost as an extension of themselves. They know its beginnings and ends, its quirks and its characteristics; they come to see patterns even in its idiosyncrasies; they finally lay down the laws of its behavior, which, if they are right, lo! it henceforth follows. Such a scientist becomes indeed a lawgiver, the god of a universe of inquiry. Is it any wonder that scientists feel such passionate attachment to the world they have virtually created? One speaks glibly of scientific revolutions, of scientific paradigms being overthrown by competing paradigms, without considering the emotional cost to those whose paradigms are overthrown. Only Wagner's Wotan, who as the *Ring* progresses sees the world he has sought to hold together disintegrate, can tell us what it is like for the scientist to find a worldview shattered by the Brünnhildes and Siegfrieds whose new science supplants the old. The old scientist-Wotan broods off stage in *Götterdämmerung* as the flames and waters consume Valhalla, the scientific edifice constructed at such terrible expense.

These remarks are, obviously, not intended to present a brief for an explicitly psychoanalytic reading of scientific works, any more than I sought to defend specifically Marxist or mythic readings. But I have hoped to suggest that one should not on a priori grounds dismiss any of these or similar readings from consideration. I maintain that one must at least attend to the artifactualist view that the scientific work, like the literary work, is shaped to a degree by the social, cultural, political, economic, and, indeed, psychological forces of the world in which it functions.

I will not now "do" a reading or a set of mythic, Marxist, and Freudian readings of scientific works to demonstrate how successfully it might be done. Whatever one thinks of such readings, it must be acknowledged that they demand considerable specialized knowledge and experience; to produce a travesty of one or all of them would serve no useful purpose. I will, however, direct attention to several scientific works whose special nature suggests that they cannot properly be understood without considering the cultural and social — even the political and economic — circumstances that influenced their direction. They are unique in that they make explicit the kind of connection that it is the rule to leave unsaid, even unthought, but that one assumes is always tacitly present. Thus they clearly voice what one would otherwise have to explicate.

5

Until the coming of quantum physics, with its uncertainty and its purely statistical laws, science had been dominated by the principle of determinism. Things happen in the world because they are caused, caused by certain antecedent events with an explicable, mechanical connection between the cause and the effect. It is the sole task of science to sort out the causes of the effects observed in the universe. Working with this agenda science proceeded remarkably. Bacon thought it would take only a few years to lay bare the secrets of the universe, and indeed by the beginning of the nineteenth century it seemed that science had succeeded in that goal, at least in principle. (Today, again, in limited areas one hears the same thing asserted.) It was at this nineteenth-century apogee of determinism that Laplace postulated his imaginary demon who, knowing the position and velocity of every mass in the universe, could calculate the universe's entire history, past and future.

Although this spirit of total determinism has its obvious methodological appeal (one cannot hope to find scientific laws if laws are not rigorously obeyed), it has less attractive philosophical, cultural, and social implications. Indeed it violates one of our most cherished notions of how the world works: our sense of our own free will. How can every event that occurs be determinable in advance (by Laplace's demon) when one has the ability to choose one's own future behavior? To be consistent, the determinist must believe that all behavior is, in fact, fully determined, regulated by natural laws, and that free will is only illusory, a kind of psychic aura that accompanies and palliates the inevitable choice. Such a view clearly says something about the social world and our reaction to it. If what happens is inevitable, then there is no room for change or improvement. In particular, it is difficult to reconcile a deterministic world and a liberal social agenda. Why work to better the lot of the indigent, say, if indigence is the result of ineluctable social circumstance, the regrettable but inevitable consequence of the working out of fixed laws?

This dilemma — determinism versus free will — scientists have sought to circumvent in various ways. Some have breached determinism itself, reached into the heart of their science and softened its iron laws. Lucretius introduced into his system the famous "swerve" — the *clinamen* — an occasional inexplicable deviation in the otherwise steady drift of atoms in the void. Newton found a little play in the gravitational mechanism that regulated the solar system and happily assigned to God the task of stepping in from time to time to get the planets back on course. These breaches of the system do not, of course, in themselves lead directly to an introduction of free will, but they suggest that the rain of atoms is not unremitting, that the universal clock is not a perfect engine, and they thereby open the door to slippage all along the line.

Other scientists, less willing to void the power of strict determinism, have been more likely to ignore the dilemma or attempt to transcend it. Over much of its history and in many of its branches, science has not involved itself with human behavior, and it has been relatively easy for scientists not so involved simply not to make the logical inferences that would lead to this particular dilemma. Many scientists, like other people, compartmentalize their lives in an effort to accommodate contradictory ideas and behaviors. What they believe and do in their work need not, then, conform with what they believe and do in their religion and their politics. More interesting, however, are the scientists who do wish to integrate their scientific doctrines with their social and political lives and who, perceiving the above dilemma, seek to transcend it. The case of one such scientist we will briefly examine.

Jacques Loeb, a German-born and -trained physiologist who came to the United States in the 1890s while still in his thirties, had a distinguished career at the Universities of Chicago and California and notably at the Rockefeller Institute, where he became virtually the apostle of biological mechanism and determinism. (He served, incidentally, as the prototype for the scientist par excellence, Max Gottlieb, in Sinclair Lewis's *Arrowsmith*; Martin Arrowsmith, the troubled young medical scientist of the novel, swears literally "by Jacques Loeb.")[46] Early in life Loeb had been interested in philosophy and had come somewhat under the spell of Schopenhauer. As historian Donald Fleming says in his introduction to a collection of Loeb's major writings, Loeb shared with Schopenhauer "not only an obsession with what Loeb called 'the problem of will' but a dogmatic conviction that freedom of the individual will was illusory. [Both] also believed, fanatically, in ripping the veil from the illusion, stripping the pretensions from the overweening automatons who fancied themselves bestriding the world."[47] At the same time, Loeb, in the tradition of European social democracy, was a socialist, who believed in the efficacy, perhaps the inevitability of social reform; and, as a Jew, he was deeply troubled by growing German militarism and nascent anti-Semitism.[48]

As biological determinist, Loeb was interested in demonstrating that the biological world was explicable simply in terms of chemical and physical interactions. Thus, in one of several lines of investigation, he studied the chemical and physical events that occur in fertilization of the egg, seeking to demonstrate that there was nothing miraculous about the beginnings of the life of the individual organism. He is perhaps best known, however, for his work on "animal tropisms," the automatic responses of simple animals to light, gravity, or chemicals in their environment. "Tropisms" are not now considered a serious model for the behavior of higher animals (indeed, even lower animals), but to Loeb they were the key to all animal behavior.

The term *tropism* is used more typically with plants, where it designates bending and twisting movements, usually directed toward light — heliotropism. Among the many types of animals whose tropic movements Loeb studied were plantlike polyps whose "stems" bend their "heads" toward the light exactly as do plants. But his examples were not limited to such marginal cases:

> Potted rose bushes or Cinerarias infected with plant lice are brought into a room and placed in front of a closed window. If the plants are allowed to dry out, the aphids (plant lice), previously wingless, change into winged insects. After this metamorphosis the animals leave the plants, fly to the window, and there creep upward on the glass. They can then easily be collected. . . .

> It can be demonstrated in these animals that the direction of their
> progressive movement is just as unequivocally governed by the source
> of light as the direction of the movement of the planets is determined
> by the force of gravity. (pp. 37–38)

This passage is drawn from an address to a psychological congress given
in 1909 and entitled "The Significance of Tropisms for Psychology." The
language of this passage reflects Loeb's major thesis, that animal tropisms
are strictly determined by physicochemical laws. With the aphids these are
laws of the photochemical action of light, coupled with the animals symmetrical structure. It is this combination that strictly orders the animals'
behavior.

> We must conclude that when two retinae . . . are illuminated with
> unequal intensity, chemical processes, also of unequal intensity, take
> place in the two optic nerves . . . . This inequality of chemical pro-
> cesses passes from the sensory to the motor nerves and eventually to
> the muscles connected with them . . . . The result of such an inequality
> of the action of symmetrical muscles of the two sides of the body is a
> change in the direction of movement on the part of the animal.
> (pp. 39–40)

A reference to the laws of planetary motion provides an example of how
fully determined behavior could seem to an observer to be the result of
will: "If a savage could directly observe the motions of the planets and
should begin to think about them, he would probably come to the conclusion that a 'will action' guides the movements of the planets just as a chance
observer is today inclined to assume that 'will' causes animals to move in
a given direction" (p. 36). Loeb's studies of animal tropisms, then, is part
of a scientific scheme to discover the laws that finally determine "will" (not,
one notes, "free will"). "The scientific solution to the problem of will
seem[s] then to consist in finding the forces which determine the movements of animals, and in discovering the laws according to which these
forces act" (p. 36).

This, therefore, *is* "The Significance of Tropisms for Psychology":
"Tropisms and tropism-like reactions are elements which pave the way for
a rationalistic conception of the psychological reactions of animals" (p. 60).
Ultimately, "it is a question of making the facts of psychology accessible
to analysis by means of physical chemistry" (p. 61). In tropisms, then, Loeb
claimed to have found the kernel process by which all animal behavior,

including ultimately human behavior, was regulated. "Tropism" became for Loeb but another name for the response of the animal automaton.

Out of a mélange of conflicting ideas — deterministic philosophy, mechanistic physiology, and social melioration — Loeb worked out his own set of beliefs with no apparent strain. Unlike Schopenhauer, Loeb "found a deep repose in the contemplation of determinism" (to quote from Fleming; p. xiii). Loeb solved the problem of will by doing away with will entirely, but the loss was no cause for grief. To Loeb, finally, strict determinism was in a curious way the ultimate source of hope for humanity.

The whole structure of Loeb's thought provided a kind of program in which his scientific work was carried out, and one cannot seriously understand that work without knowing of the program that gave it its rationale. Although in most of Loeb's scientific papers, this program is not made explicit, in 1911 he delivered an address, "The Mechanistic Conception of Life," before the First International Congress of Monists. Here in a few paragraphs he draws, at least rhetorically, the line from animal tropisms to the highest aspirations of humanity and seeks to make of the automaton an ethical being. He begins with the light-seeking tropism of marine worms:

> We may already safely state that the apparent will or instinct of these animals resolves itself into a modification of the action of the muscles through the influence of light; and for the metaphysical term "will" we may in these instances safely substitute the chemical term "photochemical action of light."

Now, at once, Loeb turns to human beings and equates their instincts with the tropisms of marine worms:

> Our wishes and hopes, disappointments and sufferings have their source in instincts which are comparable to the light instinct of the heliotropic animals. The need of and the struggle for food, the sexual instinct with its poetry and its chain of consequences, the maternal instincts with the felicity and the suffering caused by them, the instinct of workmanship, and some other instincts are the roots from which our inner life develops. (p. 32)

From here it is but a step to ethics:

> If our existence is based on the play of blind forces and is only a matter of chance; if we ourselves are only chemical mechanisms — how can there be an ethics for us? The answer is, that our instincts are the root

> of our ethics and that the instincts are just as hereditary as is the form
> of our body. We eat, drink, and reproduce not because mankind has
> reached an agreement that this is desirable, but because, machine-like,
> we are compelled to do so. We are active, because we are compelled
> to be so by processes in our central nervous system; and as long as
> human beings are not economic slaves the instinct of successful work
> or of workmanship determines the direction of their action. The
> mother loves and cares for her children, not because the metaphysi-
> cians had the idea that this was desirable, but because the instinct of
> taking care of the young is inherited just as distinctly as the morpho-
> logical characters of the female body. . . . We struggle for justice and
> truth since we are instinctively compelled to see our fellow human
> beings happy. (pp. 32–33)

Human beings, then, are automatons, but they are good automatons. They
behave well toward their fellow beings because they are programmed to
do so. The Golden Rule is not simply inscribed in their hearts; it is coded
into their nervous system and their musculature, like the heliotropism of
marine worms.

To be sure, the world is not perfect:

> Economic, social, and political conditions or ignorance and supersti-
> tion may warp and inhibit the inherited instincts and thus create a
> civilization with a faulty or low development of ethics. Individual mu-
> tants may arise in which one or the other desirable instinct is lost, just
> as individual mutants without pigment may arise in animals; and the
> offspring of such mutants may, if numerous enough, lower the ethical
> status of a community. (p. 33)

Loeb is not deterred, however, by this qualification; the system still provides for ethical behavior, however imperfectly it might be realized. It is
in this way that Loeb has, at least to his own satisfaction, achieved the
impossible — reconciled the irreconcilables, married determinism with social melioration. And he has done so by inserting a causal connection between the two; human beings will work to improve the world because
physical chemistry impels them to do so: "Not only is the mechanistic
conception of life compatible with ethics: it seems the only conception of
life which can lead to an understanding of the source of ethics" (p. 33).

What is intended by this rhetoric (one can hardly consider the long
string of unsupported assertions to be logical argument) is obvious, and
whether it succeeds in its purpose is of no concern. What is of interest,
however, is the patent situating of the science in its enabling social matrix.

What Loeb studies is the light-induced motion of marine worms and plant lice, among other things, and though one does not doubt his interest in the unique scientific problems these organisms pose, one knows that ultimately he is interested in the ethical behavior of humankind. Beyond the immediate science, concerns from the social sphere infuse the whole enterprise.

6

Strict determinism is not the only problem science poses for those who wish to write an active scenario for humanity's involvement with the universe. The famous second law of thermodynamics, with its demand for an ever-increasing measure of disorder in the world, is another. What the second law says is that for any process occurring in a closed system the ratio of the heat content to the absolute temperature always increases. What it means is that energy is always dissipated as work is done. At the same time as energy is dissipated, its converse, entropy — the measure of disorder — increases. The ultimate "closed system" is the universe as a whole, and its energy, the second law insists, is slowly but inevitably ebbing away, as entropy (disorder) equally inevitably, mounts. The resulting "heat death" of the universe casts a grim pall over the future. That chaos is destined finally to reign over all is hardly the most consoling of philosophies.

Historically, the second law was formulated not long after Laplace had brought to its final perfection the Newtonian clockwork universe. (In taking the "give" out of the Newtonian machine, Laplace, as he purportedly told Napoleon, had no further need for the "hypothesis" of God.) But the two clash in a fundamental way: the thermodynamic world of heat changes and energy consumption is all but irreconcilable with the world of dynamics, the Newtonian machine of endlessly moving masses in empty space. The Newtonian world of dynamics is reversible: the frictionless pendulum always swings into its just-traversed path. But the world of thermodynamics is irreversible: a portion of the energy consumed by the locomotive as it roars down the track is lost forever.

Interestingly, the second law has its own demonology — Maxwell's demon, an imp who sits at the portal of a divided container filled with gas and shunts the speedy molecules of gas into one chamber, the slow ones into the other.[49] As a result, one chamber contains gas that gets hotter and hotter; the other, gas that gets colder and colder — in violation of the second law. The demonic gatekeeper was Maxwell's device to illustrate his theory that heat consists in the relative motion of molecules.

The irreversibility of thermodynamics is a problem for the scientist who wishes to inhabit a world of perfect symmetries, of infinitely repeatable results. But irreversibility is not a problem for those who simply live in the world. When we mix a scotch and soda we know that the bubbles that go out will never go back in, nor will the alcohol and the water ever unmix. This is especially true of our experience with the biological world. The seed becomes the seedling; the seedling, the plant. The only way one can go back to the seedling from the plant is by way of a new seed. Our own personal histories are the most intimate example we have of biological irreversibility.

But biological irreversibility presents a new problem of its own: it seems actually to invert the second law. The second law calls for always increasing disorder, the incessant breakdown of structure; and some biological processes, like decay, appear to go along. But many, conspicuously, do not. The process of development causes the single-celled egg to convert itself into the highly complex multicellular organism. And evolution, acting over millennia, brings about quite analogous changes, often yielding organisms of bewilderingly complex structure. Even societies seem to develop, to evolve, to grow ever more elaborate and complex. Strict believers in the second law take these seeming contradictions in stride; they brush them aside as local and temporary aberrations, momentary islands of growing order bought at the expense of an accelerating disorder in the surrounding sea. But the problem remains: how can even such temporary aberrations occur when the thermodynamic pressure is all the other way? Alcohol and water always mix when brought together — their atoms seek the situations of maximum disorder. What is different about the atoms of the genome of the egg? How can they produce the ordered structure of the chicken?

Thus, a double puzzle: Newton's universe sits in time; it is bathed by time; the flow of its time is symmetrical. Swing the pendulum back, reverse the moon in its orbit, the paths remain the same; the arrow of Newton's time could have its head at either end. Not so the time of thermodynamics or the time of evolution: they are not tepid baths; they are torrents. Dissipated heat never returns; the evolved organism never devolves. These arrows shoot in only one direction, though the trajectory of one slants down to chaos, and the other aims up toward adaptation and complexity. The puzzlements here are scientific, but they are also philosophical, cultural, and social; they influence how we view our lives, how we choose to live our lives (if choose we do).

It is in the context of this multiple puzzlement that one must place the science of Ilya Prigogine, Belgian physical chemist and winner of the 1977 Nobel Prize in chemistry. The text through which we, as lay readers, can best appreciate what Prigogine is about is *Order out of Chaos*, a collaboration of Prigogine and the scientist and historian Isabelle Stengers.[50]

The Nobel committee honored Prigogine for his "contributions to nonequilibrium thermodynamics, particularly the theory of dissipative structures."[51] Until recently, Prigogine and Stengers say, much of thermodynamics has dealt with equilibrium states, stable situations of minimal energy, any small perturbations of which are met with prompt return to equilibrium conditions (pp. 122–29). But in studying systems that are far from equilibrium, Prigogine finds behaviors that seem highly anomalous, including the sudden appearance of highly ordered systems, stable or fluctuating, apparently out of nowhere — "order out of chaos" (pp. 140–53). Certain chemical solutions, for example, may switch colors back and forth — say from red to blue and back to red and so on — or they may show waves of color passing through them. The structures that form in such systems are, in effect, self-organized; Prigogine calls them "dissipative structures" because energy is consumed in maintaining their orderliness.

In some of the processes Prigogine studies, he observes "bifurcation points," moments in the reaction sequence when the system can go in any of two or more ways; the path the system follows may be determined solely by chance or by very small differences in physical conditions, which are multiplied by the system itself. But in either case, once the decision is made, it is irreversible; the system goes on to achieve whichever end state the initial choice determines. In making its choices, the system develops a history; the outcome after several bifurcations is determined not just by the initial state but by what has happened along the way (pp. 160–67). In this respect, Prigogine's systems are said to behave much as do the events in the world beyond the laboratory, including the biological and social worlds. Further, Prigogine's dissipative structures appear to resemble biological and social structures in their seeming violation of the second law (in the final analysis, this violation too is only "seeming"), because, again, one sees order increasing when it should be decreasing. Prigogine and Stengers present examples from the biological and social world whose systems behave in ways very much like the simple chemical systems Prigogine works with — aggregating slime molds, termites constructing nests, human beings building cities (pp. 181–209).

But if Prigogine's systems are models for social behavior, social behavior is implicitly a model for Prigogine's systems. The chemical systems "behave," "choose," "perceive" (pp. 161–63), "communicate" (p. 148), even "determine [their] own intrinsic size" (p. 151). It is a remarkable experience to read of Prigogine's chemical "clocks" whose molecules in synchrony switch their molecular constitution and their colors back and forth on cue like card sections in football stands. Others of his systems are like the alternate surges of cars and people at busy intersections as traffic lights change (pp. 147–48). It comes as little surprise when Prigogine and Stengers explicitly relate the "biological order" to the order shown in Prigogine's systems; their language has made the connection long before: "In the context of the physics of irreversible processes, the results of biology obviously have a different meaning and different implications. We know today that both the biosphere as a whole as well as its components, living or dead, exist in far-from-equilibrium conditions. In this context life, far from being outside the natural order, appears as the supreme expression of the self-organizing processes that occur" (p. 175).

It is a central goal of Prigogine and Stengers in *Order out of Chaos* to help resolve the puzzles referred to a moment ago — to join dynamics and thermodynamics, to connect the reversible with the irreversible, even to reconcile the upward spiral of biological evolution with the cascades of energy loss that thermodynamics demands. This they accomplish by inserting the ideas of randomness and probability into the heart of mechanics. In Prigogine's rereading of dynamics (*mis*reading, the literary critic would say, without pejoration), fully determined, reversible systems — the pendulum, the universal clock that goes backward as well as forward, the world of Laplace's demon — are the exception to the rule. *Equilibrium* suggests balance, precision, even order, and this is how one thinks of the Newtonian world of dynamics; but thermodynamic equilibrium is chaotic, confused, *dis*ordered. It is far from equilibrium where Prigogine finds true order, the molecules marching in step, turning rank on rank. Prigogine and Stengers inject this antinomy into dynamics; in their analysis of dynamics at a fundamental level, statistical causations and probabilities appear: what happens with local movement is *not* strictly determined by fundamental laws of motion; it is a chance event subject to the same kinds of uncertainty that make quantum mechanics such a puzzling system. The regularity of the pendulum is a simple, singular case, abstracted out of a much more probabilistic, uncertain general situation in which events unfold according to overall statistical patterns but individually seem to be random. This is because, if one may simplify the argument, the initial conditions of any system are too multiplex ever to be fully specified — they are simply unknowable. Laplace's demon is effectively blind; it cannot read the world system as it exists. This argument says that what *is* is totally disordered to any observing eye, which can never penetrate the patterns it contains. As the thermodynamicist says, there is an infinite entropy barrier in this, the present moment, which permits the situation to move only forward into the future. And *precisely* how it moves into the future cannot be predicted. Such behavior is not lawless, but its laws are of a new kind: laws of probability, not of certainty; statistical laws, not laws specifying individually determined behavior (pp. 257–90).

This new mode of scientific description is very different from the old, Newtonian mode:

> Classical science aimed at a "transparent" view of the physical universe. In each case you would be able to identify a cause and an effect. Whenever a stochastic [chance-ordered] description becomes necessary, this is no longer so. We can no longer speak of causality in each individual experiment; we can only speak about statistical causality. This has, in fact, been the case ever since the advent of quantum mechanics, but it has been greatly amplified by recent developments in which randomness and probability play an essential role, even in classical dynamics or chemistry. Therefore, the modern trend as compared to the classical one leads to a kind of "opacity" as compared to the transparency of classical thought. (p. 311)

"Is this a defeat for the human mind?" Prigogine and Stengers ask. Perhaps not, they answer. And they remind us that the classical world of reversibility and equilibrium (the universe like an "automaton following deterministic causal laws") never was the world of experience, with its "spontaneous activity and irreversibility." That these divergent views of reversibility and irreversibility now seem to be coming together is, as Prigogine and Stengers suggest, "a satisfying feature of the recent evolution in science that we have tried to describe" (pp. 311–12).

This "recent evolution," of course, has enormous implications as to how one views the world one inhabits. Some of these Prigogine and Stengers spell out in the peroration of *Order out of Chaos*:

The ideas to which we have devoted much space in this book — the ideas of instability, of fluctuation — diffuse into the social sciences. We know now that societies are immensely complex systems involving a potentially enormous number of bifurcations exemplified by the variety of cultures that have evolved in the relatively short span of human history. We know that such systems are highly sensitive to fluctuations. This leads both to hope and a threat: hope, since even small fluctuations may grow and change the overall structure. As a result, individual activity is not doomed to insignificance. On the other hand, this is also a threat, since in our universe the security of stable, permanent rules seems gone forever. We are living in a dangerous and uncertain world that inspires no blind confidence, but perhaps only the same feeling of qualified hope that some Talmudic texts appear to have attributed to the God of Genesis:

Twenty-six attempts preceded the present genesis, all of which were destined to fail. The world of man has arisen out of the chaotic heart of the preceding debris; he too is exposed to the risk of failure, and the return to nothing. "Let's hope it works" . . . exclaimed God as he created the World, and this hope, which has accompanied all the subsequent history of the world and mankind, has emphasized right from the outset that this history is branded with the mark of radical uncertainty. (pp. 312–13)

Here, as with Jacques Loeb, one cannot simply separate the science from its context. To say that Ilya Prigogine is a "thermodynamicist" working on "dissipative structures" is to ignore a very large portion of his thought, as he would almost surely agree. Prigogine's science is true science, pure science, but it is not science in a vacuum, science conceived apart from the culture, the society that gives rise to it, shapes it, indeed nourishes it, as he himself tells us: "The recent evolution of science gives us a unique opportunity to reconsider its position in culture in general. Modern science originated in the specific context of the European seventeenth century. We are now approaching the end of the twentieth century, and it seems that some more *universal message* is carried by science, a message that concerns the interaction of man and nature as well as of man with man" (p. 7).

But this must not be taken to mean that twentieth century science has shed its cultural dependence: "It is important to point out that the new scientific development . . . is not to be seen as some kind of 'revelation,' the possession of which would set its possessor apart from the cultural world he lives in. On the contrary, this development clearly reflects the internal logic of science and the cultural and social context of our time" (p. 309).

As these remarks might suggest, it is a major theme of Prigogine and Stengers that science generally cannot divorce itself from its cultural milieu. Thus, they cite with approval the assertion of Erwin Schrödinger that "there is a tendency to forget that all science is bound up with human culture in general, and that scientific findings, even those which at the moment appear the most advanced and esoteric and difficult to grasp, are meaningless outside their cultural context" (p. 18).

Specifically, Prigogine and Stengers relate certain developments in science to their cultural circumstances. They connect, for example, the development of modern science in the sixteen and seventeenth centuries with the "peculiar complex which, at the close of the Middle Ages, set up conditions of resonance and reciprocal amplification among economic, political, social, religious, philosophic, and technical factors" (p. 51). Noting that the mechanization of nature the new science called for was quite in line with the Christian notion of God the "designer" of the universe, nonetheless they caution: "It would be out of the question to 'prove' that modern science could have originated only in Christian Europe." Yet, clearly, "those [Christian] arguments made the speculations of modern science socially credible and acceptable, over a period of time varying from country to country" (p. 47).

For another example, Prigogine and Stengers point to the "irrationalist movement in Germany in the 1920s," which, they say, "formed the cultural background to quantum mechanics. In opposition to [Newtonian] science, which was identified with a set of concepts such as causality, determinism, reductionism, and rationality, there was a violent upsurge of ideas denied by science but seen as the embodiment of the fundamental irrationality of nature. Life, destiny, freedom, and spontaneity thus became manifestations of a shadowy underworld impenetrable to reason" (p. 6). In such a climate, one may suppose, Heisenberg, Born, and company would find their own foray into indeterminism and causality-by-chance less problematic.

This discussion of the impact of social and cultural influences on science, as on literature, began with three paradigmatic schools — myth, Marxist, and Freudian criticism. Although Prigogine and Stengers do not select any one of these schools as their point of departure, nonetheless there is evidence they would find none of them uncongenial.

Toward myth criticism they would be perhaps most sympathetic. In fact, a section of one of their chapters is labeled "The Myth at the Origin of

Science." The "myth" they refer to is the notion that the universe is explainable according to certain simple, mathematical, universal laws, ascertainable by the methods of science: "Galileo, and those who came after him, conceived of science as being capable of discovering *global* truths about nature. Nature not only would be written in a mathematical language that can be deciphered by experimentation, but there would actually exist only one such language" (p. 44). This conviction is "mythical" because, although it has the ring of absolute truth, it is in fact an assumption; there is no real *reason* to suppose that, as Newton puts it, "Nature [is] ever conformable to her self."[52] And it is this mythical conviction that Prigogine and Stengers relate to the peculiar social conditions of the late Middle Ages.

There is nothing explicitly or implicitly Marxist in Prigogine and Stengers's reading of scientific history. But the importance of economic factors in the development of this same scientific myth — indeed even the importance of the "means of production" — they do point out: "It seems hard to deny the fundamental importance of social and economic factors — particularly the development of craftsmen's techniques in the monasteries, where the residual knowledge of a destroyed world was preserved, and later in the bustling merchant cities — in the birth of experimental science, which is a systematized form of part of the craftsmen's knowledge" (p. 45).

Nor are Prigogine and Stengers avowed Freudians, although they are not inimical to Freudian readings. They cite, with some approval, Einstein's description of scientists' "flight from everyday life" and the "fetters" of their own "shifting desires" (p. 20). And they become, momentarily, true Freudians when they compare the "opacity" of modern scientific thought with the "opaque functioning of the unconscious": "Remember Oedipus," they say, "the lucidity of his mind in front of the sphinx and its opacity and darkness when confronted with his own origins." Indeed, so aware are they of the kinships of the inner world of man and the outer world of science that, they assert, one of the "satisfying" features of the developments in science they describe is the "coming together of our insights about the world around us and the world inside us" (p. 312).

Prigogine, then, is a scientist squarely in the countertradition, who denies the traditional insistence on the purity of science and its isolation from the social and cultural world it inhabits. His is an important scientific voice — though clearly not the official voice of science — asserting, proclaiming, the artifactual nature of its own utterance.

CHAPTER SEVEN

Writing as Reality

HAT STRUCTURALISTS/POSTSTRUCTURALISTS SEE IN ANY DISCOURSE IS the constant interplay of sign systems that do not so much represent an external reality as themselves constitute what we know as reality.[1] According to their instrumentality theory, writing is the instrument that brings into being the phenomenological world. But is this pattern true of scientific discourse? Does such discourse, in any sense, *constitute* the reality scientists investigate in their work? No suggestion could seem more inimical to the spirit of traditional science. Its positivist assurance that it is laying bare the true, but hidden, secrets of the world is virtually the raison d'être of traditional science.

The countertradition, as we have seen, makes its own critique of positivist science. But what is lacking, even in the countertraditional views, from the poststructuralist perspective, is the central notion of textuality — the judgment that scientists, their theories, their paradigms, their social interactions, are all embedded in textuality, shaped and formed by the textuality in which they are brought into being. Even the hermeneuticist of science — who would hold that the methodology of science is itself a reading, a decipherment of meaning of the text scientists examines in their work — sees the text as being read, scrutinized, interpreted, not itself contributing to the textuality that ultimately generates reader, reading, and read. (Only those relatively few literary critics, like Gillian Beer, who have brought contemporary critical methodologies to bear on scientific texts will adopt as part of their perspective the poststructuralist point of view.) At any rate, it is to this aspect of the question that I must now turn.

The early structuralists, working with the lives and customs of primitive peoples, uncovered the ways in which language systems, sign systems, created social meaning.[2] The contrived features of their world—their myths, their customs, their patterns of behavior—situated them in a world both natural and social. So for modern people—the structuralist asserts—do the fabrications of the social world serve to situate them, orient them, ratify their existence.

If the discourse of science is not an exception to this pattern, if science, too, is but one of the many works of humankind, then its discourse will comprise its own series of structures, carry its own weight of situating effect. Can this be so? To be sure, it must. Though there are exceptions, like the paradigm-shattering works of Einstein, the papers of the scientist are the most formulaic of writings; their rigidly prescribed patterns put the generic conventions of the western or the detective story to shame. A glance through a scientific journal reveals paper after paper with identical patterns of organization, often precisely the same headings. Every subdivision of science carries its own special, approved vocabulary, its own prescribed mode of organization of its discourse. A word or two of change here, a word or two of change there, and a new scientific paper is produced. What is said is guaranteed in advance by adherence to the accepted code, with the seal of approval, the imprimatur, applied by the referees, the certified authorities who testify to the adherence of the new entry to the official code. The new paper is new because it is a variation of the old ones; it is acceptable because it is a minute variation of them. The structure is preserved; only the names are changed (to preserve, presumably, the innocence of science). The structures of the scientists' papers, in short, are no more novelties than the retelling of primitive myths. This indeed reflects the fact that experiments, with their rigid adherence to prescribed practice, are not more truly novel than the ritual meals engaged in by primitive peoples.

Can one doubt that the patterns of scientists' discourse have their constituting effect?[3] For what purpose is the patterning if not to legitimize? The ratification by the community follows on its certification of the method spelled out in the scientific paper. That paper's adherence to the appropriate pattern asserts its claim to the validity that institutional science, with its keys to publication, financial support, promotion, and recognition, provides.

Surely the current discourse of science *constitutes* current scientific "truth"; that is its purpose. But for all its love of logic and system for its own sake, for all its dedication to truth in the abstract, science believes its truth is *about* the world. There was a precise moment in time when Galileo looked through his telescope and saw what convinced him that the Copernican system was not simply more rational than the Ptolemaic system, not merely a more satisfying mathematical construct, but a truer picture of the world he observed. This is always what scientists want, that their theories, however abstruse, be about the world. The theories, of course, remain theories; the Copernican system Galileo valued so highly, with its circular planetary orbits, never was really true, as no theory is ever absolutely true. What the discourse of science constitutes via the current theories of science is the "world" the scientist inhabits, the "world" of scientific indwelling.

It need not seem strange that the papers of scientists constitute the world for them as the myths of primitive peoples constitute their world. It has long been a commonplace of ethnographic thought that the two impulses, science and mythopoesis, derive from a common situating impulse. (We all — savage and sophisticate alike — want to know: "what is the meaning of life?") Nor need it seem strange that the scientist's discourse should consist largely of small variations on routine forms. This view is hardly news to scientists. Their education consists chiefly in learning the old ideas that they are to manipulate in their own work. It is precisely this aspect of science, science as minute variations of old themes, that constitutes Kuhn's "normal" science.

Even behind the ordinary tokens of science that are continually rearranged — the experimental accounts, the methodological descriptions — one finds, on examining the unstated assumptions and the hidden presuppositions, the same, age-old themata in their constant oppositional pairings: continuity/discontinuity, persistence/change, mathematical rigor/organic growth. Holton's *themata* are limited in number because there are only so many ways one can view the world. The themata are the expectations of the world that science fulfills, and those expectations occur again and again as different scientists seek to fulfill them.

Yet it is in the major upheavals of science, those revolutionary disruptions of the scientific system, rather than in the routine of everyday science that one can see the presence of the structuralist's bricolage.[4] For even the new systems, the apparently novel approaches, the revolutionary paradigms, are never entirely new: they are always constituted out of the debris of the old systems they displace. No scientific theory is ever born fresh, inscribed with a new point into a tabula rasa. What is new is always a chimera, constructed of already known fragments.

Science has always formulated its new ideas by taking its materials ready to hand, never constituting them fresh from pure thought. When scientists appropriate terms like *force, energy,* and *power,* like *inertia* and *momentum,* and invest them with their own specific meaning, they are simply inserting the old signifiers into new systems of signification. When Galileo speaks of *gravity,* he has in mind a property, an inherent tendency, of substances made of earth to reunite with their collective entity Earth. But the *gravity* that Newton invents is displaced; it is a force of attraction between material bodies. In reconstructing the Galilean system of the world, Newton retains the old signifier, but he inserts it into a new system of relations. And this process is not simply an antique one. When subatomic physicists wish to distinguish a family of entities by a variable property that has no counterpart in the world of ordinary dimensions, they designate the various states of the property as "flavors," just as Baskin-Robbins does the varying states of its product. One can never signify the new, the unfamiliar, without reference to the old, the familiar, the comfortable. Photons of light are neither particles nor waves, but something else entirely, yet physicists persist in calling them either particles or waves because they have nothing else to call them. Even the neologisms of the scientist are formed from antique roots: *phot-,* Greek for "light"; *-on,* "unit." This aspect of science is true bricolage, not merely the reshuffling of old ideas, but the taking of bits and pieces of old ideas and cobbling them together for the construction of supposedly new ones. Whenever science changes the spectacles by which it views the world, the new spectacles are always patched together out of the broken pieces of the old ones. Their new, clean, sharp vision is obtained through the assemblage of ill-assorted, misappropriated pieces of the old spectacles whose vision of the world had proven too astigmatic for comfort.

However convenient the antinomy of normal versus revolutionary science for expository purposes, the reality it dichotomizes resembles, as we have seen, far more a continuum. Between the minute variations of normal science and the vast conceptual upheavals of revolutionary science must come every conceivable degree of change. Indeed, such judgments must themselves be subjective. To the young scientist embarking on a fresh career, the variant insight achieved, however small an innovation it may seem in the great scheme of things, must appear the most revolutionary of events. This argument, however, is not affected by any such corrective, for the claim is that the change, great or small, revolutionary or evolutionary, is not in its ingredients wholly new. It may be a reformulation, perhaps, a revision of old ideas — but a totally new structure, a fresh fabrication employing only the most virginal of materials? No. There is always in scientific change a reassemblage, a bricolage, a repackaging of always old ingredients.

2

The appeal of method is universal. If one does it right, one will get it right. And the belief that natural philosophy, science, holds in its vaunted method the key to its success has dominated philosophies of science for millennia. From Aristotle to Descartes to Mill to Carnap, method has been cited as the road to truth. At the same time, a skeptical tradition, from Pyrrho to Hume to Derrida, has put absolute truth forever beyond reach, for all the method one may employ in seeking it. Science itself, as we have seen, wants its "truths" to be really true, but it long ago adopted the pragmatic trick of setting aside its epistemological claims while tacitly pressing them. For science to operate, for it to succeed in its endeavors, it claims it needs the comfortable assurance of the rest of us that its results are true, that the "real world" its theories depict is indeed the real world. The claim is methodological. We scientists, it goes, must operate as though our method revealed truth, for only then can it reveal "truth" — the working "truth," the provisional "truth," the pragmatic "truth" that permits our functional world of science to perform its daily miracles.

It is here, however, at this juncture, that poststructuralism levels its challenge of science. It does not, of course, claim that science does not work, merely that one does not have to label its picture of the world a true likeness in order for it to work. Let us grant science, it says, the right to assume whatever it wants to do its job, but let us not invest those assumptions with ultimate truth value (even operational truth value) they cannot inherently have.[5] It is not enough merely to argue, with the structuralists, that the ever-changing (but always similar) kaleidoscope of scientific discourse shapes or patterns the scientist's thought as it formulates a picture of the world. Rather, we must make the further claim, adopt the final disjuncture, that the world the scientist's discourse constitutes is the only "real" world that can be known, that the final, "out there" world exists, can exist, only in the world picture constructed in the scientist's work (or constructed by us in our daily lives). The Derridean argument is that physics is in its very concepts "contaminated" with metaphysics, that every discourse, including the discourse of science, is caught up in an endless play of language, a labyrinth from which there is no exit. This does not, of course, mean that there is nothing beyond language, merely that one can only perceive what one assumes is beyond language within the sphere of language. We have long ago ceased to demur at the notion that every explanation entails another explanation. Indeed, it is a comic cliché of considerable truth that the child is most annoying who counters the answer to every question with a further question. It is this infinite regress of discourse that poststructuralism makes its own.

Even if we set aside this ultimate epistemological claim of the poststructuralists that scientific discourse, like any body of discourse, is a free play of language, separated completely from a world we can never know, nonetheless I believe there is much we can adopt in the poststructuralists' view—namely, that scientific discourse represents a body of interleaving texts that in effect constitute the world they purport to describe. That that body of texts is a working body that relates to a scientific practice and operates in a particular cultural setting, however, we must also acknowledge.[6]

Certain of the poststructuralists, notably Foucault and Serres as well as others in the Anglo-American world, have directed their attention specifically to scientific discourse. We need not critically examine that work; let us, however, briefly consider the method of the deconstructionists as a valid modus for the critique of scientific discourse. It is the aim of deconstruction—one among several—to reveal within the work under scrutiny the tacit assumptions, the silent, unexpressed judgments, that govern the world the discourse organizes. By its processes (if one can so vastly simplify so complex a mechanism) by its "inversion of the hierarchy," by its "desedimentation," the deconstructionist disentangles the assemblage and reveals the problematic nature of its formulation.[7] When the task is complete, the deconstructed language lives on, its terms, however, now held "under erasure," altered in their signification by the deconstructive process itself. But this process, which at first blush may seem so unscientific, is not unlike the process the scientific revolutionary engages in when seeking to unseat an established paradigm.

The matter of paradigm shifts, following Hegel (and Engels), has been viewed as instances of dialectical reversal—thesis, antithesis, and finally, synthesis. When the new paradigm, the new view of how things are, comes to make its way in the world, it can do so only by displacing the old paradigm, the old view of things. The new must succeed at the expense of the old before a final synthesis can be achieved. The two cannot live on side by side; they are incompatible. As Galileo's Sagredo has already told us: "Eternal motion and permanent rest are such important events in nature and so very different from each other that only the most diverse consequences can depend upon them, especially when applied to such vast and significant bodies in the universe as the sun and earth. And it is impossible that one of two contradictory propositions should not be true and the other false."[8]

In the reversal, the old basic assumptions, the themata, which governed everything done under the old system, are stood upon their head. What was accidental is now crucial; what was peripheral is now central; what was minor, now major; what trivial, now determinative. What was once continuous must now be seen to be discontinuous; what once a wave, now a particle; what once a matter of mathematical rigor, now a sign of organic growth.

Galileo's Sagredo goes on to say, disingenuously and — for Galileo — dangerously:

> Now if it is further impossible to adduce in proof of the false proposition anything but fallacies, while the true one may be proved by all manner of conclusive and demonstrative arguments, how could you suppose that whichever one of you [the supporter of Copernicus or the supporter of Aristotle] approaches me in support of the true proposition would not have me convinced? I should have to be stupid indeed, warped in judgment, thick-witted, and blind to reason, not to distinguish light from darkness, jewels from coals, truth from falsity. (p. 131)

This old-fashioned view that old, false paradigms are always replaced by true, new ones twentieth-century science has repudiated. To begin with, it observes, old theories are often not discarded; they simply live on as special cases of the new one, as Newton's gravity continues to have descriptive validity for some purposes in the Einsteinian worldview. But more than that there is the problem of Sagredo's "conclusive and demonstrative arguments," for, more often than not, the two opposing views of things are incommensurable — they describe the world in competing terms that are not themselves compatible. The new system cannot logically refute the old because each is true within its own system of logic. Each draws on its own body of supporting facts, which are mere accidents or illusions in the other; each is based on its own set of assumptions, its themata, about what the world can be like and how we can come to know it.

It is when faced with this incommensurability of competing paradigms that science itself turns to deconstruction (though it does not employ the term). One may see the process at work in Galileo's *Dialogue.* First, he busily desediments the layers of accumulated musty thought that constituted the evidence for the Aristotelian-Ptolemaic world view; this he does with wit and irony and verbal skill. Indeed he uses Aristotle to unseat Aristotle from his position of authority over experience. "Does [Aristotle] not . . . declare that what sensible experience shows ought to be preferred over any argument, even one that seems to be extremely well founded?" (p. 55). And he begins the arduous task of decentering the old worldview: the vast, immobile central bulk of earth dominating its successive rotating spheres of the heavens must no longer hold; in its place, an even vaster, immobile heavenly space of stars, among which nestles our small sun, shepherding its flock of tiny planets, including the minute mote designated earth. There is here, of course, inversion of the hierarchy: the earth-dominated universe with its rim of stars becomes a star-dominated universe, containing a small accident called earth.

To be sure, most revolutionary scientists, like Galileo, do not conceive their own views to have been problematized by the very deconstructive process they have employed. For reasons as much psychological as scientific, they want their views to be correct, to describe things as they are. But we need not make this prejudice our own; we must not see the deconstructive process as one that simply replaces one set of sureties, a false set, by another, true one (as Sagredo would have it). Rather it is the system itself that has been made uncertain. The decentering of Galileo removes the earth from the center of the universe and tentatively — even Galileo is cautious about this — places the sun there (pp. 319–20). But it is centering itself that has been called into question, along with a fixed point of view. A fixed earth gives way to the fixed stars, which even Newton retains, but fixity itself is the problem. With Einstein's relativity, of course, the problematizing becomes overt, and it is argued explicitly that no one point of view can be preferred over another, no point, no structure established as fixed. (Not, of course, that the Einsteinian view is the final answer, the ultimate truth; indeed, even the idea of an ultimate truth must be itself deconstructed.)

Viewed as deconstruction, the dialectical exchange of scientific paradigms cannot quite still be seen as bricolage. Whereas earlier I suggested that the fragments of the old system persisted in the new, that the old counters were redeployed in a new game, it now seems that the old fragments have had their identity called into question, that the old counters deployed in new positions have new, uncertain values as well. The gravity that persists from Aristotle to Galileo undergoes a metamorphosis in becoming the gravity of Newton. For most of us this is still gravity, though we know, vaguely, that in the post-Einsteinian world, the term has undergone another sea change and become something else — most of us know not quite what. It is not the living on, the persistence, that now seems paramount but the revaluation. The old scientific theories that hang on within the domain of new ones occupy, like parasites under a carapace, a part of the living space of the new organism, their mode of life degenerate, their domain of applicability truncated, their meaning only approximately what it once was. The system has been deconstructed: one continues to employ its terms (*gravity*), but with new caution, "under erasure." The sense in which one employs the old terms takes note, as it were, of the old meaning, gives it a deprecating nod of recognition, before turning its face in something of a new, troubled direction.

The routine discourse of science does not seem to operate like this. Indeed, it is the apparent comfortable stability of their language that permits scientists to do their daily job. But, at the same time, science continually alters its view, and it does this far oftener, in smaller ways, than the attention to the revolutions would suggest. All such alterations, I claim, come about by operations on the language, by deconstruction, by cutting to the heart of the linguistic sign — achieving the impossible: splitting the atom of the sign, surgically slicing the signified from the signifier, then reconstituting the sign, stitching together something of a new whole, signifier and signified, word and meaning. One must note, however, the now tremulous state of the sign, its newfound incipience, its fragility, its hovering state of tentativeness; the signified still clings to the signifier — the signifier presumably may yet signify — but the act of signification now becomes to a degree ephemeral.

It is this, all of it — scientific discourse as ever-changing structure, as bricolage, as the self-deconstructing mechanism of dialectical (de)(re)-structuring — that I have in mind when averring that science in its discourse forever constitutes and reconstitutes its (dis-constituted) world. It is the kaleidoscopic structures of scientific signification that moment by moment,

like strobe-illumined flashes of dancing figures, create the constantly re-
newed, constantly destroyed, world the scientist perceives. To a degree,
this is the world that we too inhabit, for we know of our world what science
tells us, just as primitive people know of their world what their mythmakers
tell them. In a larger sense, of course, our worlds, our individual worlds,
are structured by every discourse we encounter; the intersecting worlds of
discourse formulate our world; they *are* the world, the only world we know.
The world is the world that discourse structures. (Whether there is another
world, a "real" real world, which discourse does not structure, when all of
what one *can* know is structured by discourse, is, of course, the question
one cannot seek to answer.)

3

Charles Darwin, the staid, Victorian, valetudinarian collector of
natural lore, a deconstructionist, a radical undercutter of the stability of
rational discourse?[9] The very idea seems absurd.

One knows, of course, that this shy, reclusive, gentleman-naturalist
wrote one of the nineteenth century's most revolutionary books, that his
name "rivals in infamy" those of his contemporaries Nietzsche and Marx,
that he remains today the hated target of all those who hold that God
especially and specifically, with all his lavish attention, by his own hand and
in his own image, molded and formed the human species, the lords of his
creation. Indeed, Marx proclaimed only the death of capitalism, and
Nietzsche that of God — it was Darwin who declared the death of humankind. But this is beside the point, or only part of the point. It is true that,
in a sense, evolution does deconstruct humankind, does make the position
of our species problematic in the natural biological order, but that is not
the deconstruction one sees at work in Darwin's books. Indeed, it is the
great, seldom noted irony of *Origin of Species* that when that book has finished its job there remain no more species and what are called species have
no specific origins. (For a rather different account of Darwin as deconstructionist from that presented here, the reader should consult Gillian
Beer's *Darwin's Plots*, and for a rather similar one, George Levine's *Darwin
and the Novelists*.)[10]

The work that Darwin does in the *Origin* has all the earmarks of deconstruction. He begins at once with "species."[11] What occurs is inversion
of the hierarchy. In the biology of fixed species the species is represented
by its "type," the presumed ideal physical representation of the species, the

perfect manifestation of its character. The type is all important. Quite un-important are the "real" members of the species, the living things we en-counter, which are presumed to differ in minor, unpredictable, and unimportant ways from the type. They are the accidental demonstrations of the natural state of imperfection of this sublunar sphere and are of value only insofar as they carry the evidence that permits the astute observer to infer the precise character of the type, which they are trying their earthly best to imitate. With Darwin all this must change. The species is decen-tered. The type is not simply demoted; it disappears, and the peripheral, real, variant individuals become of major concern (for it is only on them that natural selection can operate). The members of a Darwinian species are not the minor deviants from a perfect type but a collection of variant individuals, differing from one another in real, significant, determined, and predictable ways, truly individual beings (not, we would say in the jargon of our own day, clones). One is here squarely in the midst of the age-old philosophical debate between the realists, who hold with Plato that uni-versals (the Ideas) exist, are real, and the nominalists, who hold that one can have the name, the label, of the universal without the thing itself. Dar-win, then, is a nominalist. For him the type, if it exists at all, is just a name, a fiction of an ideal individual who carries in perfect form the various char-acters of the species; what is "real" for Darwin are the variants, not the type.

It is surely no coincidence that the *Origin* begins with two chapters on variation, "Variation under Domestication" and "Variation under Na-ture." Their task, among others (chapter 1 also presents man-produced variation as a model for natural selection), is to present the ubiquity of variation. Examples are added, indeed multiplied; there is hardly a page in the two chapters that is not sprinkled with the words *vary, variation*, and *variety*. And the word *type*, as used above, simply does not appear in the text. Interestingly enough, the closest Darwin comes to the idea of a pre-determined pattern affecting the character of individual organisms is when he discusses varieties produced by breeders. Here he cites Lord Somerville "speaking of what breeders have done for sheep: 'It would seem as if they had chalked out upon a wall a form perfect in itself, and then had given it existence.' "[12] The type exists in the minds of breeders and by their powers of selection they bring it into being, just as pre-Darwinian biology put the type into the mind of God and left it to nature to do its best to copy the type. But not only does Darwin aim to convince his readers of the abun-dance of variations; he wishes also to assure them of their rationality. Indeed a whole subsequent chapter is devoted to "Laws of Variation." Working without Mendelian genetics, Darwin struggles bravely, but without much success, to inject regularity into what seems to be a chaos of data; it is instructive to see the mind struggle inductively seeking to produce the general laws that will explain the apparently inexplicable. Though the results are meager, rhetorically they are enough at least to suggest that variation is not inevitably to be equated with accident.

Variation must be both real and reasonable if natural selection is to exploit it to cause species to change, to evolve, but for the reader to accept the idea that species can and have changed, Darwin must do considerably more work, must in fact desediment all the associations that have accumulated for millennia, based on the firm notion that species are fixed entities. The idea of fixed species is supported by our every experience with the world. Dandelions go to seed; the seeds fly away, land, germinate, and produce always dandelions, never oak trees. Female cats become gravid, come to term, and deliver always kittens, never puppies or elephants. And much of what biologists discover when they look more closely into nature supports the same view. Yet this is the position Darwin must challenge.

The principal point of attack is classification. And the weak spot is the differentiation of closely allied but variant forms. Are they members of separate and distinct species? individuals from closely allied subspecies? or simply variants of a single species? Taxonomists make such judgments every day. It is their professional function, and they do it with supreme authority. Generation after generation, taxonomists classify, organize, and arrange in hierarchies the living beings of the world, and over the years their judgments become "facts." The lines they draw between species, between genera, between families, orders, and classes, correspond, one cannot help but believe, with the real seams in the fabric of nature. It is this accumulation of evidence that Darwin seeks to desediment, this structure he aims to dismantle.

What makes Darwin's case is that the experts differ:

> Compare the several floras of Great Britain, of France, or of the United States, drawn up by different botanists, and see what a surprising number of forms have been marked by one botanist as good species, and by another, as mere varieties. Mr. H. C. Watson . . . has marked for me 182 British plants, which are generally considered as varieties, but which have all been ranked by botanists as species. . . . Under genera, including the most polymorphic forms, Mr. Babington

> gives 251 species, whereas Mr. Bentham gives only 112 — a difference
> of 139 doubtful forms! (pp. 127–28)

The examples continue. (Darwin employs with relish the rhetorical device
of *accumulatio*, multiplying examples long after the reader has conceded the
point.)

Significantly, Darwin reminds us that the biologist, like other scientists,
must learn to see what is "really" there; the seams in nature do not readily
reveal themselves to the untutored eye, and not every tutored eye will see
them in the same place:

> When a young naturalist commences the study of a group of organ-
> isms quite unknown to him, he is at first much perplexed in deter-
> mining what differences to consider as specific, and what as varietal;
> for he knows nothing of the amount and kind of variation to which
> the group is subject. . . . But if he confines his attention to one class
> within one country, he will soon make up his mind how to rank most
> of the doubtful forms. His general tendency will be to make many
> species, for he will become impressed . . . with the amount of differ-
> ence in the forms which he is continually studying; and he has little
> general knowledge of analogical variation in other groups and in other
> countries, by which to correct his first impressions. As he extends the
> range of his observations, he will meet with more cases of difficulty;
> for he will encounter a greater number of closely-allied forms. But if
> his observations be widely extended, he will in the end generally be
> able to make up his own mind; but he will succeed in this at the ex-
> pense of admitting much variation, — and the truth of this admission
> will often be disputed by other naturalists. (pp. 134–35)

When Darwin has finished his argument, the concept *species*, as it is normally conceived cannot be entertained. But the term cannot be abandoned;
it is simply too useful. Hence it is retained, accepted "under erasure," and
employed with only the ghost of its former meaning:

> From these remarks it will seem that I look at the term species as one
> arbitrarily given, for the sake of convenience, to a set of individuals
> closely resembling each other, and that it does not essentially differ
> from the term variety, which is given to less distinct and more fluc-
> tuating forms. The term variety, again, in comparison with mere in-
> dividual differences, is also applied arbitrarily, for convenience' sake.
> (pp. 136–37)

In this view of the biological world, individual differences shade imperceptibly into varieties and these into species. All seems to be continuity; one cannot locate the boundaries, the lines of demarcation. It is for this reason that the term *origin* too becomes problematic.[13] How can one speak of the *origin* of a *species* when the latter term is itself arbitrarily assigned? Every contemporary species has descended from ancestral species by a path of generational change, in which no generation differs from its immediately preceding generation by changes that would be identified as other than normal parental-offspring differences. Hence, there is no natural place to draw the line that separates the ancestral from the offspring species, and the origin of the offspring species must be as arbitrarily chosen as the components of the species.

The matter of origins of species had entered evolutionary thinking, or at least its public record, when in 1855, three years before he and Darwin jointly made their announcement of the evolutionary mechanism, Alfred Russel Wallace enunciated his famous Sarawak Law, which states, *"Every species has come into existence coincident both in time and space with a pre-existing closely allied species."*[14] What remained to be done — and what Wallace and Darwin did — was to erase the dividing line between the two species, parent and offspring, and show how one became converted into the other. Deconstructing the *origin* of species is at once simpler and more difficult than performing that same operation with *species*: simpler because people have no common experience with origins of species, as they do with their composition; more difficult — in Darwin's world, as still to a degree in the world today — because the Bible speaks so explicitly of the separate creation of individual species; for the average Christian of Darwin's day, and for many of today's religious fundamentalists, there could be no doubt about the origin of species: God created them precisely as we see them now.

In fact, the *Origin* deals explicitly with origins very little. The argument simply makes clear the status of the origins of species by implication. Where species gradually emerge from one another the question of the exact moment of origin of any one species becomes problematic. The bulk of Darwin's work concerns, indeed, not the origin of species but their transformation. The question of origins becomes almost infinitely postponed — one species arises from some other species, it from another, and so on ad infinitum. But the regress cannot really be infinite.

In his closing pages Darwin faces this: "It may be asked how far I extend the doctrine of the modification of species. The question is difficult to answer" (p. 751). Nevertheless, after some intervening argument, he tries: "I cannot doubt that the theory of descent with modification embraces all the members of the same great class or kingdom. I believe that animals have descended from at most only four or five progenitors, and plants from an equal or lesser number."

But one need not stop here: "Analogy would lead me one step farther, namely, to the belief that all animals and plants are descended from some one prototype."

Still: "But analogy may be a deceitful guide."

Yet: "Nevertheless all living things have much in common" (p. 752).

Finally, in the last few paragraphs of his peroration, Darwin ponders the implications of his theory vis-à-vis that of special creation:

> Authors of the highest eminence seem to be fully satisfied with the view that each species has been independently created. To my mind it accords better with what we know of the laws impressed on matter by the Creator, that the production and extinction of the past and present inhabitants of the world should have been due to secondary causes, like those determining the birth and death of the individual. When I view all beings not as special creations, but as the lineal descendants of some few beings which lived long before the first bed of the Cambrian system was deposited, they seem to me to become ennobled. (pp. 757–58)

Darwin clearly is at pains to show that his view is not un-Godly, nor is it degrading to us "lineal descendants" of those "few beings," who lived so long before the ages even geology records. And, in his final words, he repeats precisely these ideas: "There is grandeur in this view of life, with its several powers, having been originally breathed by the Creator into a few forms or into one; and that, whilst this planet has gone cycling on according to the fixed law of gravity, from so simple a beginning endless forms most beautiful and most wonderful have been, and are being evolved" (p. 759). Thus, having desedimented "species" and "origins," the *Origin of Species* continues to employ both notions in assuring its readers that its views are "noble" and "grand."

Darwin's positivist views of his own enterprise, however, are hardly compatible with my characterization of it as deconstruction. Darwin was much concerned about the radical implications of his ideas concerning human beings' place in nature and their relations with their God, but we must be more concerned with their troubling disruption of the language of biology. The decentering, the problematizing of the terms *species* and *origin*, while those terms are yet retained with altered and virtually indeterminable meaning, is a significant matter. Furthermore real species appear everywhere as not only fixed but discontinuous; Darwin's theory claims that they are neither. Indeed, he deals with the problem of discontinuity by a desedimentation much like that he employs with the idea of fixity (closely related to the decentering of the type).

Darwin argues that the geographical distribution of species today and the geological records of past species are like brief, momentary slices of a vast tangled biological web with local populations in time and space everywhere diverging into other, different local populations. But Darwin's conceived biological reality lying behind the supposed facts of the geographical and geological record is itself a construct, indescribable outside the troubled, undermined words he must use to describe it. All the *evolving/fixed*, *continuous/discontinuous* groups of organisms, be they *species/varieties/individual variants* (as one pleases), with their dubious origins, must be in Darwin's picture of the world as problematized by the descriptive language as the *fixed*, *discontinuous*, Linnaean *species* he has called into question, for it is the system of formulations that deconstruction renders problematic, not any one of those formulations. Darwin's own reading must employ the very terms he has problematized. There is, presumably, in its own ineffable reality a biological world. The Linnaean schema of that world is only that, a schema, a picture, not a reality. In deconstructing that schema and employing its language "under erasure," Darwin has given us not a real reality — certainly not a new reality — but a schema reinscribed, reformulated, an altered, troubled text in which one attempts to read the world.

Today even scientists do not insist that Darwin's language is everywhere true. (Some nonscientists would argue that it is nowhere true.) Superimposed on his language are other layers of scientific language, themselves mis- or rereadings of Darwin. There is a rereading of Darwin called the synthetic theory, which gives Darwinism the base in Mendelian genetics it so sorely lacks. There is a rereading called population genetics, which asserts that it is the evolution of populations, not that of individual organisms, to which we must attend. There is a rereading called molecular biology, which says that the molecules the genes comprise can be altered by events that are not strictly random, and there is a rereading of this rereading that urges that such molecules may be transported in toto from organism to organism, bypassing the mechanism that Darwin is at such pains to describe. None of these rereadings or misreadings show that Darwin is wrong; they merely add their own versions of the truth to the truth Darwin tells. The layers of discourse lie always on other layers of discourse, like the layers of sedimented organisms in the rock strata Darwin describes. Somewhere in the layers of language lurks the picture of what we, at this moment, (mis)take to be the real world. Undoubtedly, the debris of language will continue to sediment down (and will be desedimented from time to time); and it will continue to carry its signification, to be read, like today's, as tomorrow's reality.

4

The problem of scientific determinism — that instinctive horror that the course of our lives is regulated by the ticking of some Newtonian or Laplacian clock — is, ironically enough, not meliorated by science's recent dialectical swing to the opposite pole. Indeed, with *in*determinacy now the preferred mode of explanation (or the lack of it) in such areas as quantum mechanics, the situation is equally troubling. The idea that the world conducts itself as a series of chance events, the specific causes of which can never be determined and which in the ordinary sense are not individually caused at all but simply occur — this idea is, or would have been before the advent of modern physics, all but unthinkable. Can the world make sense if at bottom it is ruled by chance? Are not the very beginnings of science traditionally located in the attempt of Thales to find rational causes for the events that occur in the natural world? Einstein, as one so often hears, expressed our common feelings on this score: "I shall never believe God plays dice with the world."

But Einstein's plaintive, if stubborn, insistence was merely a holding action against the flooding explanatory power of the new statistical mode of causality that quantum mechanics has ever more persistently forced on science since the early decades of the century. (It works too well scientifically to be ignored.) In the older, Newtonian world — the world of Laplace's demon — every event was specifically caused, and in specifying the cause, one could confidently predict the effect. To be sure, some explanations took on a statistical character, like the description of the motion of the molecules in a volume of gas, but the behavior of the aggregate was understood to be simply the summing up of the individual behaviors. The statistical causation of quantum mechanics, however, has a new character in that individual behavior is not predictable even in principle; only aggregate behavior can be prescribed. An easy-to-grasp example of this kind of causation is observed with radioactive decay. For every unstable element there is a half-life, and in that number of seconds, or years, or millennia, half the atoms of a given sample of the element will decay; the atoms them-selves, however, appear to be identical, and there is no apparent reason one chooses, or is chosen, to decay rather than another. Similarly, quantum mechanics gives the probability of finding an electron at a given spot some-what away from the nucleus of an atom — indeed it produces a pattern of such probabilities in the space surrounding the nucleus; what it will not do is allow one to follow the path of an electron around the nucleus, as the astronomers follow the path of the moon around the earth. The problem lies not in science's ignorance, in its experimental failures, or in its lack of suitable techniques; the problem, rather, is inherent in the situation itself. In any case, it is this prescription only in terms of probability, and the concomitant undecidability, even randomness, of individual events that Einstein, like so many others, found unsatisfying in the new mode of thought. Against this background, however, there is now emerging in phys-ics a new trend, a countermove against the uncertainties and indetermi-nacies of the "modern" physics of the early part of our century. This trend might well be characterized as a postmodernism, not unlike the postmod-ernism in the arts, which seeks, among other things, to move beyond the radical problematizing so characteristic of modernism. To have survived modernism is inevitably to have reached the further, and presumably safer, shore of postmodernism. However hesitantly we must still characterize the postmodern, it is clear that, in science at any rate, it hopes to find beyond undecidability assurance of a new kind. Beyond uncertainty comes, if not certainty, at least acceptance; beyond meaninglessness comes, if not mean-ing, at least understanding — one would like to think, wisdom.

We have seen the attempt of Ilya Prigogine to arrive at a postmodern science by inserting undecidability into dynamics and seeing the result, paradoxically, as the key to a new sense of order (order out of chaos). Quite another approach is taken by the theoretical physicist David Bohm, who aims to make rational the seeming irrationalities of the quantum realm — that is, irrationalities as judged by our own macro perceptions. In the work of Bohm can be seen the struggle always entailed in the bringing into ex-istence of the new in science. I have characterized an aspect of the clash of competing scientific paradigms, the radical undercutting of the language of the paradigms themselves, as deconstruction. But my general argument is a rather different one — namely, that the discourse of science is itself constitutive, that the formulation of a scientific paradigm, and the coming of that paradigm into general scientific acceptance, is a constitutive act, an act of bringing into being.

The many worlds of science are *formed* worlds, structured worlds, worlds organized around certain principles, rules, generalizations, assertions about how the world works: $f = ma$; $E = mc^2$; variation plus natural selection brings about evolutionary change. The world one observes is chaotic, a bewildering welter of meaningless events; science, along with other bodies of discourse, invests that chaos with meaning. Indeed one can speak of the "world one observes" only when there are systems of discourse to bring the significations into existence; without them, there is no "one," no "world," no "observation." (Presumably the person without language does experience, but experiences a world very different from the world we experience.) What science does, via its discourse, is provide a framework that permits us to see a recognizable world "out there."

In ferreting out the rules of the game of the universe, science allows us to see that the game is being played, that a universe is happening around us. Suppose one encounters a group of people engaging in a series of seemingly incomprehensible acts; then someone else explains that they are playing a game and gives the rules of that game; now, what is occurring makes sense, is comprehensible. So science with its hypotheses seeks to make sense of the great game of things. When it describes the rules of the game, behold! the game comes into being; what was chaos becomes order. But the analogy is not exact. The gameplayers know the rules of their game, though the observer does not; in the game of life no one *really* knows the rules. We are all in the role of observers trying to make sense of the game. The rules that science holds to be the rules of the game make sense, make of the observed events a game, only as long as they do make sense, do make a game. When events occur, as they always do, that the rules do not account for, the game again ceases to be until new rules are devised. But the rules, however tentative, always determine the game one believes one sees. The game is ever constituted anew, but, as it were, retroactively: how scientists now see it played, they believe it has always been played, just as the players of the game we stumble upon have been adhering to their rules long before we learned them. For us, however, it is learning the rules that brings the game into being where there was none before, just as for science, learning the rules of the world brings that world into being, where before lay only chaos.

With this aim, then — to see more precisely how science, with its language, goes about constituting the world it believes it encounters — let us look at the text *Wholeness and the Implicate Order*, a work in which David Bohm seeks (and the effort is admittedly tentative) to achieve a postmodern solution to the dilemma of indeterminacy in the world of the quantum. The argument from the beginning is based on language. First, Bohm challenges (deconstructs) the scientific and the common view of reality as analyzable, as divisible, as fragmentable. This view, he says, has its origin in our habits of thought, both scientific and ordinary. "The prevailing tendency in science to think and perceive in terms of a fragmentary self-world view is part of a larger movement that has been developing over the ages and that pervades almost the whole of our society today."[15] From the fragmented state of one's mental pictures, it is but a small step to infer that the world is similarly constituted. (The articulations in one's thoughts, one always believes, correspond to the joints in the real world.)

> In scientific research and . . . in a more general context . . . , fragmentation is continually being brought about by the almost universal habit of taking the content of our thought for "a description of the world as it is." Or we could say that, in this habit, our thought is regarded as in direct correspondence with objective reality. Since our thought is pervaded with differences and distinctions, it follows that such a habit leads us to look on these as real divisions, so that the world is then seen and experienced as actually being broken up into fragments. (p. 3)

The problem here, of course, is that the whole is forever lost when one seeks to understand not the sum of the parts but their individuality. What is needed, Bohm argues, is to reinstate an earlier, prescientific view of wholeness, not fragmentation, as the essential feature of our awareness of the world. But this is not easy to achieve. "To ask how to end fragmentation and to expect an answer in a few minutes makes even less sense than to ask how to develop a theory as new as Einstein's was when he was working on it" (p. 18).

Since the problem begins with modes of thought, it is there that one must seek the answers. An analogy makes clear the approach one must follow:

> One might here consider the image of a turbulent mass of vortices in a stream. The structure and distribution of vortices, which constitute a sort of content of the description of the movement, are not separate from the formative activity of the flowing stream, which creates, maintains, and ultimately dissolves the totality of vortex structures. So to try to eliminate the vortices without changing the formative activity of the stream would evidently be absurd. Once our perception is guided by the proper insight into the significance of the whole move-

ment, we will evidently not be disposed to try such a futile approach. Rather we will look at the whole situation, and be attentive and alert to learn about it, and thus to discover what is really an appropriate sort of action, relevant to this whole, for bringing the turbulent structure of vortices to an end. Similarly, when we really grasp the truth of the one-ness of the thinking process that we are actually carrying out, and the content of thought that is the product of the process, then such insight will enable us to observe, to look, to learn about the whole movement of thought and thus to discover an action relevant to this whole that will end the "turbulence" of movement which is the essence of fragmentation in every phase of life. (pp. 18–19)

The weed of fragmentation is rooted in the language; it is from language that one must root it out. "We are, of course, often able to overcome this tendency toward fragmentation by using language in a freer, more informal, and 'poetic' way". (p. 34). But one must proceed more systematically and, at the same time, more radically. "What can be done is provisionally and experimentally to introduce a *new mode* of language" (p. 30). That new mode — dubbed the *rheomode*, from the Greek word *rhein*, "to flow" — is intended to discover "whether it is possible to create a new [linguistic] structure that is not so prone toward fragmentation as is the present one" (p. 31). At the same time, it is to be a self-conscious language, aware always of its own status *as language*, not presuming itself to be a mere transparent vehicle of thought. "We will have to be especially aware of the need for language properly to call attention to its own function at the very moment in which this is taking place" (p. 32).

The experimental rheomode is verb-centered. Bohm begins with the verb *to levate*, which describes the "spontaneous and unrestricted act of lifting into attention any content whatsoever, which includes the lifting into attention of the question of whether this content fits into a broader context or not, as well as that of lifting into attention the very function of *calling attention* which is initiated by the verb itself." From here he moves to *re-levate*, meaning to levate again; from this he develop the adjectives *re-levant* and *irre-levant*, finally, the noun *levation*. How do these forms work? As to the adjectives, it "requires an act of perception to see, in each case, whether the content thus 'lifted again' fits the observed context or not. In those cases in which this act of perception reveals a fit, we say: 'to re-levate is re-levant.' . . . Of course, in those cases in which perception reveals non-fitting, we say 'to re-levate is irre-levant.'" As to *levation*, it "signifies a sort of generalized and unrestricted totality of acts of lifting into attention" (p. 35).

The purpose of the exercise is

> to discuss what is commonly meant by "relevance" in a way that is free of fragmentation, for we are no longer being led, by the form of the language, to consider something called relevance as if it were a separate and fixed quality. Even more important, we are not establishing a division between what the verb "to levate" means and the actual function that takes place when we use this verb. That is to say, "to levate" is not only to attend to the thought of lifting an unrestricted content into attention but it is also to engage in the very act of lifting such an unrestricted content into attention. The thought is thus not a mere abstraction, with no concrete perception to which it can refer. Rather, something is actually going on which fits the meaning of the word, and one can, at the very moment of using the word, perceive the fit between this meaning and what is going on. So the content of thought and its actual function are seen and felt as one, and thus one understands what it can mean for fragmentation to cease, at its very origin. (pp. 35–36)

One may have serious reservations that this experiment, even on the face of it, demonstrates what it is intended to demonstrate, though, to be fair, the argument is extended to other verb forms in a manner we cannot pursue. But I would at this point suggest that in his attempt to unseat fragmentation and replace it with wholeness Bohm has in effect deconstructed the system — called into question the notions both of fragmentation and of wholeness. In defining his verb *to levate* he speaks of "any content" and "broader context"; does this not in itself demand fragmentation? If his "any content" is a whole, it can surely have no "broader context"; but is the "broader context" itself a whole? a "broadest context"? In a world of wholeness, can one differentiate "content" and "context"? Indeed, does a world of wholeness demand fragmentation (must a whole have parts?) or preclude it? (If all is wholeness, can there be parts?) Further, the content and the context must "fit." In a world of wholeness can any "content" not "fit" its "broader context"? In such a case one would suppose the irrelevant to be as relevant as the re-levant. What Bohm seems to have accomplished with his effort is to leave one with "wholes" and "fragments" that cannot mean what one has always thought them to mean.

In any case, however, the rheomode is an explicit coming to grips with the constitutive power of language. If the "reality" constructed by ordinary language, including the language of science, is necessarily fragmented, the "reality" Bohm intends the rheomode to produce is to be conceived holistically. (It is what Bohm subsequently calls the "holomovement"; p. 151.) If ordinary language always constitutes a world of vortices and trees, the rheomode at least aims to make a world of gurgling streams and dark forests—or better, a world simply of *world*.

The rheomode is not a working language nor is it intended to be. One can understand it only when it is embedded in the structures of our everyday language; no one, not even David Bohm, speaks rheomode. And it is, of necessity, in the framework of ordinary language that the scientific argument of *Wholeness and the Implicate Order* proceeds. That argument cannot be reviewed here in full, but several essential points, relevant to our argument, must be made.

The first deals with the matter of the "unsatisfactory" statistical mode of quantum prescription. What Bohm argues, after Einstein and in opposition to much of the world of physics today, is that this statistical causation need not be the final word; chance may not, after all, rule the world. The key to solving the quantum puzzle, according to Bohm, may well be hidden variables—factors that operate at some as yet undetermined level to produce the overall statistical results observed. To see how this can work, he again provides an analogy:

> It is well known that insurance companies operate on the basis of certain statistical laws, which predict to a high degree of approximation the mean number of people in a given class of age, height, weight, etc., that will die of a certain disease in a specified period of time. They can do this even though they cannot predict the precise time of death of an individual policyholder, and even though such individual deaths are distributed at random in a way having no lawful relationship to the kind of data that the insurance company is able to collect. Nevertheless, the fact that statistical laws of this kind are operating does not prevent the simultaneous operation of individual laws which determine in more detail the precise conditions of death of each policyholder (e.g., a man may cross a road at a particular time and be struck by a car, he may be exposed to disease germs while he is in a weak state, etc.), for when the same result (death) can be produced by a large number of essentially independent causes, there is no reason why these causes should not be distributed in just such a way as to lead to statistical laws in a large aggregate. (pp. 67–68)

This, of course, is merely to suggest the reasonableness of the search for hidden variables in the quantum domain. The argument that follows— the attempted demonstration that such hidden variables can indeed exist—

is presented in mathematical and physical terms. Only the mathematician and the physicist can assess the validity of the demonstration. (However much one may insist that science itself is structured in language, one should not lose sight of the fact that that language is language *for* the scientist.)

The matter of hidden variables may help solve the problem of quantum indeterminacy, but this approach does not in itself satisfy the need for holistic thinking that Bohm sees as the central problem of our day. It is to this end that he introduces the notion of the "implicate" order. "Reality," the world of appearances, is in this context an "explicate" order; related to it and, in a sense, transformable into it is an "implicate" order: the same reality, as it were, in posse; a variant, but intimately connected form; the same thing in identity, but a different thing in pattern. Since the two, the implicate and the explicate, are related much as are the chrysalis and the butterfly, Bohm uses the term *metamorphosis* for their interconversion.

Once again, an analogy supports the plausibility of the argument:

> A . . . striking example of implicate order can be demonstrated in the laboratory, with a transparent container full of a very viscous fluid, such as treacle, and equipped with a mechanical rotator that can "stir" the fluid very slowly but very thoroughly. If an insoluble droplet of ink is placed in the fluid and the stirring device is set in motion, the ink drop is gradually transformed into a thread that extends over the whole fluid. The latter now appears to be distributed more or less at "random" so that it is seen as some shade of grey. But if the mechanical stirring device is now turned in the opposite direction, the transformation is reversed, and the droplet of dye suddenly appears, reconstituted. . . .
>
> When the dye was distributed in what appeared to be a random way, it nevertheless had *some kind* of order which is different, for example, from that arising from another droplet originally placed in a different position. But this order is *enfolded* or *implicated* in the "grey mass" that is visible in the fluid. (p. 149)

The implicate order is needed to explain certain quantum effects, including the apparent coupling of particles spatially separated (in the explicate order), a behavior that seems to imply instant communication across an intervening (explicate) space. Such behavior seems, even superficially, less puzzling when one notes a significant feature of the implicate order: not only does it not show a part-for-part correspondence with the explicate order but, indeed, every portion of the implicate order in a sense implies the whole of the explicate order. To illustrate this particular aspect of the implicate order, the model now is the hologram (pp. 145–47, 177). It is well known that the distributed "spots" of the holographic plate carry the "message" of the image and that illuminating even a fraction of that plate will produce a complete, though diminished, image.

The key metaphor that Bohm employs to suggest the explicate-implicate relationship is *enfolding*: the egg is enfolded into the cake; the ink dot is enfolded into the medium; the explicate order, into the implicate; what is observed, into the totality of what is. What brings them out again is, of course, *unfolding*. (As with every metaphor, the correspondence is not exact: "there is no way to unfold the egg"; p. 180.)

Now, a central feature of the implicate-explicate relationship is what it does to phenomenal contiguity and continuity (an important factor in "explaining" otherwise "inexplicable" quantum effects). Bohm returns to the cylinder:

> We first insert a droplet, A, in a certain position and turn the cylinder n times. We then insert a droplet, B, in a slightly different position and turn the cylinder n more times (so that A has been enfolded by $2n$ turns). We then insert C further along the line AB and turn n more times, so that A has been enfolded by $3n$ turns, B $2n$ turns, and C by n turns. We proceed in this way to enfold a large number of droplets. We then move the cylinder fairly rapidly in the reverse direction. If the rate of emergence is faster than the minimum time of resolution of the human eye, what we will see is apparently a particle moving continuously and crossing the space. (p. 183)

What passes for simple mechanical movement in the explicate order is thus transformed (metamorphosed) into a vastly more complex set of implicate relationships. Beyond the explicate, everyday world of appearances, then, is not a single corresponding implicate pattern, but a complex set of interpenetrating implicate relationships. What all this comprises, the whole of what is, Bohm labels the holomovement, in token both of its totalizing content and its constant fluxion. (Nietzsche's Zarathustra gives, before the fact, his passionate response: "I love you, Everlasting Flow.")[16] What is *real*, what comprises the true nature of things, as opposed to what is simply *discernible* (what we encounter of the world) is the holomovement, though this is itself *"undefinable and immeasurable"* (p. 151). One is reminded inevitably of Plato's world of appearances and world of Ideas: we are again in the position of the prisoners in Plato's cave, who can see only the (explicate) shadows cast by the forever indiscernible (implicate) real.

The metaphor of enfolding is now strained to its limits: *"What is* is always a totality of ensembles, all present together, in an orderly series of stages of enfoldment and unfoldment, which intermingle and inter-pene-trate each other in principle throughout the whole of space" (pp. 183–84).

How is one to picture this? As rank after rank of billowing (implicate) sails on some multimasted sailing ship, the constantly shifting play of wind and light producing from ever-new sections of seething canvas, moving in and out, filling, slackening, surging, an always changing, subtly shifting (explicate) surface form? Or, in the metaphor Bohm employs, as river rap-ids, the complex, surging, shifting, broiling waters yielding a single surface *face*, which forever conceals and always reveals the multitude of seething movements below?

There is much more to *Wholeness and the Implicate Order* than this (for one thing, consciousness is inserted into the general structure), but only one more detail need concern us — certain cosmological considerations rel-evant to the theory. Where, one may ask, *is* the holomovement, that im-plicate world that can never be perceived or measured? It is, Bohm says, in the near infinitude of dimensions of space-time beyond those we ordi-narily know (pp. 186–89). But more than this, and astonishingly, the hol-omovement is in the very nothingness of space, for — and here one encounters the ultimate paradox — the emptiness of space is precisely full, full of energy.

> What is implied by this proposal is that what we call empty space contains an immense background of energy, and that matter as we know it is a small, "quantized" wavelike excitation on top of this back-ground, rather like a tiny ripple on a vast sea. In current physical the-ories, one avoids the explicit consideration of this background by calculating only the difference between the energy of empty space and that of space with matter in it. This difference is all that counts in the determination of the general properties of matter as they are presently accessible to observation. (p. 191)

To settle the age-old philosophical debate of void versus plenum, Bohm declares that the void has *become* plenum, "which is the ground for the existence of everything, including ourselves." ("The things that appear to our senses are derivative forms and their true meaning can be seen only when we consider the plenum, in which they are generated and sustained, and into which they must ultimately vanish.") But this plenum is not to be conceived as a simple ether, through which the bodies of the universe move.

> Rather, one is to begin with the holomovement, in which there is the immense "sea" of energy described earlier. This sea is to be understood in terms of a multidimensional implicate order, . . . while the entire universe of matter as we generally observe it is to be treated as a comparatively small pattern of excitation. This excitation pattern is relatively autonomous and gives rise to approximately recurrent, stable and separable projections into a three-dimensional explicate order of manifestation, which is more or less equivalent to that of space as we commonly experience it. (p. 192)

But this plenum, this plenitude of nothingness, is not simply the site of the phenomenal universe, the everything-we-know; it is its source.

> With all this in mind let us consider the current generally accepted notion that the universe, as we know it, originated in what is almost a single point in space and time from a "big bang" that happened some ten thousand million years ago. In our approach this "big bang" is to be regarded as actually just a "little ripple." An interesting image is obtained by considering that in the middle of the actual ocean (i.e., on the surface of the Earth) myriads of small waves occasionally come together fortuitously with such phase relationships that they end up in a certain small region of space, suddenly to produce a very high wave which just appears as if from nowhere and out of nothing. Perhaps something like this could happen in the immense ocean of cosmic energy, creating a sudden wave pulse, from which our "universe" would be born. This pulse would explode outward and break up into smaller ripples that spread yet further outward to constitute our "expanding universe." The latter would have its "space" enfolded within it as a special distinguished explicate and manifest order. (p. 192)

What has happened in all of this? Has the void become plenum? Nothing become everything? Space become, not empty, but full? There is a scientific argument not examined here (based on assumptions of the "shortest wavelength that should be considered as contributing to the 'zero-point' energy of space"). But the body of the argument is rooted in the language that is used. How? Has the pendulum of the eternal dialectic simply swung from left to right? Has *no* become *yes, stop* become *go*? Or in "inverting the hierarchy" has Bohm rendered both terms problematic?

To begin, consider a cubical vessel, a vessel full of water — literally full, so there is no room for the water to slosh around, nothing that is not water, no space that is not filled with water. But let us then fill a comparable vessel with air, atmospheric air at atmospheric pressure. Again the vessel is full;

the molecules of the various elements that compose the air bounce among themselves, dance in the void, crowding into every corner of the vessel. Then we begin to bleed off these molecules. We pump them out; slowly they attenuate; they fill the vessel still, but there are fewer and fewer of them, fewer dancing motes interspersed in the emptiness; until finally there are no more. There is nothing in the vessel now but emptiness—it is, in fact, *full* of *emptiness*. That emptiness is *there*, we all agree; it extends to every portion of the vessel—it fills the vessel as surely as the water filled the vessel we began with.

But, perhaps, David Bohm suggests, nothingness is rife with potentiality; it is a nothingness of great energy, a nothingness whose seething being throbs with nascent life; it squats there, like the water in the comparable cube, being (or nonbeing) ready for becoming. Now, the perturbations inherent to it, a chance quickening of the throbbing potential (the swerve, the clinamen of old Lucretius, the deviation in the ceaseless fall of the atoms that begins the turbulence that begets the world), and suddenly all erupts, the "very high wave" forms, the "big bang" occurs in the pregnant potentiality of the nothing, and a universe is born. "A" universe, for the nothing is everywhere, and nothing (no thing) is unique (even nothing that happens in *nothing* is unique); every portion of the nothing is equally potent, and the nothing always gives birth; out of its great potential, its *will*, its infinitude of energy waiting to be stirred into life, it engenders universes whenever and wherever the swerve comes.

The void that is empty—that great desert nothing of Democritus, the silent, chilling frost of a space utterly devoid of being—is now also a "void" that is "full." It is not only sterile, it is fecund; it is not only still, it is turbulent; it is not only cold (the absence, the sink of energy), it is hot, it is filled with its own energy (an energy we do not know because it is the ground, the zero point, from which we measure the energy we perceive); it is not only featureless, it is the site of the enfolded, interpenetrating, myriad implicate orders that constitute the holomovement, that which is really real.

One laughs at the pessimist and the optimist, with their glass that is both half empty and half full; now we have our cube, our space, our nothing, which is both fully empty and fully full. Who is the optimist, who the pessimist—Parmenides with his *plenum* or Democritus with his *void*? History has labeled Democritus the "laughing philosopher." If this characterization is correct, how he would laugh to learn that his void is both void and plenum after all (or is neither void nor plenum, if one prefers)!

One would say that void has become plenum, except that *plenum* cannot mean what it has always meant, since *plenum* must now have also the properties of *void*. And though *void* has all the properties it has always had, those properties of nothingness are only nothingness by comparison with the somethingness of the universe. In fact, one says, one proclaims, that nothingness is far more than somethingness, those tiny flecks of foam pale into insignificance on the great sea of true, ultimate reality, nothingness. *Nothing* is now the infinitude of multidimensional, surging sails beyond sails, gulfing and engulfing one another, twisting, turning, seething, shifting into an endless succession of dimension after dimension of space after space, billions of billowing folds, layering constantly in, under, and around one another, yet presenting only the one small, sunlit surface that seems to us to make a universe.

It is language that has made this miracle. Through the power of language, the empty space in, between, and around the world has now become the true home of being. The being one perceives is but the surface manifestation of true being. Indeed, through the power of language, the emptiness of space gives birth to the "reality" one comes to know; the blank page comes to have a world written on it; like the bare brow of Zeus or the smooth chest of Adam, the great emptiness, out of itself, out of its potentiality, gives birth to being, the being of everything. Lucretius, it would seem, made only one mistake: he should have put the swerve not among the atoms but in the void, for that is where one must now situate that sudden, swift move that quickens potentiality.

How easy the transformation is to achieve! How easy language makes it! *Nothing*, one now says, also means "everything." *Solid* also means only "surface." *Reality* means but "appearance" — ah! have we not always known this? There "really" is, one now says, a reality beyond, behind, within, around, "reality." It is language that impregnates nothingness and prepares it to give birth — to give birth to reality.

This is not yet truth, not yet scientific truth, but it is hypothesis. It is also a parable, for, I insist, it is always language that gives birth to a known reality — and what is the point of an unknown reality? The fabled tree of the philosophers, which falls unseen in the forest, crashing silently to earth in fall after accelerating fall, in constant flickering replay, as philosopher after philosopher contemplates its existence — that tree, waiting to be perceived, to achieve the one thing that really matters, a state of being, remains the philosophers' fiction; it has never been perceived because it never was. Yet the philosophers' fables have given that tree a life it never would have

had, however many solitary wanderers had observed its real shattering fall
in a real darkening forest. If language creates the world of perception, how
much more does it not create the worlds not directly perceived: the worlds
of philosophy and of science. It is the paradox of language that constitutes,
that brings into being, the paradox of reality.

5

We have, in a sense, returned to the starting point of this argument, the representation of reality, but we have not, all the same, come full
circle. We have, rather, arrived at the same set of relations we started from,
but viewed now, as it were, from the opposite perspective. We began with
the notion that scientific discourse, like all discourse, represents, reflects,
or copies the real. It is that relationship we now see reversed: scientific
discourse, all discourse, itself constitutes — shapes, organizes, structures,
even in a sense creates — what passes for, can only pass for, the real. We
pictured, as we began, a "discourse" and a "real," a point *A* and a point *B*.
At point *A* was a mirror; in that mirror could be seen an image of a real
structure, the real world, which itself resided at point *B*. Now, at point *A*,
we have something else, say, a motion picture projector. And at point *B* is
a *real*, but invisible, unknowable screen. In the eternal darkness, on that
screen, the projector of discourse presents the moving, changing, flickering
images called "reality."

According to the earlier perspective of representation theory, though
scientific and literary discourse both represent the world, they do so in
rather different ways. The representations of literature are fictive, but both
specific and illusory; that is, they are not true experience, however realistic
they might seem, but they come to us in the guise of true, particular, felt
experience. The representations of science, however, are true (though not
represented realistically) but general and schematic; that is, they purport,
at least, to be precisely true of the world, but generally rather than specifically true and related to true experience in a diagrammatic, nonsensory
way. They aim to give us the "real" atoms and void behind our confused
sensory images of the world. Now, when instrumentality theory asserts that
discourse in general does not so much represent reality as constitute it, it
is natural to ask whether the constitutions of literary and scientific discourse differ precisely as we earlier said their representations did. And the
answer one must surely give is yes.

The world that science constitutes is as general and schematic and true as the world that literature constitutes is specific and sensory and fictive. When one sees the world through the eyes of literature, one experiences vicariously specific events happening to specific, though not necessarily real, persons; and one infers that such events do happen to real persons, including oneself. When one sees the world through the eyes of science, however, one observes a world of general laws working themselves out through, or behind, or beyond, the bewildering world of everyday, sensory experience; one acknowledges that general world to be true, however, only insofar as one accepts the claim of science that its methods establish it as true. These two constituted worlds, the realistic, fictive world of literature and the unrealistic, true world of science, are in a larger sense neither true nor false since one has no unmediated experience with a real world beyond oneself with which to compare them.

We need not seek here a synthesis, an *Aufhebung* of representation and instrumentality theories (though soon we must relate our various theories to one another). But we must recall that our original picture of scientific representation was already sharply qualified. The representation of reality by scientific discourse, we then observed, is in fact contextually constrained. The constructs of science — its models, its laws, its explanations — are conceived within their own frameworks, their own patterns of thought, their own paradigms as the countertradition asserts; and they have, in effect, no meaning outside those frameworks, those patterns, those paradigms. Further, the scientific context is itself constituted within language — the language of mathematics and the verbal language that is our concern. Now, instrumentality theory makes the further claim that the language constructs of science themselves constitute the world that science examines and explains. What scientists know of the world exists only within the language systems that constitute their descriptions and their explanations. The magic mirror of scientific representation fabricates the images one naively believes reflect a real world (a world one can never otherwise perceive).

Yet, science, I must hasten to say, never quite loses touch with the unknowable *real*; its experiments, its observations, its measurements — its bombs going off — always demonstrate that something, related to what the scientists weave in their web of language, is *really* there — out there, beyond the web. But it is the relationship of the two that is precisely the problem. How can one know how the woven image relates to the external reality when one has no other independent access to that reality? Galileo's opponents, real or storied, had a point when they refused to look through the telescope because they could not be sure that what it revealed was a true copy of what could not be seen. Yes, the language formulations that science produces to represent the real are checkable, in part, against the real (they must be or they are not good science), but science devises the tests for checking its facts, for verifying its hypotheses, within the framework of its own theories and methodologies. Hence, the checkable facts, the confirmable hypotheses, are always provisional, always but one of several equally checkable, equally verifiable accounts. The story science tells is a true story (as the story literature tells is a fictional one), but never *the* true story, and *always* a story.

We are after all — and one more time — like Plato's prisoners in the cave: the wall shadows of our experience are all we can ever perceive of reality. From these shadows science must construe its reality; what the scientific method consists of is measuring the shadows and inferring the reality that gives rise to them. Verification, in science, consists of manipulating the unseen and unknowable real, between the fire and the wall, by means of the sightless and mindless robot arms of the laboratory and confirming that the shadows change as predicted.

Science, like Plato himself, always idealizes. But Plato's Ideal exists in a realm beyond. When science idealizes, it idealizes in the realm of the real (just as literature realizes in the realm of the unreal). Every move that science makes is to regularize, to eliminate the accidental, to smooth the curve, to generalize the law; science measures real gases but it proclaims ideal gas laws. The "laws of nature" are Platonic Ideals inhabiting the shadows of reality. Galileo ridicules the peripatetic philosophers for accepting Aristotle's view that the moon is a perfect sphere, when his telescope shows him the shadows its mountains cast. But in an analysis of the behavior of objects on the moving earth, Galileo not only considers the earth a geometrical sphere but, in an eloquent passage, justifies the practice of analyzing the imperfect, real shapes of nature in terms of the ideal shapes of geometry. (And his mechanics is flawed by an adherence to an ideal circular law of inertia.)

But here the scientist only employs the same devices we all use in apprehending our everyday world. The fuzzy ball we play tennis with is not more round than Aristotle's moon or Galileo's earth. Nor are our apples round, nor will the new tomatoes that are to be remodeled for the packers be truly square. The cubist painters discovered late what the scientist, and everyman, has known for millennia: we see nature in the shapes our geometry prescribes. In Cézanne's pictures, with mountains melting into geometrical forms, and geometrical forms emerging from mountains, we see the visual (and tactile) dialectic of nature against geometry taking place before our eyes. It is we who geometrize the world we perceive — that great buzzing, real world of atomic motes dancing in the sunbeams, of intangible fields interacting with intangible fields — but these are other images, other metaphors, other models, of the what-is-there, no more or less true than the geometric world we daily inhabit and that the scientist so minutely measures.

The world is always real — the stone that Dr. Johnson kicks, the bomb that goes off, the alarm clock that shatters one's sleep, the mystic moves of subatomic particles — but it is also always an invention because it is seen through the medium of thought. We have built our world in so many bits and pieces over so many eons that we have forgotten how it is constructed. The world was made we know not precisely when or how, but it is apprehended as a bricolage. We are what we think we are because we cannot know what we are without thought, and thought, in large part, is thought in language. Language shapes our thought, just as thought shapes our language. The world is ever a story, and science is but one of the stories of the world. This is the great dialectic of the word and the world. The word is in the world, but the world is in the word; the word is of the world, and the world is of the word; indeed the word *is* the world, and the world *is* the word.

CHAPTER EIGHT

Reading Science

HERE ARE RHETORICS OF ENDING—RHETORICS THAT SIGNAL COM-
pletion, finality, working out, bringing together, wrapping up.
Such rhetorics demand that as the writing ends the argument too
must end, must intone a final "amen." In this gamesmanship of
ending, the writer extends the closure of the argument to the great
dialogue of which it is a part. The arguments of all preceding writers are situated, contained, absorbed in the writer's own contexts.
In a triumph of assimilation, the dialectic is overthrown, the last
word is finally said, and the end-sayer alone remains, the last sur-
vivor, the king of the hill.

Here, along separate trails of argument, we have pursued successive notions of the behavior of scientific language vis-à-vis literary language and have arrived at individual conclusions. The
paths have diverged, converged, and separated again, as the discussion has taken its course. Is it time now to alter that situation,
rectify the structure, clarify the picture, bring all together in a final
concord? It would be a relatively easy matter to situate the various
lines of argument in a common ground. Our system of discourse —
scientific and otherwise — has a limited number of elements: a
writer who *expresses*, a reader who *responds*, a societal matrix that
employs and *shapes* both, a discourse that *represents*, that in itself
interests, that finally *constitutes* "reality." To combine these elements, to relate them to something like the Jakobsonian model of
discourse, would be but a step.[1]

Yet—and this is the point—in an age of massive uncertainty, doubt, disbelief, deconstruction, it is difficult to justify an argument that proceeds against a backdrop of eternal verities and asserts its own transcendent truth. One is better served, it would seem, in today's doubting world, to conceive of lines of argument not as curves developing against a predetermined space, as the curves of analytical geometry unfurl themselves against the Cartesian coordinates, but as newly emerging entities that generate their own context, create their own space as they unfold, just as, Einstein says, the masses of the universe generate their own spatial matrix by virtue of their existence. The day of the overarching framework, the prepared ground, the universally acknowledged basis for argument, seems, at least for now, to be behind us. Lacking a grand synthesis, one must aim for discrete (and discreet) analyses.

Above all we must endeavor not to be dogmatic. Our particular enemy is the traditional dogmatic assurance that scientific language is everything that literary language is not—that it is not expressive, not evocative, not interesting and so on—that it is, rather, merely the code that records the facts that science uncovers. Surely we must now accede to the countertraditional view that scientific language cannot operate that way, that no language can, that language is not, ever, a simple vehicle for nonlinguistic thought, a verbal rendition of some nonverbal beyond.

Here we tremble on the brink, feel the vertiginous pull of the abyss, as our words themselves seem to function precisely as they argue that language does not, cannot, function.[2] Always suspect today is the voice of undisputed authorial authority, especially when that voice denies the ultimate authority of the authorial voice. But for us it must be so. Users of language, even when they are analysts of language, must be or try to be or pretend to be unselfconscious in that use, even as they explicitly acknowledge that they cannot be so; otherwise, the language will cease to be language and become merely words. To use language is to assume that it functions as language, even when, indeed especially when, one is examining the uses of language. Hence one must tentatively and provisionally close one's eyes to the fact that what one says of language is of necessity true of one's own language; otherwise one is forever condemned to silence, to a void of language—a condition that the consciousness of humankind has not known for millennia.

Precisely what scientific language is, then, what its ultimate characteristics are, how it works in the last analysis, I will not claim to know. My purpose is not to end inquiry but to join it. Misconceptions, one has always supposed, must be cleared away before true conceiving can begin. To be sure, we must observe that the traditional misconceptions so courageously attacked here are rhetorical devices, received opinion insisted on as true, perhaps, by no one, but all the same permitting the argument to proceed and reflecting surely still some semblance of views the countertradition has only begun to breach. By the same token, we must acknowledge again that the various theories of the functioning of literary language that provide the springboard for this argument are themselves to a degree artifacts, having a relationship to the assumptions behind the various modes of literary criticism, but constituting for no one, perhaps, fixed firm beliefs of how language, even literary language, operates.

Thus, the various ways we have observed that scientific texts might be read we will not work into a single, joint reading, representing the sole, true mode of insight into scientific texts. It is not my purpose to say precisely *how* scientific texts are to be read so much as to insist that they *be* read, that is to say, attended to as writing, and that they be read in ways traditionally not thought possible. This task, we must observe, has hardly begun. With those in the countertradition, we have broached the subject, opened the door, taken the single step that begins the journey of a thousand miles. This point represents, then, a kind of terminus in the argument, but not so much a terminus ad quem as a terminus a quo — not an end but a beginning.

2

We can, however, go further, can claim diffidently and provisionally some advance of our own. We have sought, by way of the six theories of how texts are best construed, to compare the functioning of literary and scientific texts. With respect to a number of the theories — namely, evocation, expression, art-object, and artifact theories — we have discerned little difference in how the two function. We have, however, observed essential differences in the two with respect to representation and instrumentality theories, differences not so much in the occurrence in both cases of representation or instrumentation — that is, that reality is represented or itself constituted by the two bodies of discourse — but in the mode of that occurrence.

How did we earlier describe that difference? Regardless of whether we worked from the context of representation or instrumentality theory, we have observed that the text of science stands over and against the scientific world as generalized, schematicized, unrealized (that is, not rendered realistically), but verified (that is, certified within the canons of science), whereas the literary text stands over and against its world as particularized, sensoritized (that is, codified in terms of sensory impression), realized, but fictionalized. One may well label this aspect of discourse as "realization" — whether it be conceived as representation, the discursive representing of the preexisting real, or instrumentation, the discursive constituting of the conceptualized real; one may then characterize the two modes of realization, scientific and literary, as respectively metaphoric and metonymic. The scientific mode, with its models that, as it were, stand in for or bring into conception the real, acts metaphorically. Literary realization, on the other hand, operates by producing the particular instance of the general rule and shifts the context of experience from the direct to the vicarious register (from the real to the fictive); it is thus, in several senses of the word, metonymic. Viewed from this perspective, the axes of realization resemble the familiar metaphoric and metonymic axes of the structuralist.

Together, then, science and literature would constitute a biaxial system of coordinates, a structure, by which we would locate the real of experience. Life itself is inaccessible, incomprehensible, meaningless, but the metaphors of science and the metonymies of literature, of all art, help to make it accessible, comprehensible, meaningful. The sensory data we receive suggest to us that there is a real — a "really" real — but tell us nothing absolutely true about that real. Hence we make our scientific models of the real and contrive our literary experiences that resemble our true experiences with the real; and these help us locate the real because we cannot think of the real without them.

In the night, as we huddle around our fire on the dunes and listen to the waves come in, we tell one another stories and draw diagrams in the sand of the stars that look down, infinitely remote and forever truly beyond our ken. But we have our drawings and our stories, and they comfort us in the night.

3

These views of scientific and literary language must have their consequences. First, the argument places us squarely in the countertraditional camp. With the new historians and philosophers of science, we have accepted the context-dependence of scientific truth (though we may balk at the most extreme view that all contexts are essentially equivalent). With the new sociologists, we have taken note of the social situating of the scientific act (though, too, we have hesitated at the conversion of the context of generation into social function). In this analysis, however, the discourse of science itself has assumed center stage. It is the scientific text to which we have directed our attention, and it is the field of textuality we have focused on as it impinges on the entire enterprise of science. In short, we have asserted the primacy of science conceived as writing.

In this discussion, I have used, indiscriminately, the terms *scientific language, scientific discourse, scientific writing.* Now I must say unequivocally that, even as I did so, I meant always "writing." Nor do I use writing in a Derridean sense of archewriting, a kind of inscription in posse if not in esse; rather I mean *writing* as "writing," the inscribed, permanent, explicit record of particular language. What I wish to suggest is a contrived, studied discourse, recorded and preserved. This language must be distinguished from the ordinary, spoken language that deals with the passing trivia of everyday life: "Answer the phone." Now, linguists (some linguists, at any rate) view the essential language as that of the spoken utterance, with the written language, certainly the literary language, as an offshoot or parasite of the spoken language. Such linguists are likely to perceive scientific language, even if it happens to be written down, as falling within the general category of the "utterance" — that is, coming under the rubric of the spoken language. Presumably this reflects the view that scientific language is a working language, a language of use and function, not like literature, they would say, a language of play and fancy and imagination. Although one cannot deny that the scientific world has its daily employment of ordinary language as it does its work ("Hand me a test tube") one must hold (everything in this book argues so) that the prepared scientific document — the published paper, the report, the monograph — lies in a different category.[3] It is archival writing, intended to be part of the ongoing written documentation that traces the course of science as it proceeds. The scientific utterance is not a casual remark; it is a studied statement, part of the ever-growing archive of science. What science consists of, to repeat the figure, is stratum after stratum of written documents recording the continually changing status of current science. The documents of science encompass the progress of science; they *are* science; what science is is what scientific documents say.[4]

Whoever employs it, scientists or others, language cannot function other than as language, nor mathematics other than as mathematics. Neither do the symbols the scientists employ function other than as symbols;

they have no inherent truth value. When a chemist uses two parallel lines to represent a double bond between atoms, that does not convey upon the *real* double bond the properties of two, combined, single bonds. Indeed, a child's stick-figure drawing of a person represents that person in the same way that the chemists' structural formula represents the molecule it purports to describe. Because scientists agree to use a line to represent a bond between atoms does not privilege the scientists' representation any more than if every child in the schoolroom agrees that lines represent the arms and legs of their human figures. Thus, symbol, equation, sign, language, whatever the scientist employs is *writing*, and it is only that, but it is all of that.

Scientific writing, then, is here defined as the language of the documentation that science employs as it constructs its continuing archive. This definition does not in itself characterize scientific writing, and one must discriminate between defining characteristics and chance attributes. Much of the character commonly attributed to scientific writing is not truly defining; everything said here would insist so. Indeed, the famed objectivity of scientific writing, in particular, is part of the rhetoric of science, not an inherent quality that scientific writing has per se. Also, although I have not dealt with this in my argument, one cannot help observing that scientific writing has its historical dimension; what passes for appropriate scientific discourse in one generation is not thought so in another. Surely the character of scientific writing will change in the future in ways that one cannot now foresee. But this is part of another story.

4

If, then, science *is* writing, and if many of the distinctions commonly drawn to mark off literature from science do not hold — while other differentiae do exist — these considerations must tell us things we previously did not know about literature and about science.

Literature has for too long heard the implacable "fixed and firm" discourse of science braying at its heels, forcing it into ever more extravagant defenses of its own supposed weakness and insubstantiality. But if science is no longer the simple language of truth, then literature need not seek to be the language of fancy, or imagination, or irony, or wit, or exclusive self-reference. To note the problematics of scientific language, to observe that in being scientific it does not cease to be language, to call into question the simple truth value of that language, is merely to situate scientific language within language. The comparison of science and literature need not be invidious in either direction. Literature has no exclusive claim on imagination, expressivity, persuasiveness, creativity; science no patent on truth, reliability, functionality. The literary scholar need be no more isolated from the world than the scientist; the library shelves are no dustier than the laboratory bench. Both science and literature are about the truth of the world. And there are not two languages — the language of science and the language of poetry — but one, the language of humankind.

Although it would be naive to expect the mass defection of literary scholars from the study of poems to that of scientific texts, the recognition that their skills are not of negligible value in the true reading of scientific writings has, as earlier noted, already encouraged a number of literary scholars to direct their attention to such works. In time, then, those few scientific texts that have entered the literary canon — most notably the *Origin of Species* — will undoubtedly be joined by others. That the study of literature benefits from the broadening of its concerns need hardly be argued here (though purists will vigorously deny it); the trend of literary study — moving from the classic to the vernacular, from the antique to the contemporary and the popular — is always to suggest a broadening of concern. The masterpiece of scientific writing may be a masterpiece of writing as well as a masterpiece of science; the student of literature will surely benefit from learning how this may be. Further, since students of literature have learned to read with a concentrated attention to that process that no one else can give, their directing of attention to the writings of science can only help science become more aware of the working of its own writings.

For science, such self-consciousness concerning its own language is long overdue. For centuries, science studied everything under (and over and within) the sun but its own operation. In this century we have seen the emergence as disciplines of the history of science, the philosophy of science, and the sociology of science. Now, as the countertradition is urging, it is surely time to attend in earnest to the literature of science. Science operates within its language; indeed, science is the language it utters itself in. Surely now science must consider what it is saying, how it is saying it, and why it is saying it the way that it is.

Clearly there is much specifically that literary analysis can contribute to our understanding of the functioning of scientific texts. Thus, in a recent issue of the new *Publication of the Society for Literature and Science*, James Bono has identified four ways in which literary theory can aid in the fuller apprehension of the discourse of science: (1) by helping to "uncover how the discourse of science generates itself through acts of interpretation" — that is, in clarifying the hermeneutic aspect of scientific inquiry; (2) by examining "the narrative strategies that may inform specific scientific discourses," as Gillian Beer has done in *Darwin's Plots*; (3) by aiding the understanding of "how implicit theories of language structure scientific theories and methods," as, for example, Saussurean linguistics has shaped structuralist thought and markedly influenced ethnography; and (4) "perhaps most powerfully," by providing the " 'tools' for establishing the centrality of tropological language to any scientific discourse," affirming, in other words, the constitutive nature of scientific metaphor.[5]

When all is said and done, we are not, of course, about the business of denigrating science. The views expressed here must not be construed as an attack on science, an attempt to undercut or undermine the work that scientists do. One cannot deny that the experiments that succeed do succeed, even as one points out that their interpretation in terms of current theory is only interpretation, not brute fact. It is the fear of Simplicio in Galileo's *Dialogue* that Salviati's philosophical challenge of Aristotle's authority will not only destroy natural philosophy (science) but upset the working order of the world itself: "This way of philosophizing tends to subvert all natural philosophy, and to disorder and set in confusion heaven and earth and the whole universe." Salviati, however, is reassuring: "Do not worry yourself about heaven and earth, nor fear either their subversion or the ruin of philosophy."[6] Both science and the world, we may equally be assured, will survive any attention we give to the language by which science constitutes and reconstitutes the world. Nor need we fear, like reluctant high school students of literature, that our analysis of the language will somehow destroy the story. Shakespeare has no less appeal today than he has ever had, despite the dozen generations of scholars who have scrutinized his words. So must we believe will the discourse of science withstand any attention we may give it.

Above all, these words must not be misconstrued; to argue, as I have, that scientific discourse is more than mere representation is not to deny that it does represent, does have content. And to insist that that content is embedded in a context, a context constructed in language — to insist that the scientist's world is a world made with language — is not to say that it is less real, that it has been reduced from material status (Dr. Johnson's stone) to a mere notion (Bishop Berkeley's *idea*). It is not to dispute the content of science, not to challenge the scientific method, to assert that everything the scientist says is said with language (just as is everything the poet says).

To insist, as I have, that the voices of scientists are heard in their writings is not to praise science less but to honor scientists more. It will not render science subjective merely to point out that its practitioners inevitably express themselves as individuals. When one says that the *Principia* is uniquely Isaac Newton's, that its studied geometrical proofs and its measured Latin bear the marks of Newton's mind, one does not say that the world the *Principia* presents is anything other than it has always been admitted to be — Newton's world. This has never been *the* world; it has always been the world of Newton.

If Newton's language made his world *his* world, it also made it, for several centuries, everyone else's world. This is so because the *Principia* had readers (and, important in this case, commentators and explicators). To speak of Newton's rhetoric and to argue that there is a rhetoric of science is not to say that science has no meaning beyond "mere" rhetoric. Surely one knows enough now about how science works to perceive that the unread scientific document is simply not a part of science. If the voice of science is not heard it is not a voice. Too long have we conceived the ideal scientist in the image of the poet's meditation on Newton's statue: "with his prism and silent face, / The marble index of a mind forever / Voyaging through strange seas of thought, alone." Science itself must now be envisioned not as a structure, a Doric temple, sitting in lonely splendor on its acropolis, but as a meeting place, an arena, an agora, where a thousand competing scientists fight their battles, argue their cases, hawk their wares, struggle to be heard and heeded.

To say, as I have, that the scientific document can be an art object — crafted, shaped, formed in part for purposes of pleasure — is not to say that it cannot also function. Scientists always speak of the fun, the sheer enjoyment, of their work. They argue that they are motivated mainly by intellectual curiosity and find satisfaction chiefly in satisfying that curiosity. But they do not deny that their work can involve enormous labor and that it can serve important ends. As to "art for art's sake," the modernist movement, for all it proclaimed the self-sufficiency of art, also spawned the Bauhaus. If form follows function, perfect form follows function perfectly, and there is vast enjoyment in perceiving the way it does so. No well-turned phrase is admirable when it is inappropriate to its context, whether that context is a scientific paper or a poem. To argue that the appropriate, well-turned phrase can be as admirable in the scientific paper as in the poem can hardly be said to denigrate the paper or the poem.

Further, to observe, as I have (and as the countertradition insists), that the scientific document functions in the social, economic, political, and cultural spheres, as well as in the social world of science itself, is not to diminish the scientific content. When one says that scientists themselves constitute a society and that the functioning of that society determines in part the content of the society's dialogue, this is not to say that the dialogue has no content. When one says, borrowing Marxist terminology, that the documents of the scientist are ideological, that they function within the superstructure, it is only to place science in a context. Science would like to think that it is beyond — or above or without — politics or economics or whatever is not science. It is perhaps healthy that it should try to be so. But one must see that it cannot. The findings of science affect public policy; public policies affect science — by the allotment of funds, by the encouragement or the discouragement of activities believed to be or not to be in the public interest. To deny that this is so in any society we know is to ignore what is plain to see.

To be sure, to speak, as I have, of the discourse of science as instrumentality, as vehicle for the construction of a worldview, is in a sense to deprive science of its long-purported goal: to describe the real, objective world that exists outside of us and independent of our experience of it. But it is at the same time to give science a larger, more substantial purpose: to bring into being a world we can know through our accounts of our experiences of it. The picture that science paints of a world becomes for us the very world, the world that we cannot otherwise ever know. To weaken the tie of science to the world we cannot know is only to strengthen the tie of science to the only world we can know — the world of our experience with the world.

Finally, to distinguish, as I have, the modes of scientific and literary realization as respectively metaphoric and metonymic is not to value one over the other; rather, it is to assert that these *are* the primary modes of realization, which our culture employs in constituting the world it inhabits. These are what science and literature — indeed, art generally — do for us: tell us the story of our world.

But if these things said about the language of science are so patently true, why are they not commonplace? Why does one not always treat scientific writings as I have argued they should be treated, simply as the writings of scientists? Probably because the rhetoric of science has been so successful. When the scientists say, clearly and unambiguously, "A is B," we believe it to be unequivocally so. We do not remind ourselves that what they are really saying is that what scientists choose to call A appears to them to be that which they designate as B. Science finds this rhetoric convenient, effective, and persuasive. Many scientists undoubtedly believe the rhetoric to be true—hold that the methods of science reveal a real A and a real B, which are one and the same. Most scientists, however, are more pragmatic and argue simply that it is profitable for them to behave as though it were true, that to say "A is B" works well—until someone else comes along to say more convincingly that "A is C" or, knowing scientists, that "A' is B'."

Thus perceived, scientific rhetoric is part of the scientific method, and no inconsiderable part. When one asks that that rhetoric be examined, that it be scrutinized, studied, analyzed, one does not ask that it be abandoned. I would not challenge the language of science, only seek to understand it.

Under most circumstances we all consider that we use language simply functionally, as science believes it uses its language. When we hear one another speak, we hardly attend to what is *said*, but we think at once that we know what is *meant*. We may know that language is used expressively, persuasively, artfully, but we have gotten used to thinking of language as purely functional, as serving no purpose other than to convey meaning. So we readily accept the assertion, even the unspoken presumption, that scientific language works that way. Indeed, we are made uncomfortable, feel anxiety, whenever the merely functional, the "natural," the unselfconscious use of language, is called into question. (Again one trembles on the edge of the abyss of the self-critique of one's own language, even as one employs it.) But we must finally perceive that it is healthy to face the discomfort, to challenge the anxiety that comes when we cut away the certainty that our words simply say what we mean. Only thus can we come to know more truly what happens when we employ language.

To say these things—about language, about science, about the language of science—is not to claim that they are the final words. The last word has never been spoken, the final statement never made. The current reading of the text, or of the world, does not contain, include, surround, supplant all other possible readings. No words, even those graven in stone, are graven in stone. Words fade; they are forgotten, effaced, burnished away by time. But they return. The dialectic will always continue; only the rhetoric of the moment will pause and seem—for a time—to end.

NOTES

Chapter 1. Introduction: Science and Literature

1. Benjamin Robert Haydon, *The Autobiography and Journals of Benjamin Robert Haydon*, ed. Malcolm Elwin (New York: Coward McCann, 1950), pp. 316–19.
2. C. P. Snow, *The Two Cultures: And a Second Look* (Cambridge: Cambridge University Press, 1969).
3. For one account of this traditional view, see William K. Wimsatt, Jr., and Cleanth Brooks, *Literary Criticism: A Short History*, 2 vols. (Chicago: University of Chicago Press, 1957), 1: 71–75.
4. Cited by M. H. Abrams, *The Mirror and the Lamp: Romantic Theory and the Critical Tradition* (New York: Oxford University Press, 1953), p. 309. Nor was Wordsworth the only Romantic to perceive a kinship between literature and science. Shelley sees poetry as "that which comprehends all science, and that to which all science must be referred" (Percy Bysshe Shelley, "A Defense of Poetry," in *Shelley's Literary and Philosophical Criticism*, ed. John Shawcross [Oxford: Oxford University Press, 1909]; reprint, in *Criticism: Major Statements*, 3rd ed., ed. Charles Kaplan and William Anderson [New York: St. Martin's, 1991], p. 330). And literary realists have long seen their work as akin to science. Thus, the Goncourts declare that "today when the Novel has imposed on itself the studies and the duties of science, it can demand the freedom and immunities of science" (cited in Erich Auerbach, *Mimesis: The Representation of Reality in Western Literature*, trans. Willard R. Trask [Princeton: Princeton University Press, 1953], p. 495).
5. William Wordsworth, *The Prose Works of William Wordsworth*, 21 vols., ed. W. J. B. Owen and Jane Worthington Smyser (London: Oxford University Press, 1974), 1:141.
6. Aristotle, *Poetics*, trans. Gerald F. Else (Ann Arbor: University of Michigan Press, 1967), p. 17.
7. The passage remains, as given, in René Wellek and Austin Warren, *Theory of Literature*, 3rd ed. (New York: Harcourt Brace Jovanovich, 1962), p. 23.

211

8. George Slusser and George Guffey, "Literature and Science," in *Interrelations of Literature*, ed. Jean-Pierre Barricelli and Joseph Gibaldi (New York: Modern Language Association, 1982), pp. 176–77.

9. Leo Steinberg, "Art and Science: Do They Need To Be Yoked?" *Daedalus* 115, no. 3 (Summer 1986): 1–16.

10. Mark Kipperman, "The Rhetorical Case against a Theory of Literature and Science," *Philosophy and Literature* 10 (1986):76–77.

11. Thomas Sprat, *History of the Royal Society*, ed. Jackson I. Cope and Harold Whitmore Jones (St. Louis: Washington University Press, 1958), p. 113.

12. Herman M. Weisman, *Basic Technical Writing*, 4th ed. (Columbus: Charles E. Merrill, 1980), p. 8.

13. Roland Barthes, "Science versus Literature," in *Structuralism: A Reader*, ed. Michael Lane (London: Jonathan Cape, 1970), p. 411.

14. Sir Philip Sidney, *Sir Philip Sidney's Defense of Poesy*, ed. Lewis Soens (Lincoln: University of Nebraska Press, 1970), p. 17.

15. Wayne C. Booth, *The Rhetoric of Fiction* (Chicago: University of Chicago Press, 1961), p. 112. Or as Stanley Fish says of the presumed freedom of scientific language from emotive expression, "Isn't it the case, rather, that in any linguistic experience we are internalizing attitudes and emotions, even if the attitude is the pretension of no attitude and the emotion is a passionate coldness?" (Stanley E. Fish, "Literature in the Reader: Affective Stylistics," *New Literary History* 2 [1970]: 149). See also, e.g., Northrop Frye, *Anatomy of Criticism: Four Essays* (Princeton: Princeton University Press, 1957), p. 350.

16. Stephen J. Weininger, Introduction to *Literature and Science as Modes of Expression*, ed. Frederick Amrine (Boston: Kluwer, 1989), p. xvii.

17. G. S. Rousseau, "Discourses of the Nerve," in Amrine, *Literature and Science*, p. 33.

18. For a statement of the general proposition that the language of fundamental physics creates the world it purports to describe, see Bruce Gregory, *Inventing Reality: Physics as Language* (New York: John Wiley, 1988). For one physicist's account of his view that in some sense consciousness plays a fundamental role in the operation of the universe, see Roger S. Jones, *Physics as Metaphor* (Minneapolis: University of Minnesota Press, 1982).

19. David Bohm, *Wholeness and the Implicate Order* (London: Routledge and Kegan Paul, 1980), p. 142.

20. James Clifford and George E. Marcus, eds., *Writing Culture: The Poetics and Politics of Ethnography* (Berkeley: University of California Press, 1986), p. 2.

21. Louis F. and Mary Fieser, *Style Guide for Chemists* (New York: Reinhold, 1960), pp. 51–52.

22. Sir Isaac Newton, *Opticks, or a Treatise of the Reflections, Refractions, Inflections and Colours of Light* (1730; New York: Dover, 1952), p. 25.

23. Peter Medawar, *Pluto's Republic* (Oxford: Oxford University Press, 1982), pp. 91–92.

24. Roald Hoffmann, "Under the Surface of the Chemical Article," *Angewandte Chemie* (English ed.) 27 (1988): 1597.

25. Owen Hannaway, *The Chemists and the Word: The Didactic Origins of Chemistry* (Baltimore: Johns Hopkins University Press, 1975).

26. Frederic L. Holmes, "Scientific Writing and Scientific Discovery," *Isis* 78 (1987):220–35. For one more example of the recognition of the impact of the writing in specific texts on the history of science, see Stephen Jay Gould, *Time's Arrow, Time's Cycle: Myth and Metaphor in the Discovery of Geological Time* (Cambridge, Mass.: Harvard University Press, 1987).

27. Paul Ricoeur, *Hermeneutics and the Human Sciences: Essays on Language, Action and Interpretation*, trans. John B. Thompson (Cambridge: Cambridge University Press, 1981); Stephen Toulmin, "The Construal of Reality: Criticism in Modern and Postmodern Science," *Critical Inquiry* 9 (1982): 93–111. Hans-Georg Gadamer, the father of modern hermeneutic philosophy, stops short of reading the methodology of the natural sciences as itself hermeneutic but sees hermeneutic philosophy as providing the grounding and framework for the sciences (Hans-Georg Gadamer, *Reason in the Age of Science*, trans. Frederick G. Lawrence [Cambridge, Mass.: MIT Press, 1981]).

28. Toulmin, "Construal of Reality," p. 94.

29. Gyorgy Markus, "Why Is There No Hermeneutics of Natural Sciences? Some Preliminary Theses," *Science in Context* 1 (1987): 5–51.

30. For attempts to relate science and literature via their historicity as it is viewed in the post-Kuhnian world, see John Neubauer, "Models for the History of Science and of Literature," in *Science and Literature*, Bucknell Review 27, no. 2, ed. Harry R. Garvin (Lewisburg, Pa.: Bucknell University Press, 1983), pp. 17–37; and James M. Curtis, "Epistemological Historicism and the Arts and Sciences," in Garvin, pp. 38–60.

31. John Ziman, *Reliable Knowledge: An Exploration of the Grounds for Belief in Science* (Cambridge: Cambridge University Press, 1978), p. 3.

32. See, e.g., Robert K. Merton, *The Sociology of Science: Theoretical and Empirical Investigations*, ed. Norman W. Storer (Chicago: University of Chicago Press, 1973).

33. David Bloor, *Knowledge and Social Imagery* (London: Routledge and Kegan Paul, 1976); Barry Barnes, *Scientific Knowledge and Sociological Theory* (London: Routledge and Kegan Paul, 1974). For a review of, and representative documents from, a number of methodological and theoretical approaches to the new social study of science, see Karin D. Knorr-Cetina and Michael Mulkay, eds., *Science Observed: Perspectives on the Social Study of Science* (Beverly Hills: Sage, 1983).

34. See, e.g., Roy Wallis, ed., *On the Margins of Science: The Social Construction of Rejected Knowledge*, Sociological Review Monograph 27 (Keele, Staffordshire: University of Keele, 1979); H. M. Collins and T. J. Pinch, *Frames of Meaning: The Social Construction of Extraordinary Science* (London: Routledge and Kegan Paul, 1982).

35. Bloor, *Knowledge*, pp. 2–5.

36. See, e.g. — in addition to Latour and Woolgar (n. 37, below) — Karin D. Knorr-Cetina, *The Manufacture of Knowledge: An Essay on the Constructivist and Contextual Nature of Science* (Oxford: Pergamon Press, 1981), and Michael Lynch, *Art and Artifact in Laboratory Science: A Study of Shop Work and Shop Talk in a Research Laboratory* (London: Routledge and Kegan Paul, 1985).

37. Bruno Latour and Steve Woolgar, *Laboratory Life: The Social Construction of Scientific Facts*, Sage Library of Social Research, vol. 80 (Beverly Hills: Sage, 1979).

38. Steven Shapin and Simon Schaffer, *Leviathan and the Air-Pump: Hobbes, Boyle, and the Experimental Life* (Princeton: Princeton University Press, 1985).
39. Richard N. Boyd, "On the Current Status of the Issue of Scientific Realism," *Erkenntnis* 19 (1983): 45–90. For other varieties of scientific realism, see, e.g., Rom Harré, *Varieties of Realism: A Rationale for the Natural Sciences* (Oxford: Basil Blackwell, 1986), and Ian Hacking, *Representing and Intervening: Introductory Topics in the Philosophy of Natural Science* (Cambridge: Cambridge University Press, 1983).
40. Paisley Livingston, *Literary Knowledge: Humanistic Inquiry and the Philosophy of Science* (Ithaca: Cornell University Press, 1988).
41. See, e.g., Helen E. Longino, *Science as Social Knowledge: Value and Objectivity in Scientific Inquiry* (Princeton: Princeton University Press, 1990).
42. Latour and Woolgar, *Laboratory Life*, p. 261.
43. For the classic presentation of this classificatory scheme, see Abrams, *Mirror and the Lamp*, pp. 3–7.
44. Charles Darwin, *The Life and Letters of Charles Darwin: Including an Autobiographical Chapter*, 2 vols., ed. Francis Darwin (New York: Basic Books, 1959), 2:248.
45. James W. Souther and Myron L. White, *Technical Report Writing*, 2nd ed. (New York: John Wiley, 1977), p. 2.
46. Herbert B. Michaelson, *How to Write and Publish Engineering Papers and Reports* (Philadelphia: ISI Press, 1982), p. 3.
47. John H. Mitchell, *Writing for Professional and Technical Journals* (New York: John Wiley, 1968), p. 1.
48. Fieser and Fieser, *Style Guide for Chemists*, p. 55.
49. Albert Einstein, *Relativity: The Special and the General Theory: A Popular Exposition*, trans. Robert W. Lawson (New York: Crown, 1961), p. v.
50. Leonard Bloomfield, *Linguistic Aspects of Science*, International Encyclopedia of Unified Science, vol. 1, Foundations of the Unity of Science, no. 4 (Chicago: University of Chicago Press, 1939), pp. 46–47.
51. Cited in Gerald Holton, *Thematic Origins of Scientific Thought: Kepler to Einstein* (Cambridge, Mass.: Harvard University Press, 1973), pp. 17–18.
52. Gunther S. Stent, "Prematurity and Uniqueness in Scientific Discovery," *Scientific American*, December 1972, p. 89.
53. Bloomfield, *Linguistic Aspects*, p. 47.
54. Weisman, *Basic Technical Writing*, p. 113.
55. The more usual formulation is "contexts of discovery and of justification." See chapter 6 for my reasons for preferring the term *generation*.
56. One of the earliest is Boris Hessen, "The Social and Economic Roots of Newton's *Principia*," in *Science at the Cross Roads*, ed. N. Bukharin (London: Kniga, 1931), pp. 147–212.
57. Robert M. Young, "The Historiographic and Ideological Contexts of the Nineteenth-Century Debate on Man's Place in Nature," in *Darwin's Metaphor: Nature's Place in Victorian Culture* (Cambridge: Cambridge University Press, 1985), pp. 164–247.
58. In 1987 the University of Wisconsin Press published the first volume of a projected series on Science and Literature under the general editorship of George Levine:

George Levine, ed., Alan Rauch, asst. ed., *One Culture: Essays in Science and Literature* (Madison: University of Wisconsin Press, 1987).

59. A useful bibliography of the field is Walter Schatzberg, Ronald A. Waite, and Jonathan K. Johnson, eds., *The Relations of Literature and Science: An Annotated Bibliography of Scholarship, 1880–1980*, (New York: Modern Language Association, 1987). Among the recent reviews are G. S. Rousseau, "Literature and Science: The State of the Field," *Isis* 69 (1978): 583–91; Slusser and Guffey, "Literature and Science"; L. J. Jordanova, Introduction to *Languages of Nature: Critical Essays on Science and Literature*, ed. L. J. Jordanova (New Brunswick, N.J.: Rutgers University Press, 1986), pp. 15–47; George Levine, "One Culture: Science and Literature," in Levine, *One Culture*, pp. 3–32; Weininger, *Literature and Science*; John Christie and Sally Shuttleworth, "Introduction: Between Literature and Science," in *Nature Transfigured: Science and Literature, 1700–1900*, ed. John Christie and Sally Shuttleworth (Manchester: Manchester University Press, 1989); Stuart Peterfreund, Introduction to *Literature and Science: Theory and Practice*, ed. Stuart Peterfreund (Boston: Northeastern University Press, 1990), pp. 3–13. Recent essay collections include those by Levine, Amrine, Christie and Shuttleworth, and Peterfreund.

60. The list of critical studies properly begins with Jacques Barzun's 1941 *Darwin, Marx, Wagner*, 2nd ed. (New York: Doubleday, Anchor Books, 1958), and with Theodore Baird, "Darwin and the Tangled Bank," *American Scholar* 15 (1946): 477–86. A number of recent papers may be found in David Kohn, ed., *The Darwinian Heritage* (Princeton: Princeton University Press, 1985).

61. Stanley Edgar Hyman, *The Tangled Bank: Darwin, Marx, Frazer and Freud as Imaginative Writers* (New York: Atheneum, 1962).

62. Gillian Beer, *Darwin's Plots: Evolutionary Narrative in Darwin, George Eliot and Nineteenth-Century Fiction* (London: Routledge and Kegan Paul, Ark Paperback, 1985); George Levine, *Darwin and the Novelists: Patterns of Science in Victorian Fiction* (Cambridge, Mass.: Harvard University Press, 1988).

63. Patrick J. Mahony, *Freud as a Writer*, expanded ed. (New Haven: Yale University Press, 1987). See also, for other examples, a recent volume of papers from a symposium of the Modern Language Association discussing, besides Darwin's writings, those of Herschel, Lyell, Whewell, Lockyer, and Huxley: James Paradis and Thomas Postlewait, eds., *Victorian Science and Victorian Values: Literary Perspectives* (New Brunswick, N.J.: Rutgers University Press, 1985).

64. Paradis and Postlewait, *Victorian Science*. Another Victorian cross-cultural analysis is Peter Alan Dale, *In Pursuit of a Scientific Culture: Science, Art, and Society in the Victorian Age* (Madison: University of Wisconsin Press, 1989). The eighteenth century, too, finds its literature-science period studies; Paula R. Backscheider, ed., *Probability, Time, and Space in Eighteenth-Century Literature* (New York: AMS Press, 1979), as does the twentieth: Valerie D. Greenberg, *Transgressive Readings: The texts of Franz Kafka and Max Planck* (Ann Arbor: University of Michigan Press, 1990); (see also N. Katherine Hayes, n. 69 below). Americanists have their entries as well, e.g., John Limon, *The Place of Fiction in the Time of Science: A Disciplinary History of American Writing* (Cambridge: Cambridge University Press, 1990).

65. See Markus for a general review and discussion of the rhetoric of the scientific paper. Charles Bazerman, in *Shaping Written Knowledge: The Genre and Activity of the Ex-*

perimental Article in Science (Madison: University of Wisconsin Press, 1988), presents a book-length study and analysis. Greg Myers, in *Writing Biology: Texts in the Social Construction of Scientific Knowledge* (Madison: University of Wisconsin Press, 1990), analyzes from the perspective of the new sociologists the genres of scientific proposals, papers, and popularizations. Several historical studies of bodies of scientific papers in particular disciplines and periods may be found in Peter Dear, ed., *The Literary Structure of Scientific Argument* (Philadelphia: University of Pennsylvania Press, 1991), namely, Thomas H. Broman, "J.C. Reil and the 'Journalization' of Physiology," and Lynn K. Nyhart, "Writing Zoologically: The *Zeitschrift für Wissenschaftliche Zoologie* and the Zoological Community in Late Nineteenth-Century Germany."

66. Its leading exponent, Arthur O. Lovejoy, is best known for *The Great Chain of Being: A Study of the History of an Idea* (Cambridge, Mass.: Harvard University Press, 1936).

67. See, e.g., Michel Foucault, *The Order of Things: An Archaeology of the Human Sciences* (New York: Random House, Vintage Books, 1973).

68. See, e.g., Michel Serres, *Hermes: Literature, Science, Philosophy*, ed. Josué V. Harari and David F. Bell (Baltimore: Johns Hopkins University Press, 1982).

69. See, e.g., Rousseau, "Discourses of the Nerve"; Gillian Beer, "Discourses of the Island," in Amrine, *Literature and Science*, pp. 1–27. See also N. Katherine Hayles, *The Cosmic Web: Scientific Field Models and Literary Strategies in the Twentieth Century* (Ithaca: Cornell University Press, 1984) and *Chaos Bound: Orderly Disorder in Contemporary Literature and Science* (Ithaca: Cornell University Press, 1990).

70. For the classic statement, see Edward Kempf, "Charles Darwin: The Affective Sources of His Inspiration and Anxiety Neurosis," *Psychoanalytic Review* 5 (1918): 151–92. For a more recent presentation, see Phyllis Greenacre, *The Quest for the Father: A Study of the Darwin-Butler Controversy, as a Contribution to the Understanding of the Creative Individual* (New York: International Universities Press, 1963).

71. See, e.g., Evelyn Fox Keller, *Reflections on Gender and Science* (New Haven: Yale University Press, 1985), and Donna Haraway, *Primate Visions: Gender, Race, and Nature in the World of Modern Science* (New York: Routledge, 1989).

Chapter 2. The Problematics of Representation

1. Aristotle, *Poetics*, ed. Gerald F. Else (Ann Arbor: University of Michigan Press, 1967), p. 32.

2. For Aristotle's statement on the generality of poetry (as opposed to history), see ibid., p. 33. For a general statement on the neoclassical view, see George Saintsbury, *A History of Criticism and Literary Taste in Europe from the Earliest Texts to the Present Day*, 2nd ed., 3 vols. (New York: Dodd, Mead, 1906), 2:562. For a recent extended discussion, see William K. Wimsatt, Jr., and Cleanth Brooks, *Literary Criticism: A Short History*, 2 vols. (Chicago: University of Chicago Press, 1983), pp. 330–36.

3. For Aristotle's view that tragedy portrays people who are better than average, see Aristotle, *Poetics*, p. 18.

4. Sir Philip Sidney, *Sir Philip Sidney's Defense of Poesy*, ed. Lewis Soens (Lincoln: University of Nebraska Press, 1970), p. 9.

5. See Menachem Brinker, "Verisimilitude, Conventions, and Beliefs," *New Literary History* 14 (1983): 253–67.

6. C[harles] Si[nger], *Encyclopaedia Britannica* 1971, s.v. "History of Science."

7. I trust that it is not necessary to document fully this general remark. It is, in any case, more difficult to document absence than presence. But let me cite but one New Critical remark indicating the lack of interest in representation theory: "Any poetry which is 'technically' notable is a work of *abstractionist* art, concentrating ✓ upon the structure and the texture, and the structure-texture relation, out of a pure speculative interest" (emphasis added; John Crowe Ransom, "Criticism as Pure Speculation" in *The Intent of the Critic*, ed. Donald A. Stauffer [Princeton: Princeton University Press, 1941], p. 118). And one, even more explicit, structuralist statement: "Narrative does not show, does not imitate; the passion which may excite us in reading a novel is not that of a 'vision' (in actual fact, we do not 'see' anything)" (Roland Barthes, "Introduction to the Structuralist Analysis of Narratives," in *Image/Music/Text*, trans. Stephen Heath [New York: Noonday Press, 1977], p. 124). For some postmodernists, representation is all but unrecognizable. Thus Lyotard sees the aim of the postmodern as "not to supply reality but to invent allusions to the conceivable which cannot be presented" (Jean-François Lyotard, "Answering the Question: What Is Postmodernism?" trans. Régis Durand, *The Postmodern Condition: A Report on Knowledge* (Minneapolis: University of Minnesota Press, 1984), p. 81. And Baudrillard speaks not of representation but of simulation: "it is the generation by models of a real without origin or reality: a hyperreal" (Jean Baudrillard, *Simulation*, trans. Paul Foss, Paul Patton, and Philip Beitchman [New York: Semiotext(e), 1983], p. 2).

8. Richard Rorty, *Philosophy and the Mirror of Nature* (Princeton: Princeton University Press, 1979).

9. Plato, "The Republic," in *The Collected Dialogues of Plato Including the Letters*, ed. Edith Hamilton and Huntington Cairns, Bollingen Series 71 (Princeton: Princeton University Press, 1961), pp. 819–44.

10. For a philosophical analysis of contextualism in a larger sense, see Helen E. Longino, *Science as Social Knowledge: Values and Objectivity in Scientific Inquiry* (Princeton: Princeton University Press, 1990).

11. See, e.g., Werner Heisenberg, *Physics and Philosophy: The Revolution in Modern Science*, World Perspectives, vol. 19 (New York: Harper, 1958), pp. 167–86.

12. See chapter 6.

13. Harry F. Rosenthal, "Lost Satellite Mars Shuttle Crew's Mission," *Gainesville Sun*, February 4, 1984, p. 1.

14. See William J. Broad, "Fraud and the Structure of Science," *Science* 212 (1981): 137–41. See also, e.g., Warren E. Leary, "Harvard Retracts Immune System Data Published in *Science*," *Gainesville Sun*, November 22, 1986, p. 8A; Lawrence K. Altman, "Leading Heart-Disease Scientist Is Censured" *Gainesville Sun*, July 18, 1987, pp. 1A, 13A.

15. H. M. Collins, "The Seven Sexes: A Study in the Sociology of a Phenomenon, or the Replication of Experiments in Physics," *Sociology* 9 (1975): 205–24.

16. See, e.g., David Bohm, *Wholeness and the Implicate Order* (Boston: Routledge and

Kegan Paul, 1981), pp. 69–70; Ilya Prigogine and Isabelle Stengers, *Order out of Chaos: Man's New Dialogue with Nature* (New York: Bantam, 1984), pp. 222–26.

17. Ernest Nagel and James R. Newman, *Gödel's Proof* (New York: New York University Press, 1958), p. 6.

18. Michael Polanyi, "Life Transcending Physics and Chemistry," *Chemical and Engineering News*, August 21, 1967, pp. 54–66, and, *Personal Knowledge: Towards a Post-Critical Philosophy*, (Chicago: University of Chicago Press, 1962), pp. 381–97.

19. Francis Crick, *Of Molecules and Men* (Seattle: University of Washington Press, 1966), pp. xi-xii.

20. Polanyi, *Personal Knowledge*, pp. 393–97.

21. See, e.g., Karl R. Popper and John C. Eccles, *The Self and Its Brain* (New York: Springer, 1977), pp. 22–35.

22. Charles Darwin, *The Origin of Species by Charles Darwin: A Variorum Text*, ed. Morse Peckham (Philadelphia: University of Pennsylvania Press, 1959), p. 115.

23. Ibid., pp. 123–24.

24. Polanyi, *Personal Knowledge*, p. 101.

25. Frederic L. Holmes, "Scientific Writing and Scientific Discovery," *Isis* 78 (1987): 220–35.

26. For a different, "indexical" account of the contextual nature of science — one that emphasizes the social and the contingent, rather than the cognitive — see Karin D. Knorr-Cetina, *The Manufacture of Knowledge: An Essay on the Constructivist and Contextual Nature of Science* (Oxford: Pergamon Press, 1981), pp. 33–48. For a philosophical view, see Longino, *Science as Social Knowledge*, esp. pp. 62–82.

27. David M. Locke and S. William Pelletier, "Atisine: The Synthesis of 1-Methyl-6-ethyl-3-azaphenanthrene," *Journal of the American Chemical Society* 81 (1959): 2250.

28. Sir Isaac Newton, *Opticks, or a Treatise of the Reflections, Refractions, Inflections and Colours of Light* (1730; New York: Dover, 1952), pp. 186–91.

29. Personal communication, S. W. Pelletier. See Aaron J. Ihde, *The Development of Modern Chemistry* (New York: Harper and Row, 1964), p. 165.

30. H. J. Muller, "A Gene for the Fourth Chromosome of Drosophila," *Journal of Experimental Zoology* 17 (1914); reprint, in *Studies in Genetics: The Selected Papers of H. J. Muller* (Bloomington: Indiana University Press, 1962), p. 20.

31. Max Black, *Models and Metaphors: Studies in Language and Philosophy* (Ithaca: Cornell University Press, 1962); Mary B. Hesse, *Models and Analogies in Science* (Notre Dame: University of Notre Dame Press, 1966); James J. Bono, "Science, Discourse, and Literature: The Role/Rule of Metaphor in Science," in *Literature and Science: Theory and Practice*, ed. Stuart Peterfreund (Boston: Northeastern University Press, 1990), pp. 59–89. There is a recent general discussion of metaphor in George Lakoff and Mark Johnson, *Metaphors We Live By* (Chicago: University of Chicago Press, 1980). For a physicist's view of metaphor in physics, see Roger S. Jones, *Physics as Metaphor* (Minneapolis: University of Minnesota Press, 1982).

32. H. J. Muller, "Are the Factors of Heredity Arranged in a Line?" *American Naturalist* 54 (March-April 1920); reprint, in *Studies in Genetics*, p. 36.

33. Ibid., pp. 51–52.

34. Ibid., p. 53*n*.

35. Locke and Pelletier, "Atisine," p. 2246.

36. Muller, "Gene for the Fourth Chromosome," p. 25.

37. C. P. Snow, *The Two Cultures: And a Second Look* (Cambridge: Cambridge University Press, 1969), pp. 14–15.

38. See, e.g., Prigogine and Stengers, *Order out of Chaos*, pp. 103–29.

39. See Lawrence LeShan and Henry Margenau, *Einstein's Space and Van Gogh's Sky: Physical Reality and Beyond* (New York: Collier Books, 1983), pp. 152–56.

40. F. H. C. Crick, "On Protein Synthesis," *Symposium of the Society for Experimental Biology* 12 (1957): 138–63; cited and discussed in Horace Freeland Judson, *The Eighth Day of Creation: Makers of the Revolution in Biology* (New York: Simon and Schuster, 1979), pp. 333–40.

41. James D. Watson, *The Double Helix: A Personal Account of the Discovery of the Structure of DNA* (New York: New American Library, Signet, 1969), p. 98.

42. See Judson, *Eighth Day*, p. 47.

43. See Erwin Schrödinger, *What Is Life? The Physical Aspect of the Living Cell* (New York: Macmillan, 1945), pp. 68–69; see also Gunther S. Stent, "That Was the Molecular Biology That Was," *Science* 160 (1968): 390–95.

44. See, e.g., George Gaylord Simpson, *Biology and Man* (New York: Harcourt, Brace and World, 1969), pp. 3–31.

45. For an indication of the postmodernist attempt to achieve a "synthesis or transcension of these antitheses, which may be summed up as premodernist and modernist modes of writing," see John Barth, "The Literature of Replenishment: Postmodernist Fiction," *Atlantic*, January 1980, p. 70. Indeed, the "magic realism" of Gabriel García Márquez does not hesitate to adopt a realist manner in limning what cannot happen; see "Interview," *Playboy*, February 1983, p. 74.

46. At midcentury Erich Auerbach could still write his grand traversal of representation in Western literature, *Mimesis: The Representation of Reality in Western Literature*, trans. Willard R. Trask (Princeton: Princeton University Press, 1953).

47. Roman Jakobson, "Linguistics and Poetics," in *The Structuralists: From Marx to Lévi-Strauss*, ed. Richard T. and Fernande M. De George (Garden City, N.Y.: Doubleday, Anchor, 1972), pp. 85–95.

48. Samuel Johnson, *Rasselas and Other Tales*, ed. Gwin J. Kolb, Yale Edition of the Works of Samuel Johnson, vol. 16 (New Haven: Yale University Press, 1968), pp. 43–44.

49. Ibid.

50. T. S. Eliot, "Hamlet," in *Selected Prose*, ed. John Hayward (Harmondsworth, Middlesex: Penguin, 1953), pp. 107–08.

51. See, e.g., Ransom, "Criticism," p. 113.

52. Auerbach, *Mimesis*, p. 388.

Chapter 3. Writing without Expression

1. Louis F. and Mary Fieser, *Style Guide for Chemists* (New York: Reinhold, 1960), p. 55.

2. Gyorgy Markus, "Why Is There No Hermeneutics of Natural Sciences? Some Preliminary Theses," *Science in Context* 1 (1987): 13.

3. Ibid.

4. William Harvey, *The Circulation of the Blood and Other Writings*, trans. Kenneth J. Franklin (New York: Dutton, 1963), p. 19.

5. For a full discussion of expression theory in its heyday of Romantic criticism, see M. H. Abrams, *The Mirror and the Lamp: Romantic Theory and the Critical Tradition* (New York: Oxford University Press, 1953).

6. One well-known statement of the modernist rejection of expression theory is T. S. Eliot's "Tradition and the Individual Talent," in *Selected Prose*, ed. John Hayward (Harmondsworth, Middlesex: Penguin, 1953): "Honest criticism and sensitive appreciation is directed not upon the poet but upon the poetry" (p. 26); "Poetry is not the turning loose of emotion, but an escape from emotion; it is not the expression of personality, but an escape from personality" (p. 30).

7. Abrams, *Mirror and the Lamp*, pp. 226–62.

8. Ibid., pp. 53–56.

9. Leonard Bloomfield, *Linguistic Aspects of Science*, International Encyclopedia of Unified Science, vol. 1, Foundations of the Unity of Science, no. 4 (Chicago: University of Chicago Press, 1939), p. 47.

10. For a discussion and demonstration of the importance of shoptalk in the science laboratory, see Michael Lynch, *Art and Artifact in Laboratory Science: A Study of Shop Work and Shop Talk in a Research Laboratory* (London: Routledge and Kegan Paul, 1985).

11. See n. 9.

12. Gerald Holton, *The Scientific Imagination: Case Studies* (Cambridge: Cambridge University Press, 1978), pp. 3–24.

13. Arthur L. Robinson, "1980 Nobel Prize in Physics to Cronin and Fitch," *Science* 210 (1980): 621.

14. Holton, *Scientific Imagination*, pp. 22–24.

15. Gina Bari Kolata, "The 1980 Nobel Prize in Chemistry," *Science* 210 (1980): 888–89.

16. Ibid., p. 889.

17. Stephen Jay Gould, "Triumph of a Naturalist," *New York Review of Books*, March 29, 1984, pp. 4–5.

18. Evelyn Fox Keller, *A Feeling for the Organism: The Life and Work of Barbara McClintock* (New York: W. H. Freeman, 1983), pp. 197–207.

19. June Goodfield, *An Imagined World: A Story of Scientific Discovery* (New York: Penguin, 1982), p. 230.

20. Ibid., p. 235.

21. Michael Polanyi, *The Tacit Dimension* (Garden City, N.Y.: Doubleday, Anchor Books, 1967), pp. 3–25.

22. Goodfield, *Imagined World*, p. 229.

23. Evelyn Fox Keller, *Reflections on Gender and Science* (New Haven: Yale University Press, 1985), p. 92n.

24. Albert Einstein, "Autobiographical Notes," in *Albert Einstein: Philosopher-Scientist*, 2 vols., ed. Paul Arthur Schilpp, Library of Living Philosophers, vol. 7 (LaSalle, Ill.: Open Court, 1969), 1:9.

25. David M. Locke and S. William Pelletier, "Atisine: The Synthesis of 1-Methyl-6-ethyl-3-azaphenanthrene," *Journal of the American Chemical Society* 81 (1959): 2246.

26. R. B. Woodward, et al., "The Total Synthesis of Steroids," *Journal of the American Chemical Society* 74 (1952): 4223–24.

27. J. B. Hendrickson, "Stereochemical Implications in Sesquiterpene Biogenesis," *Tetrahedron* 7 (1959): 82.

28. Fieser and Fieser, *Style Guide for Chemists*, p. 54.

29. Historian Robert M. Young has argued that the anthropomorphism inherent in the phrase *natural selection* and emphasized in the language choices describing the process paradoxically both obscured Darwin's meaning and hastened the reception of Darwin's theory among those working to reconcile the theory with a deistic philosophical view of nature (Robert M. Young, *Darwin's Metaphor: Nature's Place in Victorian Culture* [Cambridge: Cambridge University Press, 1985], pp. 79–125). George Levine sees Darwin's personification of "natural selection" as "remythologizing the world he has tried to demystify.... For this reason, the theory itself becomes available on both sides of the argument about whether nature was meaningful and inherently value laden" (George Levine, *Darwin and the Naturalists: Patterns of Science in Victorian Fiction* [Cambridge, Mass.: Harvard University Press, 1988], p. 117).

30. Gillian Beer, *Darwin's Plots: Evolutionary Narrative in Darwin, George Eliot and Nineteenth-Century Fiction* (London: Routledge and Kegan Paul, Ark Paperback, 1985), pp. 56–64.

31. Charles Darwin, *The Origin of Species by Charles Darwin: A Variorum Text*, ed. Morse Peckham (Philadelphia: University of Pennsylvania Press, 1959), p. 155. Page numbers hereafter cited in the text refer to this edition.

32. Stanley Edgar Hyman, *The Tangled Bank: Darwin, Marx, Frazer and Freud as Imaginative Writers* (New York: Atheneum, 1962) p. 35.

33. Charles Darwin, *The Life and Letters of Charles Darwin: Including an Autobiographical Chapter*, ed. Francis Darwin, 2 vols. (New York: Basic Books, 1959), 1:485.

34. Marilyn Gaull, "From Wordsworth to Darwin: 'On the Fields of Praise,'" *Wordsworth Circle* 10 (1979): 33–48.

35. Barbara McClintock, "The Significance of Responses of the Genome to Challenge," *Science* 226 (1984): 792. Page numbers hereafter cited in the text refer to this paper.

36. Barbara McClintock, "Mutable Loci in Maize," *Carnegie Institution of Washington Yearbook* 49 (1950): 158.

Chapter 4. The Rhetoric of Science

1. See, e.g., the letter to L. Jenyns of October 12, 1845, Charles Darwin, in *The Life and Letters of Charles Darwin: Including an Autobiographical Chapter*, ed. Francis Darwin, 2 vols. (New York: Basic Books, 1959), 1:392.

2. Charles Darwin, *The Origin of Species by Charles Darwin: A Variorum Text*, ed. Morse Peckham (Philadelphia: University of Pennsylvania Press, 1959), pp. 71–72. Page numbers hereafter cited in the text refer to this edition.

3. Cicero, *De Inventione*, Loeb Classical Library, Cicero 2, trans. H. M. Hubbell (Cambridge, Mass.: Harvard University Press, 1949), p. 147.

4. A statement of the constructivist position is made in Alan G. Gross, *The Rhetoric of Science* (Cambridge, Mass.: Harvard University Press, 1990).

5. Walter B. Weimer, "Science as a Rhetorical Transaction: Toward a Nonjustificational Conception of Rhetoric," *Philosophy and Rhetoric* 10 (1977): 1–29.

6. Michael A. Overington, "The Scientific Community as Audience: Toward a Rhetorical Analysis of Science," *Philosophy and Rhetoric* 10 (1977): 143–64.

7. See, e.g., Myrna Gopnik, *Linguistic Structures in Scientific Texts* (The Hague: Mouton, 1922). For a recent review, see Gyorgy Markus, "Why Is There No Hermeneutics of Natural Science? Some Preliminary Theses," *Science in Context* 1 (1987): 5–51.

8. Herman M. Weisman, *Basic Technical Writing*, 4th ed. (Columbus, Ohio: Charles E. Merrill, 1980), p. 30.

9. Wayne C. Booth, *The Rhetoric of Fiction* (Chicago: University of Chicago Press, 1961), p. 116.

10. See Markus, "Why Is There No Hermeneutics of Natural Science?" for work along this line. For an extensive countertraditional study of the rhetoric of scientific proposals, papers, and popularizations, see Greg Myers, *Writing Biology: Texts in the Social Construction of Scientific Knowledge* (Madison: University of Wisconsin Press, 1990).

11. For a more complete discussion, see Gerald Holton, *Thematic Origins of Scientific Thought: Kepler to Einstein* (Cambridge, Mass.: Harvard University Press, 1973), pp. 431–42.

12. Evelyn Fox Keller, *Reflections on Gender and Science* (New Haven: Yale University Press, 1985), p. 126.

13. Ibid., p. 125.

14. Key statements of the reader-response position may be found in Jane P. Tompkins, ed., *Reader-Response Criticism: From Formalism to Post-Structuralism* (Baltimore: Johns Hopkins University Press, 1980). For a recent general review, see Elizabeth Freund, *The Return of the Reader: Reader-Response Criticism* (New York: Methuen, 1987). The related European development, reception theory, is summarized in Robert C. Holub, *Reception Theory: A Critical Introduction* (New York: Methuen, 1984).

15. Arnold C. Brackman, *A Delicate Arrangement: The Strange Case of Charles Darwin and Alfred Russel Wallace* (New York: Times Books, 1980).

16. For a standard account, see Curt Stern, Foreword to *The Origin of Genetics: A Mendel Source Book*, ed. Curt Stern and Eva R. Sherwood (San Francisco: W. H. Freeman, 1966), pp. v-xii.

17. For summary statements, see Augustine Brannigan, *The Social Basis of Scientific Discoveries* (Cambridge: Cambridge University Press, 1981), p. 89; Michael H. MacRoberts, "Was Mendel's Paper on *Pisum* Neglected or Unknown?" *Annals of Science* 42 (1985): 339.

18. See Brannigan, *Social Basis*, pp. 92–96.

19. Ibid. See also Onno G. Meijer, "Hugo de Vries No Mendelian?" *Annals of Science* 42 (1985): 189–232; Lindley Darden, "Hugo de Vries's Lecture Plates and the Discovery of Segregation," *Annals of Science* 42 (1985): 233–42.

20. R. A. Fisher, "Has Mendel's Work Been Rediscovered?" in Stern and Sherwood, *Origin of Genetics*, pp. 162–4.

21. Robert Olby, "Mendel No Mendelian?" *History of Science* 17 (1979): 53–72.

22. Brannigan, *Social Basis*, pp. 89–119.

23. Ibid., pp. 163–76.

24. MacRoberts, "Mendel's Paper," p. 344.

25. Ibid., pp. 343–44.

26. Gregor Mendel, "Experiments on Plant Hybrids," reprint, in Stern and Sherwood, *Origins of Genetics*, p. 2.

27. John Ziman, *Reliable Knowledge: An Exploration of the Grounds for Belief in Science* (Cambridge: Cambridge University Press, 1978), p. 12.

28. MacRoberts, "Mendel's Paper," p. 343.

29. William Bateson, *William Bateson, F.R.S., Naturalist: His Essays and Addresses: Together with a Short Account of His Life*, ed. Beatrice Bateson (Cambridge: Cambridge University Press, 1928), p. 222.

30. H. J. Muller, "Are the Factors of Heredity Arranged in a Line?" *American Naturalist* 54 (March-April 1920), reprint, in *Studies in Genetics: The Selected Papers of H. J. Muller* (Bloomington: Indiana University Press, 1962), p. 36.

31. Ibid., p. 51.

32. See, e.g., the often-cited letter to Asa Gray, in *Life and Letters*, 1:437–38.

33. Galileo Galilei, *Dialogue Concerning the Two Chief World Systems — Ptolemaic and Copernican*, 2nd ed., trans. Stillman Drake (Berkeley: University of California Press, 1967), pp. 72–79. Page numbers hereafter cited in the text refer to this edition.

34. Leopold Infeld, *Albert Einstein: His Work and Its Influence on Our Times* (New York: Charles Scribner's Sons, 1950), p. 23.

35. Holton, *Thematic Origins*, p. 168. Page numbers hereafter cited in the text refer to this edition.

36. Albert Einstein, "On the Electrodynamics of Moving Bodies," in *Annalen der Physik* 17 (1905), reprint, in *The Principle of Relativity: A Collection of Original Memoirs on the Special and General Theory of Relativity*, trans. W. Perrett and G. B. Jeffrey (1923; New York: Dover, 1952), pp. 37–38. Page numbers hereafter cited in the text refer to this edition.

37. Albert Einstein, *Relativity: The Special and the General Theory: A Popular Exposition*, trans. Robert W. Lawson (New York: Crown, 1961), p. v. Page numbers hereafter cited in the text refer to this edition.

38. Einstein, "The Foundation of the General Theory of Relativity," *Annalen der Physik* 49 (1916), reprint, in *Principle of Relativity*, p. 114.

39. Einstein, "Cosmological Considerations on the General Theory of Relativity," *Sitzungsberichte der Preussischen Akad. d. Wissenschaften*, 1917, reprint, in *Principle of Relativity*, pp. 179–80.

40. Einstein, Foreword to Galileo, *Dialogue*, pp. vi-xx.

41. In this regard, the *Australian Journal of Chemistry* professes a more enlightened attitude than that of many science journals: "The Journal prides itself on its tolerance, and editorial interference is restricted to the removal of solecisms, ambiguities, and the more irritating manifestations of long-windedness" (inside back cover, all issues, as of vol. 43 [1990]). It then adds, in striking reminiscence of the Fiesers: "The supreme rule is: use language that drives your story forward, rather than slowing it down." I am indebted to David Loewus for calling this instance to my attention.

Chapter 5. The Art of Artless Prose

1. Herman M. Weisman, *Basic Technical Writing*, 4th ed. (Columbus, Ohio: Charles E. Merrill, 1980), p. 113.
2. See chapter 1, nn. 21–4.
3. H. F. Heatwole, "Modern Biology: Art Form and Survival Imperative," in *A University Perspective*, ed. R. A. de Fossard (Sydney: John Wiley and Sons Australasia, 1970), p. 41.
4. For a very brief statement of the art-object critical position, see Vernon Hall, Jr., *A Short History of Literary Criticism* (New York: New York University Press, 1963), pp. 172–77. For a more extended discussion, see Murray Krieger, *The New Apologists for Poetry* (Bloomington: Indiana University Press, 1963).
5. E. H. Gombrich, *Art and Illusion: A Study in the Psychology of Pictorial Representation*, Bollingen Series 35, vol. 5 (Princeton: Princeton University Press, 1969), pp. 314–20.
6. See, e.g., René Wellek and Austin Warren, *Theory of Literature*, 3rd ed. (New York: Harcourt Brace Jovanovich, 1962), pp. 226–37.
7. See, e.g., David Daiches, *Critical Approaches to Literature* (Englewood Cliffs, N.J.: Prentice-Hall, 1956), pp. 129–57.
8. See John Crowe Ransom, "Criticism as Pure Speculation," in *The Intent of the Critic*, ed. Donald A. Stauffer (Princeton: Princeton University Press, 1941), pp. 92–124.
9. See Boris Eichenbaum, "The Theory of the 'Formal Method,'" in *Russian Formalist Criticism: Four Essays*, trans. Lee T. Lemon and Marion J. Reis (Lincoln: University of Nebraska Press, 1965), p. 116.
10. Ibid., p. 120.
11. Stanley Edgar Hyman, *The Tangled Bank: Darwin, Marx, Frazer and Freud as Imaginative Writers* (New York: Atheneum, 1962), p. 34.
12. Hayden White, e.g., gives a tropological reading of the *Origin*, describing it as "a history of nature meant to be understood literally but appealing ultimately to an image of coherence and orderliness which it constructs by linguistic 'turns' alone" (Hayden White, "The Fictions of Factual Representation," in *The Literature of Fact: Selected Papers from the English Institute*, ed. Angus Fletcher [New York: Columbia University Press, 1976], pp. 21–44).
13. The word, as has often been noted, is from James Joyce, *Finnegan's Wake* (New York: Viking, 1939), p. 383: "*Three quarks for Muster Mark!*"
14. Aldous Huxley, *Literature and Science* (New Haven: Leete's Island Books, 1963), p. 12.
15. N. R. Hanson, "Hypotheses Fingo," in *The Methodological Heritage of Newton*, ed. Robert E. Butts and John W. Davis (Toronto: University of Toronto Press, 1970), pp. 14–33.
16. Isaac Newton, *Sir Isaac Newton's Mathematical Principles of Natural Philosophy and His System of the World*, trans. Florian Cajori (Berkeley: University of California Press, 1947), p. 547.
17. Isaac Newton, *Opticks, or a Treatise of the Reflections, Refractions, Inflections and Colours of Light*, 4th ed. (1730; New York: Dover, 1952), p. 350.
18. Ibid., pp. 280–81.

19. Indeed, for extended "tropological" readings of Copernicus and Kepler, see Fernand Hallyn, *The Poetic Structure of the World: Copernicus and Kepler*, trans. Donald M. Leslie (New York: Zone Books, 1990).

20. Galileo Galilei, *Dialogue Concerning the Two Chief World Systems — Ptolemaic and Copernican*, 2nd ed., trans. Stillman Drake (Berkeley: University of California Press, 1967), pp. 5–6.

21. For a discussion of irony in Renaissance scientific writings, especially those of Copernicus, see Hallyn, *Poetic Structure*, pp. 35–52. Note the frequent references to ironic disjuncture between preface and text, e.g., p. 51.

22. Giorgio de Santillana, *The Crime of Galileo* (Chicago: University of Chicago Press, 1955), pp. 125–44.

23. For a succinct statement of the various positions on the matter, see Stillman Drake, Foreword to Jerome J. Langford, *Galileo, Science and the Church*, rev. ed. (Ann Arbor: University of Michigan Press, 1971), p. xii.

24. Galileo, *Dialogue*, pp. 130–31.

25. For a somewhat different reading of *Double Helix* and "Molecular Structure," with emphasis on the irony of the latter, see Alan G. Gross, *The Rhetoric of Science* (Cambridge, Mass.: Harvard University Press, 1990), pp. 54–65.

26. J. D. Watson and F. H. C. Crick, "Molecular Structure of Nucleic Acids: A Structure for Deoxyribose Nucleic Acid," *Nature* 171 (1953): 737–38.

27. James D. Watson, *The Double Helix: A Personal Account of the Discovery of DNA* (New York: New American Library, 1969), p. 102. Page numbers hereafter cited in the text refer to this edition.

28. Horace Freeland Judson, *The Eighth Day of Creation: Makers of the Revolution in Biology* (New York: Simon and Schuster, 1979), p. 180.

29. For a typical discussion of the interest in irony by the New Critics, see Daiches, *Critical Approaches*, pp. 160–62.

30. Victor Shklovsky, "Art as Technique," in Lemon and Reis, *Russian Formalist Criticism*, pp. 13–22.

31. See Elder Olson, "An Outline of Poetic Theory," in *Critics and Criticism: Ancient and Modern*, ed. R. S. Crane (Chicago: University of Chicago Press, 1952), pp. 546–66.

Chapter 6. The Putative Purity of Science

1. For a classic statement of the distinction, see Karl Popper, *The Logic of Scientific Discovery* (New York: Basic Books, 1959), pp. 31–32.

2. Augustine Brannigan, *The Social Basis of Scientific Discoveries* (Cambridge: Cambridge University Press, 1981), pp. 163–76.

3. For a classic statement of this position, see Leonard Bloomfield, *Linguistic Aspects of Science*, International Encyclopedia of Unified Science, vol. 1, Foundations of the Unity of Science, no. 4 (Chicago: University of Chicago Press, 1939), pp. 46–47. See also Gunther S. Stent, "Prematurity and Uniqueness in Scientific Discovery," *Scientific American*, December 1972, p. 89.

4. For a directly contrary view, see Helen E. Longino, *Science as Social Knowledge: Values and Objectivity in Scientific Inquiry* (Princeton: Princeton University Press, 1990),

pp. 62–82. But Longino's intersubjective objectivity has been considerably rede-
fined, as she would agree: "Even though the resulting picture [from her contextual
analysis] of objectivity differs from what we are used to, our intuition that scientific
inquiry at its best is objective is kept intact by appealing to the spirit of criticism
that is its traditional hallmark" (p. 82).

5. For the most significant work of the best-known contemporary myth critic, see
Northrop Frye, *Anatomy of Criticism: Four Essays* (Princeton: Princeton University
Press, 1957). For a recent review of the field, see John B. Vickery, "Literature and
Myth," in *Interrelations of Literature*, ed. Jean-Pierre Barricelli and Joseph Gibaldi
(New York: Modern Language Association, 1982). For recent brief reviews of Marx-
ist and Freudian criticism, respectively, see Terry Eagleton, *Marxism and Literary
Criticism* (Berkeley: University of California Press, 1976), and Elizabeth Wright,
Psychoanalytic Criticism: Theory in Practice (New York: Methuen, 1984).

6. Evelyn Fox Keller, *Reflections on Gender and Science* (New Haven: Yale University
Press, 1985), esp. pp. 17–20. See also Donna Haraway, *Primate Visions: Gender, Race,
and Nature in the World of Modern Science* (New York: Routledge, 1989). For feminist
critiques of science less focused on discourse, see Sandra Harding, *The Science Question in Feminism* (Ithaca: Cornell University Press, 1986), and Longino, *Science as
Social Knowledge*.

7. See Harding, *Science Question*, pp. 38–41.

8. Lyotard speaks of two "grand narratives" that once served to provide justification
for science: one, akin to the Promethean vision, shows "humanity as the hero of
liberty," with science as the grand emancipator; the other sees "life" and "spirit"
in the "ordered knowledge . . . contained in the empirical sciences" (Jean-François
Lyotard, *The Postmodern Condition: A Report on Knowledge*, trans. Geoff Bennington
and Brian Massumi [Minneapolis: University of Minnesota Press, 1984], pp. 31–
37).

9. Sigmund Freud, *The Interpretation of Dreams*, trans. James Strachey (New York:
Avon Books, 1965), pp. 549–50, 647–60.

10. See Keller, *Reflections*, pp. 33–42.

11. Stanley Edgar Hyman, *The Tangled Bank: Darwin, Marx, Frazer and Freud as Imaginative Writers* (New York: Atheneum, 1962), p. 28.

12. Ibid., p. 29.

13. Ibid., pp. 34–43.

14. Gillian Beer, *Darwin's Plots: Evolutionary Narrative in Darwin, George Eliot and
Nineteenth-Century Fiction* (London: Routledge and Kegan Paul, Ark Paperback,
1985), pp. 104–45.

15. Gerald Holton, *Thematic Origins of Scientific Thought: Kepler to Einstein* (Cambridge,
Mass.: Harvard University Press, 1973), p. 112.

16. Ibid., pp. 17–20.

17. For a recent discussion, see Eric Charles White, "Contemporary Cosmology and
Narrative Theory," in *Literature and Science: Theory and Practice*, ed. Stuart Peterfreund (Boston: Northeastern University Press, 1990), pp. 91–112.

18. Jacques Barzun, *Science: The Glorious Entertainment* (New York: Harper and Row,
1964).

19. Barry Barnes and Donald MacKenzie, "On the Role of Interests in Scientific

Change," in *On the Margins of Science: The Social Construction of Rejected Knowledge*, Sociological Review Monograph 27, ed. Roy Wallis (Keele, Staffordshire: University of Keele, 1979), p. 61.

20. Bruno Latour, *Science in Action: How to Follow Scientists and Engineers through Society* (Cambridge, Mass.: Harvard University Press, 1987), pp. 145–76.

21. Boris Hessen, "The Social and Economic Roots of Newton's *Principia*," in *Science at the Crossroads*, ed. N. Bukarhin (London: Kniga, 1931), pp. 147–212. For a recent assessment, see Barry Barnes, *Scientific Knowledge and Sociological Theory* (London: Routledge and Kegan Paul, 1974), pp. 104–08.

22. For a detailed analysis, see David Dickson, *The New Politics of Science* (New York: Pantheon, 1984).

23. For a counterproposal for a weak program for the social study of science, which aims to inject a committed meta-analysis into the realm of policymaking, see Daryl E. Chubin and Sal Restivo, "The 'Mooting' of Science Studies: Research Programmes and Science Policy," in Karin D. Knorr-Cetina and Michael Mulkay, eds., *Science Observed: Perspectives in the Social Study of Science* (Beverly Hills: Sage, 1983), pp. 53–83.

24. Professor George Wald: "Well, here is a Nobel Laureate who thinks these words [of Senator Richard Russell, 'If we have to start over again from Adam and Eve, I want them to be American'] are criminally insane" (Richard Todd, "George Wald: The Man, *the* Speech," *New York Times Magazine*, August 17, 1969, p. 28); see also Philip M. Boffey, "Dissent Spreads to Nobelists, Industrial Scientists," *Science* 168 (1970): 1325.

25. See, e.g., R. C. Lewontin, Steven Rose, and Leon J. Kamin, *Not in Our Genes: Biology, Ideology, and Human Nature* (New York: Pantheon, 1984), pp. 101–06.

26. Ibid., pp. 89–91.

27. See Keller, *Reflections*, p. 91.

28. Albert Einstein, "Principles of Research," *Ideas and Opinions*, trans. Sonja Bargmann (New York: Dell, 1973), p. 220.

29. See, e.g., the discussion in B. A. Farrell, *The Standing of Psychoanalysis* (Oxford: Oxford University Press, 1981), pp. 26–46.

30. Freud himself confesses as much in the preface to the second edition of *The Interpretation of Dreams*, p. xxvi.

31. Peter Medawar, *Pluto's Republic* (Oxford: Oxford University Press, 1982), pp. 143–44.

32. For a recent discussion, see Ralph Colp, Jr., *To Be an Invalid: The Illness of Charles Darwin* (Chicago: University of Chicago Press, 1977).

33. Freud, *Interpretation of Dreams*, pp. 311–546, esp. pp. 385–419.

34. Cited by Aaron J. Ihde, *The Development of Modern Chemistry* (New York: Harper and Row, 1964), p. 310.

35. John H. Wotiz and Susana Rudofsky, "Kekulé's Dreams: Fact or Fiction?" *Chemistry in Britain* 20 (1984): 722.

36. O. B. Ramsay and A. J. Roche, "Kekulé's Dreams: Separating the Fiction from the Fact," *Chemistry in Britain* 20 (1984): 1093–94.

37. Ihde, *Development of Modern Chemistry*, p. 306.

38. Ibid., p. 312.

39. Cited (and challenged) by Edward Farber, "Dreams and Visions in a Century of Chemistry," in *Kekulé Centennial*, Advances in Chemistry Series 61 (Washington, D.C.: American Chemical Society, 1966), p. 138.
40. Cited in ibid., p. 136.
41. Ibid., pp. 136–37.
42. For a succinct account, see Sigmund Freud, *Encyclopaedia Britannica*, 11th ed., reprint, 1971, s.v. "Psychoanalysis."
43. Evelyn Fox Keller, *A Feeling for the Organism: The Life and Work of Barbara McClintock* (New York: W. H. Freeman, 1983), p. 34.
44. Keller, *Reflections*, pp. 69–126.
45. For an extended contemporary discussion, see Jean Laplanche, *Life and Death in Psychoanalysis*, trans. Jeffrey Mehlman (Baltimore: Johns Hopkins University Press, 1976).
46. Cited by Donald Fleming, introduction to Jacques Loeb, *The Mechanistic Conception of Life*, ed. Donald Fleming (Cambridge, Mass.: Belknap Press, Harvard University Press, 1964), p. xxxiii.
47. Ibid., p. xiii. Page numbers hereafter cited in the text refer to this edition of Loeb's writings.
48. Ibid., pp. xiv-xv.
49. For a recent reading of Maxwell's demon and entropy, see N. Katherine Hayles, "Self-Reflexive Metaphors in Maxwell's Demon and Shannon's Choice: Finding the Passages," in Peterfreund, *Literature and Science*, pp. 209–37.
50. Ilya Prigogine and Isabelle Stengers, *Order out of Chaos: Man's New Dialogue with Nature* (New York: Bantam Books, 1984). Page numbers hereafter cited in the text refer to this edition. For a more critical reading of *Order out of Chaos*, see N. Katherine Hayles, *Chaos Bound: Orderly Disorder in Contemporary Literature and Science* (Ithaca: Cornell University Press, 1990), pp. 91–114.
51. Cited in Itamar Procaccia and John Ross, "The 1977 Nobel Prize in Chemistry," *Science* 198 (1977): 716–17.
52. Sir Isaac Newton, *Opticks, or a Treatise of the Reflections, Refractions, Inflections and Colours of Light* (1730; New York: Dover, 1952), p. 76. See also pp. 376, 397.

Chapter 7. Writing as Reality

1. Among the many collections of structuralist critical writings are Michael Lane, ed., *Structuralism: A Reader* (London: Jonathan Cape, 1970); Richard Macksey and Eugenio Donato, eds., *The Structuralist Controversy: The Languages of Criticism and the Sciences of Man* (Baltimore: Johns Hopkins University Press, 1972); and Richard T. and Fernande M. De George, eds., *The Structuralists: From Marx to Lévi-Strauss* (Garden City, N.Y.: Doubleday, Anchor Books, 1972). Useful reviews are Jonathan Culler, *Structuralist Poetics: Structuralism, Linguistics and the Study of Literature* (Ithaca: Cornell University Press, 1975), and, briefer, Terence Hawkes, *Structuralism and Semiotics* (Berkeley: University of California Press, 1977). The poststructuralist critical scene can hardly be briefly reviewed, but for the Derrideans, Harold Bloom et al., *Deconstruction and Criticism* (New York: Seabury Press, 1979), contains some key writings, and Christopher Norris, *Deconstruction: Theory and Practice* (New York:

Methuen, 1982), is a good introductory review. For Foucault, a key text that outlines the methodology and its rationale is Michel Foucault, *The Archaeology of Knowledge: And the Discourse on Language*, trans. A. M. Sheridan Smith (New York: Pantheon, 1972). The Lacanian approach, for reasons of space not otherwise referred to here, may be found in Jacques Lacan, *Speech and Language in Psychoanalysis*, trans. Anthony Wilden (Baltimore: Johns Hopkins University Press, 1968), and *Ecrits: A Selection*, trans. Alan Sheridan (New York: W. W. Norton, 1977).

2. The work of Claude Lévi-Strauss is perhaps best introduced by his first major work to appear in the United States, *The Savage Mind* (Chicago: University of Chicago Press, 1966).

3. For an extended discussion, see Gyorgy Markus, "Why Is There No Hermeneutics of Natural Sciences? Some Preliminary Theses," *Science in Context* 1 (1987): 37–43.

4. For the classic introduction of the term, see Lévi-Strauss, *Savage Mind*, pp. 16–22.

5. See, e.g., Jacques Derrida, "Structure, Sign, and Play in the Discourse of the Human Sciences," in Macksey and Donato, *Structuralist Controversy*, pp. 247–72.

6. For a presentation of the philosophical position that the texts of science and technology are governed by intertextual constitutivity — "Science and technology, like any textual assemblage, is apprehended and comprehended only through its use. And use orders a different concentration of significance or value according to the cultural topography into and out of which it is inscribed" (p. 135) — see Gayle L. Ormiston and Raphael Sassower, *Narrative Experiments: The Discursive Authority of Science and Technology* (Minneapolis: University of Minnesota Press, 1989).

7. For these processes at work, see Jacques Derrida, *Of Grammatology*, trans. Gayatri Chakravorty Spivak (Baltimore: Johns Hopkins University Press, 1974), pp. 3–26.

8. Galileo Galilei, *Dialogue Concerning the Two Chief World Systems — Ptolemaic and Copernican*, 2nd ed., trans. Stillman Drake (Berkeley: University of Califonia Press, 1967), pp. 130–31. Page numbers hereafter cited in the text refer to this edition.

9. Here, as elsewhere, I have selected as examples instances of scientific discourse particularly suited to illustrate the points I sought to make. In some cases these are among the high dramas of science — reflecting clashing paradigms or the overturning of long-held beliefs — but my general argument is that the more mundane language of everyday science itself exhibits the same properties, though perhaps not so strikingly or so accessibly. Indeed, as noted earlier, studies of the daily life of the scientist are the work of ethnographers of various stripe, and more literary studies of everyday scientific discourse are now being done — e.g., Greg Myers, *Writing Biology: Texts in the Social Construction of Scientific Knowledge* (Madison: University of Wisconsin Press, 1990), and Charles Bazerman, *Shaping Written Knowledge: Essays in the Growth, Form, Function, and Implications of the Scientific Article* (Madison: University of Wisconsin Press, 1988). In this book I might have adopted as "tutor text" some such routine scientific paper as Bill Pelletier's and mine on the synthesis of the degradation product of atisine, employing it to illustrate (perhaps somewhat tediously) the various approaches taken. Here, e.g., the focus would be on the natural-products chemist's deconstruction of the "organic" (read: vitalistically produced) character of organic materials. In the process the hierarchy natural/synthetic is inverted, with the natural no longer valorized over the synthetic, but with the system itself destabilized and the boundary natural/synthetic no longer quite clear.

In its practice as well as its discourse, chemistry now reflects this deconstruction: thus, the natural substance may be separated and purified by the techniques of the synthetic chemist, and the synthetic substance produced "naturally" with the aid of bioengineered organisms.

10. Gillian Beer, *Darwin's Plots: Evolutionary Narrative in Darwin, George Eliot and Nineteenth-Century Fiction* (London: Routledge and Kegan Paul, Ark Paperback, 1985), pp. 62, 97; George Levine, *Darwin and the Novelists: Patterns of Science in Victorian Fiction* (Cambridge, Mass.: Harvard University Press, 1988), pp. 84–118.

11. To a considerable degree this argument is anticipated in Levine, *Darwin and the Novelists*, pp. 98–99.

12. Charles Darwin, *The Origin of Species by Charles Darwin: A Variorum Text*, ed. Morse Peckham (Philadelphia: University of Pennsylvania Press, 1959), p. 106. Page numbers hereafter cited in the text refer to this edition.

13. For Levine on this point, see *Darwin and the Novelists*, pp. 95–7.

14. Alfred Russel Wallace, "On the Law Which Has Regulated the Introduction of New Species," reprint, in Arnold C. Brackman, *A Delicate Arrangement: The Strange Case of Charles Darwin and Alfred Russel Wallace* (New York: Times Books, 1980), p. 314.

15. David Bohm, *Wholeness and the Implicate Order* (London: Routledge and Kegan Paul, 1981), p. 15. Page numbers hereafter cited in the text refer to this edition.

16. Friedrich Nietzsche, *Thus Spoke Zarathustra: A Book for All and No One*, trans. Marianne Cowan (Los Angeles: Henry Regnery, Gateway Editions, 1957), p. 273.

Chapter 8. Reading Science

1. Roman Jakobson, "Linguistics and Poetics," in *The Structuralists: From Marx to Lévi-Strauss*, ed. Richard T. and Fernande M. De George (Garden City, N.Y.: Doubleday, 1972), pp. 85–95.

2. Nothing, in my view, has so bedeviled poststructuralist discourse as its agonizing over the self-reflexive nature of its critique of discourse. For a discussion of self-reflexive concerns in the new sociology of science, see Steve Woolgar, ed., *Knowledge and Reflexivity: New Frontiers in the Sociology of Knowledge* (Beverly Hills: Sage, 1988).

3. One must, of course, acknowledge the importance of shoptalk in the everyday interactions of scientists — interactions that form the bedrock for the ultimate social construction of scientific knowledge. For an important demonstration of the functioning and importance of shoptalk, see Michael Lynch, *Art and Artifact in Laboratory Science: A Study of Shop Work and Shop Talk in a Research Laboratory* (London: Routledge and Kegan Paul, 1985).

4. I do not, of course, deny the existence of a scientific practice, which is ineluctably bound up with its discourse. (Again I allude to Polanyi's pulmonary radiologist, who can learn one only in company with the other.) To be sure, certain philosophical realists have based their claims for scientific realism on assertion of the primacy of scientific practice; see, e.g., Ian Hacking, *Representing and Intervening: Introductory Topics in the Philosophy of Natural Science* (Cambridge: Cambridge University Press, 1983), and Rom Harré, *Varieties of Realism: A Rationale for the Natural Sciences* (Oxford: Basil Blackwell, 1986). Thus, Harré describes scientific discourse as a kind of froth floating on the ocean of scientific practice: "Science is an activity: it is some-

thing people *do*. Some, but not all of that doing is thinking, and yet a more minor part of it is producing discourses in which the results of making those manipulations and doing that thinking are recorded." Surely one cannot argue that the "thinking" is done in some language apart from that of the "discourses," and as I hope to have shown, even the "manipulations" are not only describable but conceivable only within the context the "discourses" generate. I do not argue that the two do not interpenetrate, that the relationship is not dialectical. Thus, the discourse helps determine the practice, and the practice also makes its way into the discourse; it is what the "methodology" sections of scientific papers are all about. Further, I will concede that it is likely that an element of each sequesters itself off from the other, that there is a degree of practice that remains unrecorded or uncoded into any language (hence the difficulty of making scientific experiments repeatable), just as there is an element of the language (perhaps the "textuality" of the poststructuralists) that derives not from the *materia* it describes or constructs but from its own essence. Finally, I argue for the primacy of discourse in the dialectic of discourse and practice (as the Marxist would argue for the primacy of the material base in the dialectic of base and superstructure), yet I do so largely to free science from the thrall of the conceived hegemony of its practice, and I would hold no serious quarrel with anyone who saw the two in a more precarious balance.

5. James J. Bono, "Literature, Literary Theory, and the History of Science," *Publication of the Society for Literature and Science* 2 (November 1986): 8–9.

6. Galileo Galilei, *Dialogue Concerning the Two Chief World Systems — Ptolemaic and Copernican*, 2nd ed., trans. Stillman Drake (Berkeley: University of California Press, 1967), p. 37.

INDEX